Encyclopaedia of

DEWEY DECIMAL CLASSIFICATION

Encyclopaedia of
DEWEY DECIMAL CLASSIFICATION

Volume 2

Edited by
Ram Shobhit Singh

ANMOL PUBLICATIONS PVT. LTD.
NEW DELHI - 110 002 (INDIA)

ANMOL PUBLICATIONS PVT. LTD.
H.O.: 4374/4B, Ansari Road, Daryaganj,
New Delhi-110 002 (India)
Ph.: 23278000, 23261597
B.O.: No. 1015, Ist Main Road, BSK IIIrd Stage
IIIrd Phase, IIIrd Block,
Bangalore - 560 085 (India)
Visit us at: www.anmolpublications.com

Encyclopaedia of Dewey Decimal Classification

First Edition, 2008
ISBN 978-81-261-3673-5 (Set)

PRINTED IN INDIA

Printed at Mehra Offset Press, Delhi.

Contents

Preface

The Dewey Decimal Classification (DDC) system is the world's most widely used library classification system. The 22nd edition of the DDC enhances the efficiency and accuracy of your classification work in ways no previous editions have done. The DDC evolves continually to keep up with recorded knowledge. The Dewey Decimal Classification (DDC) system uses simple decimal notation to divide recorded knowledge into 10 main classes, 100 divisions and 1,000 sections. DDC 22 Summaries provides a complete list of these groupings. Browsing the summaries is fast and easy way to become familiar with the DDC's structure. It also uses some aspects of a faceted classification scheme, combining elements from different parts of the structure to construct a number representing the subject content (often combining two subject elements with linking numbers and geographical and temporal elements) and form of an item rather than drawing upon a list containing each class and its meaning.

Except for general works and fiction, works are classified principally by subject, with extensions for subject relationships, place, time or type of material, producing classification numbers of no less than three digits but otherwise of indeterminate length with a decimal point before the fourth digit.

Books are placed on the shelf in increasing numerical order; the whole number to the left of the decimal is in counting order, while the digits to the right of the decimal are compared one digit at a time, with a blank coming before zero. When two books have the same subject, and therefore the same classification number, the second line of the call number, which usually has the first letter or first several letters of the author's last name (or the title if there is no identifiable author), is placed in alphabetical order.

It is a common misconception that all books in the DDC are nonfiction. The DDC has a number for all books, including those that generally become their own section of fiction. If DDC rules are strictly followed, American fiction is classified in 813. Most libraries create a separate fiction section to allow shelving fiction in a more generalised fashion than Dewey provides for, or to avoid the space that would be taken up in the 800s.

Although the scheme is one of the major internationally recognized classification systems, yet there is hardly a book on the subject that may highlight special features of the successive editions of DDC. The present book is primary aimed to fill up that void.

—Editor

1

DDC System and Fundamental Laws

Throughout the history of the world, there have continually been attempts made to record culture by people who saw the importance of preserving the knowledge of their own civilization. The degree and nature of this activity varied as did the peoples; and have ranged from simple cave paintings to more sophisticated systems of classification seen in ancient institutions, such as the Alexandrian Museum and Library. Cultural relevancies and temporal developments have always been deciding factors in determining the kinds of subjects that were compiled, primarily on tablets, scrolls, and books; how they were interpreted; and the fashion in which they were classified, but some things may be said in general about the historical development of knowledge and how two of its principle characteristics make classification quite easy under the Dewey Decimal system.

Specifically, this essay, will look at the fundamental fact that the universe of knowledge is forever expanding and how the Dewey Decimal Classification system hospitably integrates that reality. Also discussed will be the historically acceptable fashion of setting knowledge down in an hierarchical order and its relevancy within the Dewey Decimal System. What is the DDC20 and how does it classify the universe of knowledge?

An Overview of the Dewey Decimal Classification System

Melvil Dewey was born on December 10, 1851 in Adam's Centre in New York State (Wiegand 1996,4). His extensive diaries are filled with his hopes, fears, dreams, and decisions, and show that by the time he reached eighteen years of age, he had made the decision to "... devote my life to Education" (Wiegand 1996,12). During his years at Amherst College, his conviction that free schools and free libraries were the right of everyone, was cemented (Wiegand 1996,19). His involvement with the library at Amherst, coupled with his strongly held views on the power of books, led him to investigate the cataloguing of libraries to make them easier to use. Melvil Dewey first published his classification system in 1876 (Wiegand 1996,32), and although it has expanded and seen many changes, it has survived and flourished.

Principally, a classification system has historically been used to develop some order out of the ever expanding world of knowledge, and more specifically, as Wynar states: "the ultimate aim of any classification system is to lead the patron to the items required" (Wynar 1992,317). That was the dream of Melvil Dewey. He wanted to have a hand in the education of the masses and he fulfilled it by developing a system which put related topics in an hierarchical order from general to specific as needed. His was a faceted system, which developed facets or the characteristics of division. The facets are mutually exclusive and exhaustive so that every topic may be accounted for (Wynar 1992,320 21). Some are very specific, while others are more general and can be applied to many subjects. Most importantly, Dewey's system depends upon recurring facets, such as Periods (Wynar 1992,320). He did not classify under subjects his hierarchical system organized the universe of knowledge into "traditional academic disciplines or fields of study" (DDC20 1989,xxvi).

He used ten such fields, numbering them from 000 to 900, with the first digit representing its main class. Each main class was then divided into ten separate divisions, with numbers running from zero to nine and each division divided into sections or subdivisions, also using the zero to nine numerical sequence. An example may help to illustrate the system. Using the number 931, one can say that the nine represents the main class, the three, the separate division, and the one, a distinct section (DDC20 1989,xxviii). To the right of the third number goes a decimal point, which can theoretically continue to divide the number by ten to make a place for very specific topics.

This is Dewey's most important contribution to the field of classification: with the use of hierarchical divisions, which are subdivided with the decimal system, division can continue indefinitely, thus, allowing for new areas to be added (Wynar 1992,328). By using the decimal system, Dewey allowed for pure notation and relatively close shelf proximity for books on related topics (Wynar 1992,327). Since there is no "single place for a given subject,... the Relative Index assembles the disciplinary aspects of a subject in one place" (DDC20 1989,xxvii). For example, if you look up "Birth", you will find notations as varied as 392.12 and 808.80354 under the heading. The Relative Index is an integral part of the system.

The Principles

Dewey's system made relative location possible and did away with all the inherent problems of rigidly fixed location methods (Evans & Heft 1994,431 33). Books could be shelved anywhere a librarian wanted them without altering their order. This was an extremely progressive advancement since knowledge is always growing. The continually increasing base of knowledge is the foremost consideration in employing a catalogue system because it is the one constant that can be relied upon (Abrera 1974,30).

Examples would be the fast growing fields of genetics and computer technologies. Also, Sociology used to be 301, now it is 301 307 (DDC20 1989,xiii). It needed a broader range to reflect new societal concerns. The DDC20 can incorporate any new areas developed, since its structure of decimals allows for infinite additional notations. It does so with 'hospitality' (Abrera 1974,33), having the ability to include any additions easily and quickly. The DDC20 is very adaptable to expanding horizons of information. As Phyllis A. Richmond states:

The system must he hospitable to all knowledge, including things that never were, such as phlogiston; things that never shall be, like utopias; and things that are impossible, like the square root of minus one (Bengtson & Hill 1990,18).

Next to consider is the common procedure of beginning with general knowledge and working towards specific, in an hierarchical system of ordering. This can be traced primarily to Aristotle, who identified classes and sub classes.

By arranging them in an hierarchy, he was able to see relationships between objects or concepts (Abrera 1974,21 29). He moved from the general to the specific or from the extension to the intention. This had great possibilities for library classification and is actually what lies behind Dewey's whole system.

As Wynar stresses, "[n]o matter what scheme is chosen, or how large the library, the purpose of classification is to bring related items together in a helpful sequence from the general to the specific" (Wynar 1992,317). For example, 700 represents the Arts, while 702 is Miscellany of fine and decorative arts, and 735.21 is Sculpture from 1400 1799. With Dewey, one can get as specific as needed, with the infinite notation system, just by adding another number. Remember, when using hierarchical classifications, one must always make natural and logical decisions in sub-dividing (Wynar 1992,317).

Conclusion

The Dewey Decimal system has like most things, good and bad parts. It is very adaptable for small libraries because "it stresses hierarchies of subject matter..." (Wynar 1992,323), but its numbers can become long, making them difficult to remember, and even more difficult to fit on book spines (Evans & Heft 1994,433).

Also, Wynar makes the point that along with all the positives of being flexible enough to accept new topic areas, there is the work and expense of making those changes in a library setting (Wynar 1992,325). Overall, the DDC20 has a long history because it is a valuable tool in the classification of knowledge, it is used extensively throughout world, and is flexible enough to make it the only choice for many institutions.

The University of Texas at Arlington Libraries

The Special Collections Division of The University of Texas at Arlington Libraries has been collecting archival and manuscript materials since the 1960s. In this twenty-five-plus year period, the division has grown from a two-person operation collecting and processing the records of Texas labour unions and officials to a highly visible division of the library with ten full-time staff, seven student employees, and a much broadened collecting focus.

Also during this period, the division has grown, extending its administrative umbrella over several once-separate and autonomous units, each processing archival and manuscript collections in its own way. The need to bring consistency to the division's archival arranging, describing, and cataloging practices has, in part, prompted the writing of this processing manual.

In 1994, Special Collections staff members, Jane Boley, Marcelle Hull, Shirley Rodnitzky, and Gerald Saxon, met to discuss the drafting of this manual. All agreed that a processing manual would benefit the division in many ways:

The manual, as mentioned above, would bring consistent processing practices to the division for the first time. Special Collections staff has always adhered to high standards of modern archivy, but each archivist in the division described collections in a different way. In today's automated environment, descriptive practices in particular should be consistent so that online cataloging records and finding aids are helpful to users.

The manual would serve as a training tool and reference source for the division's student employees, volunteers, and new hires assigned archival responsibilities.

The manual would be used as a textbook in the History Department's graduate classes on archival science. The holdings of Special Collections are often used for processing projects by graduate students in the programmeme. The processing manual, used as a textbook for graduate students in the archives class, will ensure that their processing is consistent with the division's standards and methods.

The processing manual, then, will have both an internal function (for Special Collections' students and staff) and an external one (for UT Arlington graduate students). Moreover, the authors of the manual realize that it is an organic document, one subject to change and revision as archival practices shift and new methods and technologies are introduced. What probably will not change are the underlying assumptions the authors brought to the manual's writing. The reader should be aware that these assumptions include the following:

1. The ideal level of processing is not the same for every collection. It is the processor's responsibility to determine the most practical processing scheme.
2. The research value of each collection should determine its level of processing.
3. Staff should do only enough work on collections to make them usable for researchers.
4. The archival principles of provenance and original order should determine arrangement.
5. It is unlikely that any collection will ever be "reprocessed" so processors should consider their work on each collection to be final.
6. The manual is designed as a guide. It cannot answer every question or consider every possibility in the archival enterprise. Processors with questions not addressed in the manual should consult their colleagues on the staff or in the broader archival community.
7. The overall goals in processing are to preserve the material with enduring value in the collection, arrange the collection in a logical way, describe the arrangement in a well-written finding aid, and make sure all appropriate forms are completed.

Special Collections is committed to providing effective access to all of its holdings and actively encourages its collections be used. In order to provide the best possible service to users, it is important that as many of our collections as possible be processed, open, and available for research. Processors must always keep in mind that they should not do more work on a collection than is necessary to make it usable because the extra work done on one collection will detract from the work that can be done on others.

While many have said that processing is largely a matter of common sense, the authors of the manual believe that the procedures and methods discussed herein will make our processing methods more efficient, more consistent, and ultimately, of course, more helpful to researchers.

This processing manual has served Special Collections staff and others well since it was first produced in 1995. It has gone through several revisions, as text was clarified, typos corrected, new procedures and practices incorporated, and archival standards have changed.

The manual, until now (2001), has never been available electronically. We believe by making the manual available over the UT Arlington Library web page that practicing archivists at UT Arlington and beyond can benefit as will graduate students and others. Special thanks must go to Shirley Rodnitzky, who coordinated the efforts in Special Collections to revise the manual yet again and to see that it is mounted on the web.

Basic Principles of Processing

In some ways, the processing of an archival collection is like putting together a jigsaw puzzle because the archivist is trying to fit all of the different pieces together to get a clear picture of the whole. Archivists over the years have formulated a few basic principles to help guide them in their work of arranging and describing collections. These principles are provenance, the sanctity of original order, and the concept of levels of control. There have been a number of attempts to arrange archives in other ways, but these attempts have ended in failure and disruption of collections.

1. *Provenance*. Simply defined, provenance means that the archives of a given records creator must not be intermingled with those of other records creators. Archivist Fredric Miller has said that "provenance is the fundamental principle of modern archival practice." It is important to understand that provenance is identified primarily with the creator rather than the donor, if the two are different. For example, if Jane Smith donated the papers of her grandmother, Sarah Norton, the papers would be the Sarah Norton Papers because she created them.
2. *Original Order*. This principle states that records should be maintained in the order in which they were originally kept while in active use. It is not the order imposed on the material by someone who was not involved with the records while they were in active use. If the order has been destroyed over time or in the transfer/packing process, then it is the archivist's obligation to reconstitute it if possible. If the original order of a collection cannot be discerned or if the original order was capricious and incomprehensible, then the archivist must impose a reasonable and logical order on the collection.
3. *Levels of Control*. The concept of levels of control is not a theoretical principle, but rather a way of implementing provenance and original order in the management and processing of records. Perhaps best explained by Oliver Wendell Holmes, the concept recognizes that most modern archival work involves progressively grouping and describing sets of records along a continuum, going from the largest and most general to the smallest and most specific. Not all collections need to be arranged and described at the same level. The collection's size, research value, basic structure, and other factors will dictate the level to which it should be arranged and described. The various levels of control are:

a. *Collection Level*: Generally, small collections (collections consisting of two manuscript boxes or less), more than large ones, lend themselves to a single arrangement and only a collection-level description. Single items maintained as discrete collections, such as a diary, ledger book, scrapbook, etc., also should be described at only the collection level.

b. *Series Level*: A series consists of records which have been brought together in the course of their active life to form a discrete sequence. This sequence may be a discernable filing system (arranged alphabetically, chronologically, numerically, topically, or some combination of these) or it may be a grouping of records on the basis of similar function, content, or format. For collections with no apparent order or discernable former order, the archivist may create series based on the same considerations—chronology, topics, function, and record type. In any case, the series level is probably the most important one in arrangement because here the archivist expresses the character of the collection by the series into which it has been divided. For the most part, processing depends on establishing series for collections or uncovering the series that the records creator used. Moreover, the series cannot be isolated before the archivist has studied the entire collection. After the series have been established in a collection, the archivist then arranges the series by placing the most important one first, followed by the other series in descending order of importance. A series may also be divided into subseries based on form, record type, physical class of the records, or filing arrangement. See diagram at the end of this chapter for examples of subseries.

c. *File Unit Level*: A file unit is an aggregation of documents brought together, usually for convenience in filing, in such away that the documents may be treated as a unit. File units are often placed in chronological sequence when they document a regular activity, such as minutes of meetings. The order may be alphabetical when the units document programmemes, topics, organizations, or people; for example, case files arranged by the name of the client or correspondence arranged by the name of the individual to receive the letter. The arrangement of file units may also be by some internal classification system, usable only if the archivist can find a key or codebook to the system. Also remember that not only do the file units themselves have to be arranged according to some logical plan, but the individual documents within each unit must also be logically arranged.

d. *Item Level*: An item is a single document or manuscript within a collection. The smaller, or more important, or more disheveled the collection, the more likely is the archivist to work it item by item. Single items are placed together in file units. Generally, items in files have either a chronological or alphabetical arrangement. For example, if one has a series of correspondence, arranged alphabetically in file units by the name of the individual to whom the correspondence is addressed, then the letters in each file unit would probably be arranged in chronological order. While archivists sometimes have to handle and arrange every item in a collection, it is extremely rare that they describe a collection at the item level, unless the collection is very small or very important. Time constraints restrict the description of a collection at such a minute level.

The levels of control deal with the arranging, ordering, and describing of a collection. According to T. R. Schellenberg, archival processing "is largely a process of grouping individual documents into meaningful units and of grouping such units in a meaningful relation to one another." For a graphic look at a collection's organizational arrangement, see the following example provided by Dr. David Gracy, professor of archival enterprise at The University of Texas at Austin.

Accessioning

Incoming archives and manuscript collections are accessioned to obtain basic intellectual control over the material. The same process is followed for donated and purchased collections. Each addition to Special Collections should be accessioned as follows:

1. Enter the collection information in the Accession Log Book: record the arrival date; assign an accession number; write a brief description; list the name and address of donor; record the size of collection; and note location. If purchased, the amount paid should be entered in the Log Book.

Beginning with the year 2000 the accession number consists of four digits for the year of accession then a dash, followed by the consecutive number of the accession for that year. For example, the first collection accessioned in 2000 is recorded as 2000-1. This number serves as a location number until processing has been completed and a permanent collection number is assigned.

2. Complete the Accession Form as accessioning steps are being performed. As you fill out the Accession Form, the collection should be examined for preservation problems. Rehousing in acid-free folders may be performed for selected parts of the collection at this time. It is also necessary to record on the form, and perhaps a separate sheet of paper, pertinent facts about the collection and its creator to facilitate the writing of the collection-level description.

3. After the collection has been examined and the Accession Form completed, assign a level of processing number for the collection. See the appendices for a description of the assignment of levels of processing.
4. Create a holding file for the paper records for this accession and any correspondence pertinent to the acquisition. Use legal size acid-free folders with a one-third cut tab. A label with the collection name only should be typed for the folder.
5. Rehouse the collection in acid-free records centre boxes, or manuscript boxes, and shelve it with the unprocessed archives by accession number. Small manuscript collections may be housed in the Garrett Archives and assigned a GA number. A box by box inventory may be compiled at this time for large collections. This will be decided on a case by case basis.
6. Write a collection-level description for every new collection. It is useful to researchers and staff members for a quick overview of a collection. A copy of the description, prepared by the archivist who accessions the collection, is added to the holding file, to the *Guide Addenda* at the reference desk, and a copy is given to the *Guide* editor. The description will be updated by the processing archivist to include the final location number and information regarding material discovered during processing. The collection-level description is a one paragraph summary that includes:
   - o Accession number/location number (in bold).
   - o Name of person with birth and death dates or name of organization (in bold).
   - o Title (*i.e.*, papers, records, collection, etc.) with inclusive dates and bulk dates, if applicable.
   - o Number of boxes and amount of material in linear ft.; number of folders or for small collections number of items.
   - o Biographical or historical summary.
   - o Types of material (a list, not a sentence.)
   - o Scope and content statement, including major subjects with dates, if possible, and primary correspondents, if applicable.
   - o Restriction/preservation statement, if applicable.
   - o Acquisition statement and date of acquisition.
   - o Inventory/finding aid available, if applicable.
7. Each donation to Special Collections must have a signed Transfer of Title form and a completed Donor Record form. Send a thank you letter along with the Transfer of Title form to the donor for his signature, and the date, along with

a stamped self-addressed envelope. Upon its return to Special Collections, it is signed by a university representative, dated, and placed in the Transfer of Title holding file. A photocopy of the completed Transfer of Title will be sent to the donor.

The Donor Record is an in-house document, which must be co-signed by a designated individual from the Acquisitions and Cataloging Services Department of the UT Arlington Library and an archivist from Special Collections. The signed and dated Donor Record is then filed in the division's Donor Record holding file.

8. After a new collection is accessioned, the following details should be recorded on the shelflist: accession number/collection number; the collection name; the number and type of boxes; the size of the collection in linear feet, inches, or number of items; and the storage room and shelf location numbers if appropriate. This information is then recorded online in the Special Collections shelflist file. The shelflist file can also be used to locate empty spaces for storage of new collections. A paper copy, which is available at the reference desk, is updated monthly.

Arrangement

Arrangement is the process of organizing archival and manuscript material in accordance with accepted archival principles. The two basic principles are provenance and original order. Provenance means that records from one creator or one donor cannot be intermingled with records from another creator or donor even if the subject matter is the same. The principle of original order requires that materials in a collection be kept in their original order whenever possible. The order of the records reveals information about the creator of the collection and how the documents were used and about the relationships between the files themselves.

Arrangement of a collection consists of the following steps: research on the collection, survey of records pertaining to the collection, formulation of a processing plan, physical arrangement, processing and rehousing of materials, and labelling of file folders and boxes.

A. *Research:* Before work can begin on processing a collection, it is helpful to know as much as possible about the subject of that collection. If the collection consists of personal papers, try to obtain a biography of that person, find out the dates of important events in that person's life, or determine noteworthy activities the person was engaged in. If the collection consists of the records of an organization, obtaining information may be more difficult. Check the holdings of the library for a history of the organization or for oral history interviews with members of the corporate body. If the sources mentioned above are not available either for an individual or for an organization—which is frequently the case—information will have to be obtained from the collection itself. The types of documents that are particularly useful for this purpose are resumes, obituaries, newspaper clippings, diaries, correspondence, annual reports, minutes, and charters.

B. *Survey* : It is very important to examine all records pertaining to a collection before processing begins. The processor should first check the transfer of title to see whether any restrictions apply to the use of the collection. Correspondence in the holding file should be read to learn whether there are special instructions from the donor with regard to disposal of material in the collection (such as duplicates) or other matters. The Special Collections Guide, the Accession Log Book, and the donor file should also be consulted to find out whether other processed or unprocessed material has been received from the same donor or creator. Accession records will also provide information on the exact size of a collection so that no boxes will be overlooked when the collection is moved from the storage area to the processing area.

After this basic information has been obtained, the collection should be assigned the title, which is a combination of the creator's name plus one of the following terms: papers, records, or collection. Ordinarily collections are named for the person or organization that created the records, not for the donor. (For information on determining the correct form of the name, refer to the chapter on Cataloging.) The title of a collection is determined usually by the creator. For example, if the material was created by a person, the collection is titled "papers." If the material was created by an organization, the collection title is "records." If the material was artificially formed around a particular subject, person, or by a collector, the collection is titled "collection." If the entire collection is made up of only one document type, it can be titled more specifically, for example, "photographs," "minutes," and so forth. Following are a few examples of names and titles taken from the Special Collections Guide: Betty Andujar Papers, McKinney Family Papers, Texas AFL-CIO Records, Fort Worth Driving Club Records, Garry Mauro Christmas Card Collection, Rebel Theme Controversy Collection, W. A. Ransom Grade Books, and Lubbock Central Labour Council Minutes.

C. *Processing Plan* : With the preliminary work completed, the archivist is ready to devise a processing plan. (Archival students should submit a preliminary plan to their supervisor—see form at end of this chapter.) The first task is to obtain an overview of the collection. This is best done by setting the boxes on a table (or tables), opening each box, and quickly examining the contents of each box. If a careful box-by-box contents list was prepared at the time the collection was accessioned, an intellectual grasp of the contents can be obtained by a perusal of the written list. Scanning the actual contents of a collection, however, accomplishes several purposes. It helps the archivist to become more familiar with the collection and to note either mentally or on paper the logical sequence of the records and eventually to work out a plan for arranging the material. It also provides the archivist with many clues as to the task that lies ahead: Are file folders neatly arranged, are they poorly arranged, or are there no file folders? Do the folders have labels? Do folder titles actually reflect the contents? Are the papers in the folders in order? Are they folded? Are there few or many newspaper clippings, reels of film, photographs or fragile documents or artifacts that will require special attention? Is there any evidence of mildew, insect or rodent damage? Are there oversize documents, government documents, books, or other materials in the collection that may have to be handled separately or transferred to other areas of the library? Although these problems will be addressed later by the processor (and are discussed more fully in the sections on description and preservation), they are nonetheless considerations that must be factored into the final decision on how the collection is to be arranged.

D. *Physical Arrangement* : The primary task of the processor is to discover the creator's file order and to insure that it is systematically implemented. It bears repeating that a basic rule of archival management is that ideally the original order of the materials in a collection should not be altered or should be altered as little as possible. All too frequently, however, collections do not arrive in good order or sometimes have no order whatsoever. In these instances, the archivist has to impose order on the materials so that they will be easily accessible to the researcher.

There are four basic methods of arranging archival and manuscript collections: alphabetically by topic, in series by document type, chronologically, or in series by function of the creator. The arrangement of a collection will be determined largely by the size and content of the collection. For example, the file folders in a small collection (two or three manuscript boxes) might be arranged alphabetically by subject.

If a collection contains only one or two types of material, it might be preferable to arrange the collection into document types, such as correspondence, minutes, and financial records and thereunder chronologically. Some collections, such as the papers of legislators, lend themselves to chronological arrangement because the activities of the creator of the records are centred around specific time periods (*i.e.* terms in office).

Very large collections also can be made more manageable if the records are arranged in series, which in turn are arranged chronologically, alphabetically, or by order of importance. Arrangement of records by function of the creator groups together documents that relate to a specific activity of the creator.

Collections that are moderate to large in size (five or more manuscript boxes) are usually made more manageable by dividing the materials into series. For example, the papers of an individual might require a separate series for personal records, business records, and political records.

The records of an organization might be divided into the different components of that organization, such as Department of Equal Opportunity, Education Department, Public Relations Department. If a particular document type dominates the collection, the series could be formed around those record types, such as correspondence, financial records, minutes, personnel applications, grievances, etc.

It is virtually impossible to make a general statement on how a collection should be arranged because each collection is unique, and each one has to be evaluated on its own characteristics. After the basic principles governing provenance and original order have been taken into consideration, the primary objective of the archivist should be to arrange the material in the most user-friendly manner possible. Material should be arranged so logically that the researcher can quickly find needed information.

E. *Processing, Rehousing, and Labelling:* When the plan for arranging a collection has been determined, the task of processing can begin. At this stage the processor works with one file folder at a time.

Careful attention should be given to the physical condition of the documents.

For example:

1. Remove paper clips and rubber bands.
2. Replace rusted staples with rust proof staples, if necessary. Remove excess staples and replace with one staple only.
3. If necessary, remove metal spirals from notebooks or remove pages and discard notebook cover and spirals. Photocopy cover onto acid-free paper if it contains needed information.
4. Flatten folded documents. If a document is too large for a legal-size folder and too valuable to remain folded, transfer to an oversize box.
5. Place photographs and negatives in polyester or polypropylene sleeves or in acid-free envelopes.
6. Place a sheet of bond paper on each side of documents on coloured paper (such as labour union handbills or yellow carbon copies) to prevent staining of adjacent documents.
7. Encapsulate fragile documents or place in polyester sleeves.

8. Trim newspaper clippings and photocopy them onto acid-free paper. Discard the original clipping.

This is also the time to discard duplicates and to decide whether those records with little value should be retained. Envelopes are often discarded as well (especially from voluminous 20th century collections), although some archivists prefer to file them with their related correspondence. Other documents that should be removed from the collection at this time are copies of periodicals or newspapers that are available elsewhere in the library and federal or state documents that should be transferred to the government publications department.

When all of these concerns have been taken care of, arrange the contents of each folder in numerical, alphabetical or chronological order as appropriate. If material is placed in chronological order, undated material should be placed after dated material. Then transfer the contents of the folders to new, acid-free folders and label each folder. Write the headings on each folder with a No. 2 pencil, including the following information: collection, series, box, and folder numbers and folder title and dates. Note that if there is more than one series in a box the folder numbers do not start over with the new series, but continue in numerical order. Also folder numbers start over with number 1 in each new box, even if the series continues from the previous box.

See the front of the accession log for the next collection number. Record this number on the accession form, in the log, on all pertinent records, and on each folder in the collection. Ideally, no more than 50 sheets or 10 photographs should be put in a file folder. If necessary, divide the contents and place the material in additional folders, using the same heading for each folder. The folders can now be transferred from record centre storage boxes to acid-free, lignin-free manuscript boxes. They should be arranged in their prescribed order and placed snugly in the manuscript box. Folders should not be stuffed into the box so that they are difficult to remove, nor should they be so loosely packed that in time the material will slump and bend. At this time the archivist may begin writing the container list.

Temporary labels can be clipped to each manuscript box after it is filled, but later when the processing has been completed and the finding aid written, permanent labels should be typed and affixed to each box. These labels should include the collection number, collection name, and box number. If the collection, or a portion of it, is housed in an oversize box, the box label should indicate the oversize box number, the collection name, and the collection number.

By the time the finding aid is completed, the archivist will have worked with the material in each folder in the collection several times. It is a good idea to develop the habit of taking notes on the collection during the course of these processing procedures. The notes will be useful to the archivist later when preparing the description of the collection. They should include information on the earliest and latest dates of the records in the collection, on each series within the collection, dates of and facts about important events, the purpose and history of an organization, biographical information, a record of name changes (of an organization), and when the changes occurred, and any other information about the collection that would be helpful to the researcher and to the cataloguer.

Preservation

Preservation is an ongoing activity, performed in the course of accessioning and arranging a collection, or even after arrangement is completed. Most archivists define preservation as the actions taken to stop, prevent, or retard deterioration of archival and manuscript materials as well as improve the condition or change the format to preserve the intellectual content.

Preservation is very time consuming. The sheer bulk of modern records justifies a hard look at the amount of preservation work to be done for each collection. A processor will not do elaborate preservation work. The division's policy is to keep work to a minimum and focus efforts on preserving the information value of records rather than preserving documents as artifacts.

Custom housings or extensive repairs should only be undertaken for special items by a trained staff member or outside conservator. The following procedures are undertaken to insure the proper housing and preservation of a manuscript or archival collection.

A. *Housing the Collection:* Transfer all material to acid-free, lignin-free folders and boxes. All folders should be the same size as the box. To accommodate the most common sizes of paper, store documents in legal size folders in legal size boxes. If every item in a collection is letter size, letter-size folders and boxes may be used. Unfold any documents that have previously been stored folded or rolled. If a specific item is too large for a legal-size folder, place a "document removed" form in its place and transfer it to a folder in GO (Garrett Oversize in Bay D). Size the folder to the drawer, not to the item to keep it from shifting in the drawer. If several items from a collection need oversize storage, insert "document removed" forms in the appropriate original locations and put everything in an acid-free, lignin-free flat oversize box. Do not, however, store bulky items with papers or photographs. Use a box that will accommodate the largest document. Cut folders the size of the box, even though items going into the box will be smaller. Separate the oversize box from the collection and place it in the shelving area reserved especially for oversize box storage when processing is completed. A unique box number is assigned to all oversize boxes.

Materials transferred to an oversize box should be listed on the inventory in a separate series with the oversize box numbers noted. If materials in oversize boxes were never part of another series, then "document removed" forms are unnecessary.

Folders are designed to house from one to fifty or more items. How many documents are stored in a folder is a matter of judgment and depends on their age and importance. Folders that house very old manuscripts have as little as one or as many as fifteen documents. Archival collection folders will accommodate up to one-half inch of material comfortably. More than a half inch of documents is unwieldy and in time possibly damaging to the contents of the folder. Crease the folder along the proper scoring line according to the bulk of the contents so that the folder rests on its flat edge in the document box. A folder with only a few items need not be creased. Use your judgment.

Document boxes should not be overfilled so that the box bulges and files are difficult to retrieve. However, neither should a box be under filled so that the contents buckle or slump. Use a half-size document box for small collections or for housing materials of less than two and a half inches in bulk at the end of a collection. If a standard five-inch box must be under filled (in GA for example), crease and insert an acid-free document box spacer (found in the archival supply shelving area) behind the folders to fill up the extra space or until another collection is placed in that box.

B. *Contaminants :* Collections are usually received with one or more types of contaminants attached to some of the papers. Rubber bands, ribbon, twine, and plastic folders should be removed from the materials. Metal paper clips, brads, rusty staples, metal spirals in notebooks, fasteners of any type, or metal straps which rust and damage paper should be removed. A wire cutter is useful in cutting the spirals from notebooks. Put notebook contents in a folder and discard any blank pages. Note number of pages discarded. Metal fasteners may be replaced with plastic coated paper clips or stainless steel staples. A safer alternative is to place previously fastened pages loose in a separate file folder, or in a folder with other items but separated by a sheet of acid-free paper on each side. A note can be written in pencil on the top sheet to describe the content or number of pages that were originally fastened.

In very large archival or manuscript collections, staples, which are not rusting do not have to be removed. Staples do not rust as quickly as paper clips, and they can be replaced if or when time allows with stainless steel staples.

Cellophane tape, masking tape, and rubber cement or glue cause great damage to documents. They discolour with age and leave permanent stains. Removal from documents is difficult and time consuming and should not be attempted by a staff member without expertise or without consultation with a trained conservator. If the document is old or valuable, it might be worthwhile to attempt tape removal. Otherwise it is best to leave the item alone, isolate it, or construct custom housing for it to avoid causing more damage, which may result from the attempt to repair it.

Avoid the use of Post-it notes on any item of known permanent value, such as material entrusted to archival care. Aging tests indicate that the note's colour tends to transfer to the sheets on which the notes are affixed. Adhesive residue from the note may remain on the sheet after the note is removed. Attempts to rub off the residue will do more harm than good, as the adhesive becomes further embedded in the substance to which it has been attached. Use of these self-stick notes should be limited to non-valuable, non-archival materials. Strips of acid-free paper may be used in place of Post-it notes for most archival processing needs.

C. *Paper :* Newsprint, manila paper, and construction paper are extremely acidic. They darken with age, become brittle, and stain any papers with which they come in contact. Documents printed or written on highly acidic paper include newspaper clippings, telegrams, carbons, copies on thermofax paper, and school writing tablets.

Text on highly acidic paper should be photocopied onto acid-free paper. However, quantities of newspaper clippings of secondary importance, for example, would be too time-consuming to photocopy. Separate the clippings from other paper documents into their own folders. Photocopy any item that is badly deteriorated or on poor quality paper. Letter size, legal size, and oversize acid-free paper is available. Discard the original item unless it has value as an artifact, for exhibition, or is handwritten. Such items are encapsulated in mylar with a sheet of acid-free paper as a neutralizing backing. Sometimes a photocopy of a brittle encapsulated item is also made and researchers are encouraged to use it instead of the original.

D. *Oversize Material:* Oversize documents and other items (above 8 1/2" x 14") will not fit into a legal-size document box when unfolded or encapsulated. Examples are legal or financial documents, muster rolls, certificates, diagrams, photographs, scrapbooks, albums, posters, galley sheets, etc. Items in this category are stored flat in large flat, acid-free, lignin-free document boxes or in an acid-free folder sized to fit the box or oversize drawer. Smaller bound volumes such as diaries, journals, albums, scrapbooks, etc., which are no more than a half inch thick can be stored in an acid-free folder or envelope. It is acceptable to store such items spine down in document boxes without folders if necessary. They may be wrapped individually in mylar or acid-free paper depending on condition. A label can be attached to the mylar or paper covering. Oversize bound volumes are not usually stored in a box with other documents or photographs. If they are heavy enough to shift, they will cause damage to the other items. Old volumes with leather bindings should be wrapped in acid-free paper, spun polyester, or mylar and boxed together if the bindings have red rot.

E. *Photographs, Audio Tapes, and Films :* Photographs mounted on acidic pages of an old album or scrapbook present a special problem. Each album and its contents must be evaluated individually. Albums of this type can be photographed or photocopied page by page to maintain a record of the original historical arrangement and descriptions. The photos can then be removed and stored in separate folders or envelopes. Often the best solution is to interleave the pages with acid-free paper between the pages to neutralize the harmful effects of the original pages and keep the item intact. If the album cannot accommodate the bulk added by protective sheets, disbinding may be required. Loose sheets can then be boxed.

Photographs, oral history tapes, films, video tapes, and artifacts should be separated from the paper part of the collection and stored in separate folders, series, or document boxes so that their unique formats may be accommodated. Photographs 8" x 10" and under can be stored either in archival folders interleaved with acid-free paper (non-buffered if they are colour or albumen prints), in acid-free envelopes, in albums, or in mylar or polypropylene sleeves or pages designed for storage of photographs. Rolled photographs may be stored rolled if absolutely necessary or may be humidified, flattened, and wrapped with an acid-free board support for storage. Negatives and photographs are never stored in the same envelope, sleeve, or folder although they can be stored in the same box.

Slides and photographic negatives should be housed in archival slide and film protectors designed for the individual size and format. Photographs over 8" x 10" and mounted photographs must be stored flat in oversize boxes. Cased photographs, such as tintypes, daguerreotypes, or glass negatives, need custom containers to protect them. Such containers can be made or purchased. They may be protected by wrapping them in tissue paper and storing them horizontally in flat storage document boxes. Microfilm storage boxes are also useful for smaller cased photographs.

When housing a large collection of photographs, put no more than ten photographs or approximately a quarter inch in each folder. This is a general rule of thumb adhered to by most photographic archivists. Interleaving the prints with acid-free paper is optional. However, if the prints are on acidic board, have clippings attached to the verso, or if any kind of transferable marker or ink was used by the original owners to write identifications, acid-free paper should be considered to protect adjacent prints. Fragile prints should be stored in sleeves and filed singly in folders. Very fragile prints should be stored flat with a piece of supporting mat board and a Mylar enclosure. Consider the value of the material. The more valuable or unique it is, the more carefully it should be housed.

Photographs stored vertically must be stored in full boxes or in polypropylene pages in a firm notebook to retard curling. Never affix a gummed label on the front or back of a photo. Information about a photo is placed on its verso in pencil and only along its border. Information can be written on a piece of interleaving paper placed behind the photo or on the envelope or folder in which it is stored. Excessive photocopying of photographic prints of any kind should be avoided. Copy prints should be made of frequently photocopied photographic materials.

F. *Basic Techniques for Repairing Documents:* Simple repairs and conservation steps are undertaken on manuscript and archival materials keeping in mind that any repair should be durable, reversible, but harmless to the item being treated. Consultation with specific staff members in the Preservation Department or with a professional conservator is advised for complicated preservation or storage problems. Learn to distinguish between repairs that you are capable of doing with the equipment on hand and that which is best left to the experts!

1. To remove staples use a microspatula, especially on old manuscript materials. Bend up the prongs on the verso of the paper group, then lift off the top of the staple at the front of the document with the microspatula. Staple removers on modern documents in good condition are acceptable if done carefully.
2. To clean soiled documents, use the powder from a document cleaning pad or cleaning powder. Rub the powder gently in a circular motion with your fingertips. Brush dirt into a waste container. A soft eraser may be used for stray marks. Do not use cleaning powder on documents written in pencil or on chalk drawings. This technique is primarily for soiled printed materials.
3. To flatten curled documents or photographs, place them on the rack in the humidifier. Be sure that there is fresh, warm water in the container beneath the rack. Close the lid tightly. Let your document remain in the humidifier for several hours or overnight. Remove documents and place them between sheets of blotter paper under the heavy boards of the flattening table. Leave overnight to dry. Let the blotter paper dry between uses. Thin soft items will take only a few hours to humidify whereas heavy, rolled materials may take a few days. Check your document each day that it is being humidified. Over humidified documents sag and do damage to themselves and other items in the humidifier from being exposed to too much humidity for too long.

4. Before washing any document, clean the surface first to remove any loose dirt. Gently test a small area of each colour of ink for solubility with a Q-tip dipped in water. If any colour lifts off the item, it should not be washed. Wash documents in a shallow amount of cool, clean water in a flat photo tray. Put a sheet of screening or woven polyester in the bottom of the tray and on top of the item to support the wet document. Allow it to soak for approximately 30 minutes. Check frequently.

   When the tape or glue is loose, gently remove it with your finger. Remove the document from the tray by lifting the item sandwiched between the screening or polyester and allow it to drip dry for several minutes. Blot excess water between two sheets of blotter paper, then place it between two dry blotters and flatten it. Do not wash documents that have water soluble inks, watercolours, or chalk. Wash items to remove oils, water soluble dirt, glue, stains, or tape and to flatten very wrinkled or creased, brittle paper. Don't take a chance with precious, valuable, irreplaceable documents. There are other washing methods that use specific chemicals that only a trained conservator should attempt. If in doubt, leave it alone!

5. To remove scotch, cellophane, or masking tape from an item, without washing it use a small scalpel or microspatula and 200 proof alcohol. Blot the tape on the verso of the item with 200 proof alcohol, let it sit a few minutes to loosen and carefully remove the tape. Use an eraser or a tacky remover to remove the residual adhesive. This procedure is extremely time consuming and can be tricky. Do it only if the tape seems newly attached and easy to remove. Don't remove tape on a dirty item using this method, because the liquid will leave tide marks (wavy dark water lines.) It is beneficial to clean or wash the item first. Test the ink beforehand as in the instructions above. Consult recommended sources before attempting washing or tape removal.

6. To flatten creased or wrinkled materials, spray the verso with a light spray of water and dry between sheets of blotter paper under weights. If the item is delicate or a photograph, spray the blotter paper that will be in contact with the unprinted verso and flatten.

7. To mend tears in documents, use document repair tape on the reverse side of the document and only along tears that have no writing or printing if possible. Japanese mending tissue and rice paste or methyl cellulose glue are used to mend older manuscripts. Photographs can also be mended using Japanese mending tissue or document repair tape on the reverse side.

8. Encapsulation is used to protect brittle, torn, or fragile but frequently used items. To encapsulate a document, cut a piece of 3 mil mylar at least one inch larger than the document on all sides. Lay one sheet of mylar on a clean surface. Clean the mylar with a soft cloth to remove dust and create a static charge. Place the document at the centre of the mylar and use a soft weight on the document to keep it from shifting. Place a strip of 1/4" 3M encapsulation tape along each side of the document approx. 1/8" from the item leaving a gap at the corners. Place the second sheet of mylar on top of the document as you remove the weight. Place the weight on top of the three items and clean the top sheet of mylar with a soft cloth. Reach under each edge in turn and remove the protective paper from the tape, letting the mylar fall quickly in place to seal. Press out the air after removing each piece of tape with a squeegee or cloth to create more static and clean any dust off the mylar. Trim the borders to 1/4" and round the corners.
9. We do not have the facilities or chemicals to deacidify documents. At best highly acidic items should be encapsulated with a piece of acid-free, buffered paper backing.
10. To kill mold, put the document in the sun for several hours. When mold is dry, brush or vacuum it off. Do this outdoors and use a protective facemask and gloves. Mold is dangerous to handle and can cause health problems for anyone who handles infected items. Isolation of the item from other library materials is necessary until a decision is made to reproduce the item and discard it. To remove a moldy odour, place a document in a plastic garbage bag with a small box of charcoal briquettes. Seal the bag and leave it for a week. Consult reference materials at the end of this section for more detail on handling various types of mold infected documents.

Fill out the division's Conservation/Preservation Form when repairs are complicated or beyond your knowledge or experience. The form should be given to the staff archivist responsible for basic book and paper repairs and custom housing for archival and manuscript material. The repairs will be completed as time allows. Contact the archivist personally for rush jobs and explain the problem. If it is beyond the archivist's expertise and the repair is necessary, the item will be referred to an outside conservator. A sample copy of the form is at the end of this chapter.

For greater detail and more information on specific preservation techniques, consult the recommended works listed below. The above methods are intended to serve only as an introduction to the basic preservation techniques used in the division. What you do depends on your training and the value of the material. Workshops in basic preservation techniques are offered by AMIGOS Library Services, SAA, and SSA and are a valuable experience. They not only teach repair techniques, but also teach what not to do and when to ask for help.

Description

The finding aid is compiled specifically to describe the arrangement and contents of a collection and to comment on its research potential. It serves the researcher seeking information about a person, family, or corporate body; serves the staff in locating desired materials; and serves the donor as a record of material deposited. The finding aid should be written in clear, concise language, in a tone free of value judgments, personal bias, or professional jargon.

Use Microsoft Word 2000, 12 point Times New Roman font, in creating the finding aid and all related documents. The preferred page setup is one inch margins all around. If the finding aid is compiled in two separate files, title page through note to researcher in one file and the container list in another file, headers are then easier to insert and revise in the container list. *Do not change the Word filename extensions from the default. All Word documents should have the.doc extension.* The standard finding aid includes the following parts:

Title page Table of Contents (optional) Biographical/Historical Sketch Series Description (optional) Scope and Content Note Provenance Restrictions (optional) Literary Rights Statement Note to the Researcher (optional) Container List Materials Removed List (optional) Appendices (optional) Index (optional)

Each part will be discussed separately accompanied by brief examples. Sample finding aids are included in the appendices.

A. *Title Page the Title Page should Include:* Name and dates of the collection Amount of material in linear ft. Restrictions if any Collection Number Name of processor Date of preparation of finding aid Citation Libraries identification
B. *Table of Contents:* If a finding aid is more than twelve pages or has several series, a table of contents may be included for easy access. Add series and subseries titles to the title page.
C. *Biographical or Historical Sketch;* The purpose of the sketch or history is to give the researcher a brief, general introduction to the person or organization that created the collection. Prepare a sketch or history in narrative form that highlights major events in the past of the person or organization primarily during the period represented by the collection. The description may include limited background data. If more than one person or organization is very important to the collection, prepare a short biography or history for them also.

Write your text in clear, concise language including accurate data. Your text may range anywhere from two paragraphs to two pages at most.

Books or useful articles by or about the person or organization, which would be useful to the researcher, should be listed in bibliographic format and follow the narrative.

Consult *The Chicago Manual of Style* or Kate Turabian's *A Manual for Writers of Term Papers, Theses, and Dissertations* for the standard style of entry. If more than a few items are listed, they may be placed on a separate page.

D. *Series Description:* The series description introduces the arrangement of the collection and provides a concise statement of the files within each series. The series description should include the following elements in this order: title, inclusive and bulk dates, quantity in linear feet with number of boxes or folders, arrangement, and a very brief summary of contents or principal subjects. Series should be listed in order of importance, if possible, otherwise alphabetically. A series description is optional, depending on the size of the collection and number of series. Bold the series title headings as shown below. Subseries, if they exist, can be described within the series description, such as when financial records are divided into subseries by record type.

E. *Scope and Content Note:* The scope and content note is an expanded version of the series description and briefly describes the content of the collection but with sufficient detail to provide the researcher with a good understanding of the collection's general characteristics, strengths, and weaknesses or gaps. It also may include a statement regarding the original condition of the collection, a summary of the archivist's processing and preservation decisions, and the amount and types of materials that were removed from the collection.

Describe in essay form and at a minimum note the document types and/or subjects represented with inclusive dates, the extent of the materials, primary correspondents, and significant or unusual items. Describe these major elements in the order in which the materials are physically arranged. Information regarding significant aspects of a person's or organization's past should be related to the description of the papers or records. The scope and content note is the archivist's opportunity to relate the collection and its relevance to the creator and, if possible, to the events at the time of its creation.

Summarize the research value of the collection and point out important gaps. One or two pages are usually sufficient.

F. *Provenance Statement:* The provenance statement describes how, from whom, and when the collection or materials were acquired. This information may be found in the manuscripts holding file documented in correspondence and recorded on the Accession Form. Include the original accession number or numbers.

G. *Restrictions:* If the donor or the library has restricted access to all or part of a collection, the specific terms of the agreement should be described clearly here. Check both the holding file and the Transfer of Title for the statement of restrictions if any.

Material may be withheld from use for a variety of reasons. In addition to the donor's restrictions, the archivist, during processing, may find material that would be damaging to the creator or to others mentioned in the collection. Be especially alert for sensitive information about persons other than the donor, for correspondence or reports that are marked confidential or seem to have been written with the understanding they would be kept confidential, especially if written by someone other than the donor.

Procedures for protecting restricted materials:

1. Organize the restricted material along with the other material.
2. If a single item or folder is being restricted, put it in an envelope, seal it, and add a label with the terms of the restriction on it. If the entire folder is being restricted, write the folder title, dates, box number and folder number on the envelope as well. Put a red dot on the envelope and on the box that the folder is in.
3. If an entire box is being restricted, seal it shut with a label that describes the terms of the restriction. Put a red dot on the box.

H. *Literary Rights Statement:* Include a statement indicating where a researcher should obtain permission to publish materials from the collection. If the donor did not sign the literary rights over to the university, then he/she should be contacted for permission. The usual statement follows.

I. *Note to the Researcher:* Add a note with any other pertinent information such as cross references to other collections in the Division, special handling or preservation problems, or any special instructions to alert the researcher that something about this collection is unusual.

J. *Container List:* Prepare a list of the folder titles that were created or determined during the arrangement of the collection. The heading at the top of each page of the container list should include the collection number, collection title, colon, and the words "Container List" (on the top line in boldface type and in caps), double space and follow it by the series title (in bold) if there is one. Use the header feature in Word rather than manually inputting these titles on each page. Changes and additions to the text will be easier to manage. An additional heading at the top of each page should include the box number (underlined), and below the box number the folder, title, dates, and description headings (underlined). A page number should be inserted on the bottom centre of each page except the title page. See the heading example at the bottom of this page and complete finding aid examples in the appendices.

K. *Materials Removed List:* Compile a list of books, periodicals, graphics, broadsides, pamphlets, maps, and art objects, etc., (in bibliographic format) that were removed from the collection to be catalogued for a different location within the Special Collections Division. Do not include items removed to oversize locations, but do include items, which because of their format, will be accessed easier if they are catalogued individually. Place the list at the end of the finding aid. A description of materials removed from the collection and returned to the donor, transferred to the Central Library, or deaccessioned should be prepared and filed in the holding file.

L. *Appendices:* Include any information (if readily available) that would be useful to researchers such as family trees, organization charts, lists of awards, chronologies, a map showing routes travelled, a photograph (photocopy), etc.

M. *Index:* If the container list is large and particular information would be difficult to find, create an alphabetical index listing names, subjects, titles, and formats.

N. *Guide Entry:* Write a guide entry for the collection after the finding aid has been completed. The guide entry is basically a revision of the collection-level description described. The accession number is changed to the permanent collection number. One or all of the elements of the collection-level description may need to be revised. A statement regarding the availability of a finding aid should be added. Depending on the collection, a restriction/preservation statement may or may not be needed. However, the format remains the same.

The Guide entry does not become a part of the finding aid. File a copy of the guide entry in the collection's holding file, add a copy to the *Guide Addenda*, and give a copy to the *Guide* editor. Also, send an electronic copy of the entry to the LAII who will revise the minimal level description that is in the UT Arlington Library Catalogue. See the example at the end of this chapter. Use Microsoft Word 2000, Times New Roman font, 12 point, for the text.

Review and Final Steps

A copy of the finding aid may be circulated to each archivist for review or an e-mail message may be sent to the staff announcing the completion of the finding aid. The purpose of the review process is to maintain conformity to standards, catch typing errors, factual errors, and omissions. Style is generally a matter of individual preference and should be determined by the finding aid compiler. The review is also a process for informing co-workers about collections now open and available for research. It gives the archivist an opportunity to receive feedback before the finding aid is finalized.

Archival students should save the finding aid to a 3 1/2" high density disk. Label the disk with the collection number and name, the word processing software name, the version used, the date created, and each file name. An example would be: AR317 Basil Clemons Microsoft Word 2000, June 2000. Finding aid, press release, cataloging worksheet, and guide entry The archivist that receives the disk will save the finding aid to the Q drive under SPCO, Finding Aids, and then file the disk in the collection's holding file. Make two or three copies of the finding aid and velobind them. Place a copy in the collection's holding file, a copy (in a labelled folder) in the file cabinet in the reference area, and send a letter and a copy to the donor, if applicable. Update the accession log and accession form with the new location/collection number(s). Create the box labels and shelve the collection. Delete the title from the unprocessed collections shelflist and add the new finding aid title to the Finding Aids Tracker database. This database is an in-house ACCESS document on which are maintained a list of completed finding aids and a shelflist of unprocessed collections.

OCLC Cataloging Worksheet Instructions

The "Archives and Manuscripts Cataloging Worksheet" should be filled out by the processor during the writing of the finding aid to a collection or shortly thereafter. However, completing the worksheet as the finding aid is compiled allows one to pull and photocopy pertinent information as work on the collection progresses. Limit descriptions and subject headings to the most important. Subject headings are used to identify pertinent material in a collection and to enable the researcher to find related material.

A character limit for each OCLC record requires that the record be concise. Give the completed worksheet to the librarian with the responsibility for archival and manuscript cataloging. The information provided about the processed collection will enable the cataloging librarian to prepare the MARC record for OCLC and Voyager in the shortest possible time.

OCLC and Voyager records are additional finding aids that provide local and remote access to primary sources in the Special Collections Division. A copy of the worksheet follows this explanation.

A. Collection Name (a main entry and a title)

1. The main entry is the name of the primary person, family, or corporate body responsible for creating or collecting and maintaining a body of materials

over a period of time. A main entry can be an individual, family, organization, labour union, school or university, association, government, business firm, church, or a sports team to name a few. Only one name can be entered as the main entry; if there is more than one creator, enter the most important one here. Other names can be noted in the historical information, the description, and with the subject headings.

2. The name chosen should be the most commonly used form of the name. Note also other forms of the name if used by an individual, *i.e.*, formal name, nicknames, etc., in the space provided. The additional forms of the name are used for cross-references and to establish the authority record if there is none. For example: James Earl Carter is known as Jimmy Carter. His papers would be the Jimmy Carter Papers.
3. Supply birth and death dates if known.
4. If an organization's records reveal various name changes, the latest form of the name should be used unless there are very few items in the collection with that name. Attach a photocopy of the organization's letterhead or if not available, a photocopy of another item with the official name to the worksheet. If possible, provide the cataloguer with the various name changes or different forms of the main entry that appear in the collection with the dates when they were used.
5. Use the form of the materials as the title following the main entry. Papers, records, or collection are the most commonly used titles, but photographs, correspondence, diaries, journals, etc., may be used if the entire collection is composed of a single document type. If the collection was created by two persons and no one person can be identified as more prominent or predominating, both names can be entered under the title and there would be no main entry. Descriptive titles may be used if applicable.

Examples: Trussell Family Papers Berachah Home Collection George W. Armstrong Papers Rebel Theme Controversy Collection University of Texas at Arlington, Office of the President Records Texas AFL-CIO Records Longshoreman's Association, Local 851 Minutes Progressive Party Photographs and Recordings Collection Amalgated Transit Union, Local 694 Records Walter Prescott Webb Collection Fowler-Rowland-Steward Family Photographs John and Ann Vanderlee Collection

B. *Dates* :Supply inclusive dates; the earliest and latest dates taken from the items in a collection. If dates are scattered in the collection, but most of the materials are grouped within a limited date range, supply these dates as well. For example, 1903-1949 (bulk 1929-1945). Do not use the dates of transcribed documents or dates recorded on research notes as dates pertaining to the collection unless the actual documents or photocopies of the documents are in the collection. Use ca. or c. for circa dates example: ca. 1910 or c. 1910.

C. *Biographical / Historical Information:* Summarize the biographical/historical sketch written for the finding aid, reducing it to four sentences or less. Identify a person's major occupation or accomplishments and place of primary activity. Family relationships may be included. This note may be omitted or very brief for very well known people. Provide an organization's incorporation date and ending date if it no longer exists, name or describe founders, list name changes and dates, major function, and location.

Examples: The Austin Labour Temple was established December 21, 1922, in Austin, Texas. The Association was composed of individuals and representatives of local unions united for the purpose of erecting and operating a building to be used as a meeting place for its members. The original building was in use from 1923 until 1959, when the structure was sold and razed.

Graves, a resident of Collin County, Texas, was a second lieutenant in Captain J. W. Throckmorton's Company K, Sixth Texas Cavalry, Ross' Texas Brigade, during the Civil War.

The Francois Santerre family emigrated from France in 1856 to join La Reunion Colony, a socialist experiment founded in 1855 by the Societe de Colonisation Europeo-Americaine. The colony, located a few miles west of Dallas, Texas, dissolved after only two years, but several families, including the Santerres, remained at the site or in the area.

D. *Description:* Condense the information from the scope and content note of the finding aid for this section. Summarize the document types first, in order of importance. Then give a summary statement regarding the contents of the collection. Major or well-known correspondents or other persons responsible for producing the materials should be noted. Records from other organizations or additional subjects that are noteworthy or abundant as well as unusual items should also be noted. Major correspondents, organizations, and subjects described in this section will also be listed on the verso of the cataloging worksheet in the appropriate section. Do not list any name or organization on the verso if it is not mentioned in the description.

Examples: Correspondence, financial documents, legal documents, clippings, constitution, and printed material. Texas AFL-CIO office files that contain the correspondence of the president, Hank Brown, and members of the executive board. Correspondents include Jim Wright and Ralph Yarborough. Also includes legal records of the Texas State Federation of Labour, 1952-1956, and material on right-to-work laws.

Correspondence and financial documents. Records relate to the supply and maintenance of Fort Ewell and Fort Merrill. Typescript transcription. Lieutenant Graves' diary describes his military training and the company's movements through Texas, Arkansas, and Mississippi. It also describes Graves' wounding at Corinth, Mississippi, and his experiences after being taken prisoner. Included is a muster roll of Company K.

E. *Subject headings (people / organizations):* Enter names of the creators, frequent or well-known correspondents, names of individuals and organizations who are the subject of a significant amount of correspondence or a significant amount of research. To provide verification of each organization or corporate name listed, attach a photocopy of a letterhead or another official document representing each name change.

F. *Subject headings (topics):* Limit choices to major themes reflected in the collection. Do not include a subject heading for everything or everybody in the collection. Avoid dead ends. It should be obvious from the finding aid where the information referred to in the subject entries can be found. Topical subject headings include geographical place names, historic events, occupations, and general terms. See the attached list of Library of Congress subject headings used frequently in Special Collections.

G. *Size of the Record:* List subjects in order of importance. Usually a maximum of approximately fifteen subjects (topical and people/organizations) is the most that will fit on the record. OCLC has a size limit per record. In the MARC format most variable fields also have a size limit. These limits vary from time to time and cannot be stated here definitively. Therefore, the more concise the Biographical/Historical Information and Description sections are, the more subject headings can be included in the record.

Publicity and News Releases

Preparing news releases about new acquisitions and recently processed collections is an important part of the archival enterprise. Once a significant collection has been acquired and accessioned, the archivist will want to write a general news release about the acquisition. The decision to write a release should be made on a collection-by-collection basis. Not all collections merit releases. The release should be relatively brief (no more than three pages double-spaced or two pages single-spaced) and include the following information:

A. Releases for New Acquisitions

Name of the Collection

Information about the collection, including size, bulk dates, items or series of particular interest, and strengths of the collection (be truthful; do not exaggerate)

Name of the Donor (if applicable) and When it was Donated

Reason why the donor chose Special Collections; provide a quote from the donor if possible or a quote from the Assistant Director for Special Collections or the archivist handling the collection. Information on whether the collection is open or closed until it is processed; if the latter, give an estimate on when processing may be completed (if possible)

Information on Whom to Contact about the Collection; Include Complete Name, Address, Fax and Telephone Numbers

Once the release has been written, double-check it for any grammatical and factual errors. If appropriate, have the donor review and revise the release before it is mailed to ensure that all of the information is correct. After this is done, send the release to the addresses in the division's news release database and make sure a copy is sent to the university's News Service. Also, target other publications for releases, such as scholarly journals and organizational newsletters specializing in subjects covered by the collection. This will require some research, but it is well worth it. Ask the donor for appropriate addresses too. Often the donor is your best source for specialized addresses. Make sure a copy of the news release is placed in the collection holding file for possible future reference. It is not to be included in the finding aid.

B. *Releases for Newly Opened Collections:* A news release should also be written when important collections are processed and open for research. As mentioned above, the decision to write a release should be made on an individual basis. The more significant and important a collection, the more likely a release should be written and distributed. The release should follow basically the same format and include much of the same information as outlined above. The release for a processed collection, however, may be slightly longer than one for a new acquisition because the collection is more familiar.

The archivist distributing the release should keep the considerations discussed above in mind when identifying and targeting media and scholarly channels for it. Also, consider mailing releases at a time when the collection relates to a particular holiday or celebration. For example, send releases about a labour collection near Labour Day; mail one about an African American collection during Black History Month, etc. Newspapers in particular are always looking for a "hook" for stories about these observances. News about archives and historical materials makes a great "hook."

The second example that follows is of a release for a recently processed collection.

News Release

The Special Collections Division of the University of Texas at Arlington Libraries is pleased to announce the acquisition of the personal papers of A. C. Greene, noted journalist, historian, and radio and television commentator. A generous donation by Greene and the support of the University of Texas System Board of Regents made the acquisition of the papers possible. The Green papers include sixty cubic feet of material and consist of the writer's personal papers and the historical materials he has amassed during his lifetime. Greene's personal papers are by far the most important of the two groups and the most voluminous.

Among his papers are a thirty-year collection of daily journals maintained by Greene; voluminous correspondence with various literary figures, including most Texas writers of the 1960-1990 period; much material about his involvement with the Texas Institute of Letters, an organization for which he served as vice president, president, and newsletter editor; personal material reflecting his childhood, education, and military service during World War II; notes, drafts, second sheets, corrections, letters, and manuscripts for many of his books and for his *"Texas Sketches"* syndicated column; photographs, posters, awards, and broadsides reflecting his life and work; and extensive correspondence with Angus Cameron, senior editor for Alfred A. Knopf and former editor for J. Frank Dobie. The historical materials Greene has collected are also a part of the acquisition. These include the records of the George M. and George E. Dilley Foundry located in Palestine, Texas (1880s-1930s); extensive files relating to the Texas YMCA and Red Cross during World War II; notebooks, unpublished poetry, and essays of Maude E. Cole, Greene's grandmother and an accomplished poet; and extensive sources and manuscripts relating to Texas railroads.

A. C. Greene was born in Abilene, Texas, in 1923. After serving in the military during World War II, he graduated cum laude in history from Abilene Christian College in 1948 and spent many years as a reporter and editor for newspapers in Abilene (*Abilene Reporter-News*) and Dallas (*Dallas Times Herald*). In 1968 he left his editorial position at the *Times Herald* to pursue a career as a writer and to enrol in the American Civilization programmeme at the University of Texas at Austin. He left the university shortly after receiving a prestigious Dobie-Paisano Fellowship and after publishing his highly regarded first book, *A Personal County*, in 1969. To date Greene has written eighteen books, scores of magazine articles, and numerous screenplays. Most of his works focus on the history and literature of Texas.

Since the deaths of J. Frank Dobie and Lon Tinkle, it has been Greene, more than anyone else, who has been called upon to define and interpret Texas to a national and international audience. Greene has won a number of regional and national awards, and has recently retired as Resident Professor of Texas Studies at the University of North Texas. He and his wife, Judy, live in Salado, Texas, where he continues to write. The Greene papers document the life and work of Greene and the development of the Texas literary scene in the second half of the twentieth century, according to Gerald Saxon, assistant director for Special Collections at the University of Texas at Arlington. "Because of his notoriety, personality, and outspokenness," Saxon said, "Greene has led the effort in the popular and academic press to define and promote regional literature. Greene's own creative work, in addition to his role as literary booster and lightning rod for Texas letters, will draw researchers now and in the future to his collection."

News Release

Women. Women's history. Women's issues. Feminism. If you are interested in any of these topics, the most recent collection open for research at UT Arlington can help address these interests. The Special Collections Division of the University of Texas at Arlington Libraries is pleased to announce the opening of the UT Arlington Women's Centre Records. The collection includes eleven boxes plus oversize materials, and dates from 1974-1989, with the bulk of the materials spanning 1974-1984. The collection focuses on the work of the UT Arlington Women's Centre in the area of women's issues and advancement. The importance of the collection can be seen in the overall evolution of the Women's Centre and its commitment to the advancement of women. From the sanctioning of the Centre for Women's Studies in 1974, the struggle for women in the academic arena is reflected in these records.

As the Centre for Women's Studies grew to encompass the Women's Centre and the Displaced Homemakers Centre, the evolution of women's issues broadened and vied to hold a permanent place in the academic world as well as a place for women in the community to seek aid and assistance. Providing counselling, continuing education, seminars, workshops, training and job placement, the Women's Centre sought to answer the needs of all women. Of particular interest will be the series of materials on WomanFair, the second annual convention for the South Central Women's Studies Association that was held at UT Arlington in 1980. These materials contain many original works, such as poetry, plays, and art, and attracted many prominent women from different fields, such as education, business, law, and government.

WomanFair brought these professional women together to bring awareness as to what the role of women could be in society. The different panels and workshops that took place during WomanFair represent a diverse and unique look at the interests and concerns to women in the early 1980's. The area of women's studies and women's issues continues to be one of growth as more researchers and scholars address the role of women in society, past and present. As the interest in women's issues grows, the need for understanding how women have come to be in the position they hold in society will grow as well. The UT Arlington Women's Centre Records will help address this understanding and aid in the overall picture of women, their issues, and place.

The Canon Law

General Notions and Divisions

Canon law is the body of laws and regulations made by or adopted by ecclesiastical authority, for the government of the Christian organization and its members. The word *adopted* is here used to point out the fact that there are certain elements in canon law borrowed by the Church from civil law or from the writings of private individuals, who as such had no authority in ecclesiastical society. Canon is derived from the Greek *kanon*, *i.e.* a rule or practical direction (not to speak of the other meanings of the word, such as list or catalogue), a term which soon acquired an exclusively ecclesiastical signification.

In the fourth century it was applied to the ordinances of the councils, and thus contrasted with the Greek word *nomoi*, the ordinances of the civil authorities; the compound word "Nomocanon" was given to those collections of regulations in which the laws formulated by the two authorities on ecclesiastical matters were to be found side by side. At an early period we meet with expressions referring to the body of ecclesiastical legislation then in process of formation: *canones, ordo canonicus, sanctio canonica*; but the expression "canon law" (*jus canonicum*) becomes current only about the beginning of the twelfth century, being used in contrast with the "civil law" (*jus civile*), and later we have the "Corpus juris canonici", as we have the "Corpus juris Civilis".

Canon law is also called "ecclesiastical law" (*jus ecclesiasticum*); however, strictly speaking, there is a slight difference of meaning between the two expressions: canon law denotes in particular the law of the "Corpus Juris", including the regulations borrowed from Roman law; whereas ecclesiastical law refers to all laws made by the ecclesiastical authorities as such, including those made after the compiling of the "Corpus Juris".

Contrasted with the imperial or Caesarian law (*jus caesareum*), canon law is sometimes styled pontifical law (*jus pontificium*), often also it is termed sacred law (*jus sacrum*), and sometimes even Divine law (*jus divinum*: c. 2, De privil.), as it concerns holy things, and has for its object the wellbeing of souls in the society divinely established by Jesus Christ.

Canon law may be divided into various branches, according to the points of view from which it is considered:

- If we consider its sources, it comprises Divine law, including natural law, based on the nature of things and on the constitution given by Jesus Christ to His Church; and human or positive law, formulated by the legislator, in conformity with the Divine law. We shall return to this later, when treating of the sources of canon law.
- If we consider the form in which it is found, we have the written law (*jus scriptum*) comprising the laws promulgated by the competent authorities, and the unwritten law (*jus non scripture*), or even customary law, resulting from practice and custom; the latter however became less important as the written law developed.
- If we consider the subject matter of the law, we have the public law (*jus publicum*) and private law (*jus privatum*). This division is explained in two different ways by the different schools of writers: for most of the adherents of the Roman school, *e.g.* Cavagnis (Instit. jur. publ. eccl., Rome, 1906, I, 8), public law is the law of the Church as a perfect society, and even as a perfect society such as it has been established by its Divine founder: private law would therefore embrace all the regulations of the ecclesiastical authorities concerning the internal organization of that society, the functions of its ministers, the rights and duties of its members. Thus understood, the public ecclesiastical law would be derived almost exclusively from Divine and natural law. On the other hand, most of the adherents of the German school, following the idea of the Roman law (Inst., I, i, 4; "Publicum jus est quad ad statuary rei Romanae spectat: privatum quad ad privatorum utilitatem"), define public law as the body of laws determining the rights and duties of those invested with ecclesiastical authority, whereas for them private law is that which sets forth the rights and duties of individuals as such. Public law would, therefore, directly intend the welfare of society as such, and indirectly that of its members; while private law would look primarily to the wellbeing of the individual and secondarily to that of the community.
- Public law is divided into external law (*jus externum*) and internal law (*jus internum*). External law determines the relations of ecclesiastical society with

other societies either secular bodies (the relations therefore of the Church and the State) or religious bodies, that is, interconfessional relations. Internal law is concerned with the constitution of the Church and the relations subsisting between the lawfully constituted authorities and their subjects.

- Considered from the point of view of its expression, canon law may be divided into several branches, so closely allied, that the terms used to designate them are often employed almost indifferently: common law and special law; universal law and particular law; general law and singular law (*jus commune et speciale*; *jus universale et particulare*; *jus generale et singulare*). It is easy to point out the difference between them: the idea is that of a wider or a more limited scope; to be more precise, common law refers to things, universal law to territories, general law to persons; so regulations affecting only certain things, certain territories, certain classes of persons, being a restriction or an addition, constitute special, particular, or singular law, and even local or individual law. This exceptional law is often referred to as a privilege (*privilegium, lex privata*), though the expression is applied more usually to concessions made to an individual. The common law, therefore, is that which is to be observed with regard to a certain matter, unless the legislator has foreseen or granted exceptions; for instance, the laws regulating benefices contain special provisions for benefices subject to the right of patronage. Universal law is that which is promulgated for the whole Church; but different countries and different dioceses may have local laws limiting the application of the former and even derogating from it. Finally, different classes of persons, the clergy, religious orders, etc., have their own laws which are superadded to the general law.
- We have to distinguish between the law of the Western or Latin Church, and the law of the Eastern Churches, and of each of them. Likewise, between the law of the Catholic Church and those of the non-Catholic Christian Churches or confessions, the Anglican Church and the various Eastern Orthodox Churches.
- Finally, if we look to the history or chronological evolution of canon law, we find three epochs: from the beginning to the "Decretum" of Gratian exclusively; from Gratian to the Council of Trent; from the Council of Trent to our day. The law of these three periods is referred to respectively as the ancient, the new, and the recent law (*jus antiquum, novum, novissimum*), though some writers prefer to speak of the ancient law, the law of the Middle Ages, and the modern law (Laurentius, "Instit.", n.4).

Canon Law as a Science

As we shall see in treating of the gradual development of the material of canon law, though a legislative power has always existed in the Church, and though it has always been exercised, a long period had necessarily to elapse before the laws were reduced to a harmonious systematic body, serving as a basis for methodical study and giving rise to general theories. In the first place, the legislative authority makes laws only when circumstances require them and in accordance with a definite plan. For centuries, nothing more was done than to collect successively the canons of councils, ancient and recent, the letters of popes, and episcopal statutes; guidance was sought for in these, when analogous cases occurred, but no one thought of extracting general principles from them or of systematizing all the laws then in force.

In the eleventh century certain collections group under the same headings the canons that treat of the same matters; however, it is only in the middle of the twelfth century that we meet in the "Decretum" of Gratian the first really scientific treatise on canon law. The School of Bologna had just revived the study of Roman law; Gratian sought to inaugurate a similar study of canon law. But, while compilations of texts and official collections were available for Roman law, or "Corpus juris civilis", Gratian had no such assistance. He therefore adopted the plan of inserting the texts in the body of his general treatise; from the disordered mass of canons collected from the earliest days, he selected not only the law actually in force (eliminating the regulations which had fallen into desuetude, or which were revoked, or not of general application) but also the principles; he elaborated a system of law which, however incomplete, was nevertheless methodical. The science of canon law, *i.e.* the methodical and coordinated knowledge of ecclesiastical law, was at length established.

Gratian's "Decretum" was a wonderful work; welcomed, taught and glossed by the decretists at Bologna and later in the other schools and universities, it was for a long time the textbook of canon law. However his plan was defective and confusing, and, after the day of the glosses and the strictly literal commentaries, it was abandoned in favour of the method adopted by Bernard of Pavia in his "Breviarium" and by St. Raymund of Pennafort in the official collection of the "Decretals" of Gregory IX, promulgated in 1234. These collections, which did not include the texts used by Gratian, grouped the materials into five books, each divided into "titles", and under each title the decretals or fragments of decretals were grouped in chronological order.

The five books, the subject matter of which is recalled by the well-known verse: "judex, judicium, clerus, connubia, crimen" (*i.e.* judge, judgment, clergy, marriages, crime), did not display a very logical plan; not to speak of certain titles that were more or less out of place. They treated successively of the depositaries of authority, procedure, the clergy and the things pertaining to them, marriage, crimes and penalties. In spite of its defects, the system had at least the merit of being official; not only was it adopted in the latter collections, but it served as the basis for almost all canonical works up to the sixteenth century, and even to our day, especially in the universities, each of which had a faculty of canon law. However, the method of studying and teaching gradually developed: if the early decretalists made use of the elementary plan of the gloss and literal commentary, their successors in composing their treatises were more independent of the text; they commented on the titles, not on the chapters or the words; often they followed the titles or chapters only nominally and artificially. In the sixteenth century they tried to apply, not to the official collections, but in their lectures on canon law the method and division of the "Institutes" of Justinian: persons, things, actions or procedure, crimes, and penalties (Institutes, I, ii, 12).

This plan, popularized by the "Institutiones juris canonici" of Lancellotti (1563), has been followed since by most of the canonist authors of "Institutiones" or manuals, though there has been considerable divergence in the subdivisions; most of the more extensive works, however, preserved the order of the "Decretals". This was also followed in the 1917 code. In later times many textbooks, especially in Germany, began to adopt original plans. In the sixteenth century too, the study of canon law was developed and improved like that of other sciences, by the critical spirit of the age: doubtful texts were rejected and the *raison d'être* and tendency or intention of later laws traced back to the customs of former days. Canon law was more studied and better understood; writings multiplied, some of an historical nature, others practical, according to the inclination of the authors. In the universities and seminaries, it became a special study, though as might be expected, not always held in equal esteem. It may be noted too that the study of civil law is now frequently separated from that of canon law, a result of the changes that have come over society. On the other hand, in too many seminaries the teaching of ecclesiastical law is not sufficiently distinguished from that of moral theology. The publication of the new general code of canon law will certainly bring about a more normal state of affairs.

The first object of the science of canon law is to fix the laws that are in force. This is not difficult when one has exact and recent texts, drawn up as abstract laws *e.g.* most of the texts since the Council of Trent, and as will be the case for all canon law when the new code is published. But it was not so in the Middle Ages; it was the canonists who, to a large extent, formulated the law by extracting it from the accumulated mass of texts or by generalizing from the individual decisions in the early collections of decretals. When the law in force is known it must be explained, and this second object of the science of canon law is still unchanged. It consists in showing the true sense, the reason, the extension and application of each law and each institution.

This necessitates a careful and exact application of the triple method of exposition, historical, philosophical, and practical: the first explains the law in accordance with its source and the evolution of customs; the second explains its principles; the last shows how it is to be applied at present. This practical application is the object of jurisprudence, which collects, coordinates and utilizes, for more or less analogous cases, the decisions of the competent tribunal. From this we may learn the position of canon law in the hierarchy of sciences. It is a judicial science, differing from the science of Roman law and of civil law inasmuch as it treats of the laws of an other society; but as this society is of the spiritual order and in a certain sense supernatural, canon law belongs also to the sacred sciences. In this category it comes after theology, which studies and explains in accordance with revelation, the truths to be believed; it is supported by theology, but in its turn it formulates the practical rules toward which theology tends, and so it has been called "theologia practica", "theologia rectrix".

In as far as it is practical the science of canon law is closely related to moral theology; however, it differs from the latter which is not directly concerned with the acts prescribed or forbidden by the external law, but only with the rectitude of human acts in the light of the last end of man, whereas, canon law treats of the external laws relating to the good order of society rather than the workings of the individual conscience. Juridical, historical, and above all theological sciences are most useful for the comprehensive study of canon law.

Sources of Canon Law

This expression has a twofold meaning; it may refer to the sources from which the laws come and which give the latter their judicial force (*fortes juris essendi*); or it may refer to the sources where canon law is to be found (*fortes juris cognoscendi*), *i.e.* the laws themselves such as they occur in the texts and various codes. These sources are also called the material and the formal sources of canon law. We shall consider first the sources under the former aspect.

The ultimate source of canon law is God, Whose will is manifested either by the very nature of things (natural Divine law), or by Revelation (positive Divine law). Both are contained in the Scriptures and in Tradition. Positive Divine law cannot contradict natural law; it rather confirms it and renders it more definite.

The Church accepts and considers both as sovereign binding laws which it can interpret but can not modify; however, it does not discover natural law by philosophic speculation; it receives it, with positive Divine law, from God through His inspired Books, though this does not imply a confusion of the two kinds of Divine law. Of the Old Law the Church has preserved in addition to the Decalogue some precepts closely allied to natural law, *e.g.* certain matrimonial impediments; as to the other laws given by God to His chosen people, it considers them to have been ritual and declares them abrogated by Jesus Christ. Or rather, Jesus Christ, the Lawgiver of the spiritual society founded by Him (Con. Trid., Sess. VI, "De justif.", can. I), has replaced them by the fundamental laws which He gave His Church. This Christian Divine law, if we may so call it, is found in the Gospels, in the Apostolic writings, in the living Tradition, which transmits laws as well as dogmas. On this positive Divine law depend the essential principles of the Church's constitution, the primacy, the episcopacy, the essential elements of Divine worship and the Sacraments, the indissolubility of marriage, etc.

Again, to attain its sublime end, the Church, endowed by its Founder with legislative power, makes laws in conformity with natural and Divine law. The sources or authors of this positive ecclesiastical law are essentially the episcopate and its head, the pope, the successors of the Apostolic College and its divinely appointed head, Saint Peter. They are, properly speaking, the active sources of canon law. Their activity is exercised in its most solemn form by the ecumenical councils, where the episcopate united with its head, and convoked and presided over by him, with him defines its teaching and makes the laws that bind the whole Church.

The canons of the Ecumenical councils, especially those of Trent, hold an exceptional place in ecclesiastical law. But, without infringing on the ordinary power of the bishops, the pope, as head of the episcopate, possesses in himself the same powers as the episcopate united with him. It is true that the disciplinary and legislative power of the popes has not always, in the course of centuries, been exercised in the same manner and to the same extent, but in proportion as the administration became centralized, their direct intervention in legislation became more and more marked; and so the sovereign pontiff is the most fruitful source of canon law; he can abrogate the laws made by his predecessors or by Ecumenical councils; he can legislate for the whole church or for a part thereof, a country or a given body of individuals; if he is morally bound to take advice and to follow the dictates of prudence, he is not legally obliged to obtain the consent of any other person or persons, or to observe any particular form; his power is limited only by Divine law, natural and positive, dogmatic and moral. Furthermore, he is, so to say, the living law, for he is considered as having all law in the treasury of his heart ("in scrinio pectoris"; Boniface VIII. c. i, "De Constit." in VI). From the earliest ages the letters of the Roman pontiffs constitute, with the canons of the councils, the principal element of canon law, not only of the Roman Church and its immediate dependencies but of all Christendom; they are everywhere relied upon and collected, and the ancient canonical compilations contain a large number of these precious "decretals" (*decreta, statuta, epistolae decretales,* and *epistolae synodicae*).

Later, the pontifical laws are promulgated more usually as constitutions, Apostolic Letters, the latter being classified as Bulls or Briefs, according to their external form, or even as spontaneous acts, "Motu proprio". Moreover, the legislative and disciplinary power of the pope not being an in communicable privilege, the laws and regulations made in his name and with his approbation possess his authority: in fact, though most of the regulations made by the Congregations of the cardinals and other organs of the Curia are incorporated in the Apostolic Letters, yet the custom exists and is becoming more general for legislation to be made by mere decrees of the Congregations, with the papal approval. These are the "Acts of the Holy See" (Acta Sancte Sedis), and their object or purpose permitting, are real laws.

Next to the pope, the bishops united in local councils, and each of them individually, are sources of law for their common or particular territory; canons of national or provincial councils, and diocesan statutes, constitute local law. Numerous texts of such origin are found in the ancient canonical collections. At the present day and for a long time past, the law has laid down clearly the powers of local councils and of bishops; if their decrees should interfere with the common law they have no authority save in virtue of pontifical approbation.

It is well known that diocesan statutes are not referred to the sovereign pontiff, whereas the decrees of provincial councils are submitted for examination and approval to the Holy See (Const. "Immensa" of Sixtus V, 22 Jan., 1587). We may liken to bishops in this matter various bodies that have the right of governing themselves and thus enjoy a certain autonomy; such are prelates with territorial jurisdiction, religious orders, some exempt chapters and universities, etc. The concessions granted to them are generally subject to a certain measure of control.

Other sources of law are rather impersonal in their nature, chief among them being custom or the unwritten law. In canon law custom has become almost like a legislator; not in the sense that the people are made their own lawgiver, but a practice followed by the greater part of the community, and which is reasonable and fulfils the legal requirements for prescription and is observed as obligatory, acquires the force of law by at least the tacit consent of the legislator. Under such circumstances custom can create or rescind a legal obligation, derogate from a law, interpret it, etc.

But it must be remarked that in our days, owing to the fully developed body of written law, custom plays a much less important part than did the practices and habits of early Christian times, when there was but little written law and even that seldom of wide application.

The civil law of different nations, and especially the Roman law, may be numbered among the accessory sources of canon law. But it is necessary to explain more exactly its role and importance. Evidently secular law cannot be, strictly speaking, a source of canon law, the State as such having no competence in spiritual matters; yet it may become so by the more or less formal acceptation of particular laws by the ecclesiastical authorities.

We pass by in the first place the laws made by the mutual agreement of both parties, such as the legislation of the numerous assemblies in the Visigothic kingdom, and the Frankish kingdom and empire, where the bishops sat with the lords and nobles. Such also is the case of the concordats of later ages, real contracts between the two powers. In these cases we have an ecclesiastico-civil law, the legal force of which arose from the joint action of the two competent authorities. It is in a different sense that Roman law, Germanic law, and in a lesser degree modern law, have become a subsidiary source of canon law.

It must be remembered that the Church existed for a long time before having a complete and coordinated system of law; that many daily acts of its administration, while objectively canonical, were of the same nature as similar acts in civil matters, *e.g.* contracts, obligations, and in general the administration of property; it was quite natural for the Church to accommodate itself in these matters to the existing flows, with out positively approving of them. Later when the canonists of the twelfth century began to systematize the ecclesiastical law, they found themselves in presence, on the one hand, of a fragmentary canon law, and on the other hand of the complete methodical Roman code; they had recourse to the latter to supply what was wanting in the former, whence the maxim adopted by the canonists and inserted in the "Corpus Juris", that the Church acts according to Roman law when canon law is silent (cap. 1. "De novi op. nunc.", X, i, V, tit. xxxii). Moreover, in the Teutonic kingdoms the clergy followed the Roman law as a personal statute.

However, in proportion as the written canon law increased, Roman law became of less practical value in the Church (cap. 28, X, "De priv.", X, lib. V, tit. xxxiii). Canon law, it may be said, adopted from Roman law what relates to obligations, contracts, judiciary actions, and to a great extent civil procedure. Other Roman laws were the object of a more positive recognition than mere usage, *i.e.* they were formally approved, those, for instance, which though of secular origin, concerned ecclesiastical things, *e.g.* the Byzantine ecclesiastical laws, or again laws of civil origin and character but which were changed into canonical laws *e.g.* the impediment of marriage arising from adoption.

The juridical influence of Teutonic law was much less important, if we abstract from the inevitable adaptation to the customs of barbarous races, yet some survivals of this law in ecclesiastical legislation are worthy of note: the somewhat feudal system of benefices; the computation of the degrees of kindred; the assimilating of the penitential practices to the system of penal compensation (*wehrgeld*); finally, but for a time only, justification from criminal charges on the oath of guarantors or co-jurors (De purgatione canonica, lib. V, tit. xxxiv).

Modern law has only a restricted and local influence on canon law, and that particularly on two points. On the one hand, the Church conforms to the civil laws on mixed matters, especially with regard to the administration of its property; on some occasions even it has finally adopted as its own measures passed by the civil powers acting independently; a notable case is the French decree of 1809 on the "Fabriques d'église". On the other hand, modern legislation is indebted to the canon law for certain beneficial measures: part of the procedure in criminal, civil, and matrimonial cases, and to some extent, the organization of courts and tribunals.

Historical Development of Texts and Collections

Considered under the second aspect, the sources of canon law are the legislative texts, and the collections of those texts whence we derive our knowledge of the Church's laws. In order to appreciate fully the reasons for and the utility of the great work of codification of the canon law, recently begun by order of Pius X, it is necessary to recall the general history of those texts and collections, ever increasing in number up to the present time. A detailed account of each of the canonical collections is here out of place; the more important ones are the subject of special articles, to which we refer the reader; it will suffice if we exhibit the different stages in the development of these texts and collections, and make clear the movement to wards centralization and unification that has led up to the present situation.

Even in the private collections of the early centuries, in which the series of conciliary canons were merely brought together in more or less chronological order, a constant tendency towards unification is noticeable. From the ninth century onwards the collections are systematically arranged; with the thirteenth century begins the first official collections, thenceforth the nucleus around which the new legislative texts centre, though it is not yet possible to reduce them to a harmonious and coordinated code. Before tracing the various steps of this evolution, some terms require to be explained. The name "canonical collections" is given to all collections of ecclesiastical legislative texts, because the principal texts were the canons of the councils. At first the authors of these collections contented themselves with bringing together the canons of the different councils in chronological order; consequently these are called "chronological" collections; in the West, the last important chronological collection is that of Pseudo-Isidore. After his time the texts were arranged according to subject matter; these are the "systematic" collections, the only form in use since the time of Pseudo-Isidore.

All the ancient collections are private, due to personal initiative, and have, therefore, as collections, no official authority: each text has only its own intrinsic value; even the "Decretum" of Gratian is of this nature. On the other hand, official or authentic collections are those that have been made or at least promulgated by the legislator. They begin with the "Compilatio tertia" of Innocent III; the later collections of the "Corpus Juris", except the "Extravagantes", are official. All the texts in an official collection have the force of law. There are also general collections and particular collections: the former treating of legislation in general, the latter treating of some special subject, for instance, marriage, procedure, etc., or even of the local law of a district. Finally, considered chronologically, the sources and collections are classified as previous to or later than the "Corpus Juris".

Canonical Collections in the East: Until the Church began to enjoy peace, the written canon law was very meagre; after making full allowance for the documents that must have perished, we can discover only a fragmentary law, made as circumstances demanded, and devoid of all system. Unity of legislation, in as far as it can be expected at that period, is identical with a certain uniformity of practice, based on the prescriptions of Divine law relative to the constitution of the Church, the liturgy, the sacraments, etc. The clergy, organized everywhere in the same way, exercised almost everywhere the same functions. But at an early period we discover a greater local disciplinary uniformity between the Churches of the great sees (Rome, Carthage, Alexandria, Antioch, later Constantinople) and the Churches depending immediately on them. Further it is the disciplinary decisions of the bishops of the various regions that form the first nucleus of local canon law; these texts, spreading gradually from one country to another by means of the collections, obtain universal dissemination and in this way are the basis of general canon law.

There were, however, in the East, from the early days up to the end of the fifth century, certain writings, closely related to each other, and which were in reality brief canon law treatises on ecclesiastical administration the duties of the clergy and the faithful, and especially on the liturgy. We refer to works attributed to the Apostles, very popular in the Oriental Churches, though devoid of official authority, and which may be called pseudo-epigraphic, rather than apocryphal. The principal writings of this kind are the "Teaching of the Twelve Apostles" or "Didache", the "Didascalia", based on the "Didache"; the "Apostolic Constitutions", an expansion of the two preceding works; then the "Apostolic Church Ordinance", the "Definitio canonica SS.

Apostolorum", the "Testament of the Lord" and the "Octateuch of Clement"; lastly the "Apostolic Canons". Of all this literature, only the "Apostolic Canons" werein cluded in the canonical collections of the Greek Church. The most important of these documents the "Apostolic Constitutions", was removed by the Second Canon of the Council in Trullo (692), as having been interpolated by the heretics. As to the eighty-five Apostolic Canons, accepted by the same council, they rank yet first in the above-mentioned "Apostolic" collection; the first fifty translated into Latin by Dionysius

Exiguus (c. 500), were included in the Western collections and afterwards in the "Corpus Juris".

As the later law of the separated Eastern Churches did not influence the Western collections, we need not treat of it, but go on to consider only the Greek collection. It begins early in the fourth century: in the different provinces of Asia Minor, to the canons of local councils are added those of the ecumenical Council of Nicea (325), everywhere held in esteem. The Province of Pontus furnished the penitentiary decisions of Ancyra and Neocæsarea (314); Antioch; the canons of the famous Council "in encaeniis" (341), a genuine code of metropolitan organization; Paphlagonia, that of the Council of Gangra (343), a reaction against the first excesses of asceticism; Phrygia, the fifty-nine canons of Laodicea on different disciplinary and liturgical matters. This collection was so highly esteemed that at the Council of Chalcedon (451) the canons were read as one series. It was increased later by the addition of the canons of (Constantinople (381), with other canons attributed to it, those of Ephesus (431). Chalcedon (451), and the Apostolic canons.

In 692 the Council in Trullo passed 102 disciplinary canons, the second of which enumerates the elements of the official collection: they are the texts we have just mentioned, together with the canons of Sardica, and of Carthage (419), according to Dionysius Exiguus, and numerous canonical letters of the great bishops, SS. Dionysius of Alexandria, Gregory Thaumaturgus, Basil, etc. If to these be added the canons of the two ecumenical councils of Nicea (787) and Constantinople (869) we have all the elements of the definitive collection in its final shape. A few "systematic" collections may be mentioned as pertaining to this period: one containing fifty titles by an unknown author about 535; another with twenty-five titles of the ecclesiastical laws of Justinian; a collection of fifty titles drawn up about 550, by John the Scholastic, a priest of Antioch.

The compilations known as the "Nomocanons" are more important, because they bring together the civil laws and the ecclesiastical laws on the same subjects; the two principal are the Nomocanon, wrongly attributed to John the Scholastic, but which dates from the end of the sixth century, with fifty titles, and another, drawn up in the seventh century, and afterwards augmented by the Patriarch Photius in 883.

The Canonical Collections in the West to Pseudo-Isidore: In the West, canonical collections developed as in the East, but about two centuries later. At first appear collections of national or local laws and the tendency towards centralization is partially effected in the ninth century. Towards the end of the fourth century there is yet in the West no canonical collection, not even a local one, those of the fifth century are essentially local, but all of them borrow from the Greek councils.

The latter were known in the West by two Latin versions, one called the "Hispana" or "Isidorian", because it was inserted in the Spanish canonical collection, attributed to St. Isidore of Seville, the other called the "Itala" or "ancient" (Prisca), because Dionysius Exiguus, in the first half of the sixth century, found it in use at Rome, and being dissatisfied with its imperfections improved it. Almost all the Western collections, therefore, are based on the same texts as the Greek collection, hence the marked influence of that collection on Western canon law.

(1) At the end of the fifth century the Roman Church was completely organized and the popes had promulgated many legislative texts; but no collection of them had yet been made. The only extra-Roman canons recognized were the canons of Nicea and Sardica, the latter being joined to the former, and at times even cited as the canons of Nicea. The Latin version of the ancient Greek councils was known, but was not adopted as ecclesiastical law. Towards the year 500 Dionysius Exiguus compiled at Rome a double collection, one of the councils, the other of decretals, *i.e.* papal letters. The former, executed at the request of Stephen, Bishop of Salona, is a translation of the Greek councils, including Chalcedon, and begins with the fifty Apostolic canons; Dionysius adds to it only the Latin text of the canons of Sardica and of Carthage (419), in which the more ancient African councils are partially reproduced. The second is a collection of thirty-nine papal decretals, from Siricius (384) to Anastasius II (496-98). Thus joined together these two collections became the canonical code of the Roman Church, not by official approbation, but by authorized practice. But while in the work of Dionysius the collection of conciliary canons remained unchanged, that of the decretals was successively increased; it continued to incorporate letters of the different popes till about the middle of the eighth century when Adrian I gave (774) the collection of Dionysius to the future Emperor Charlemagne as the canonical book of the Roman Church. This collection, often called the "Dionysio-Hadriana", was soon officially received in all Frankish territory, where it was cited as the "Liber Canonum", and was adopted for the whole empire of Charlemagne at the Diet of Aachen in 802. This was an important step towards the centralization and unification of the ecclesiastical law, especially as the Latin Catholic world hardly extended beyond the limits of the empire, Africa and the south of Spain having been lost to the Church through the victories of Islam.

(2) The canon law of the African Church was strongly centralized at Carthage; the documents naturally took the form of a collection, as it was customary to read and insert in the Acts of each council the decisions of the preceding councils. At the time of the invasion of the Vandals, the canonical code of the

African Church comprised, after the canons of Nicea, those of the Council of Carthage under Bishop Gratus (about 348), under Genethlius (390), of twenty or twenty-two plenary council under Aurelius (from 393 to 427), and the minor councils of Constantinople. Unfortunately these records have not come down to us in their entirety; we possess them in two forms: in the collection of Dionysius Exiguus, as the canons of a "Concilium Africanum"; in the Spanish collection, as those of eight councils (the fourth wrongly attributed, being a document from Arles, dating about the beginning of the sixth century). Through these two channels the African texts entered into Western canon law. It will suffice to mention the two "systematic" collections of Fulgentius Ferrandus and Cresconius.

(3) The Church in Gaul had no local religious centre, the territory being divided into unstable kingdoms; it is not surprising therefore that we meet no centralized canon law or universally accepted collection. There are numerous councils, however, and an abundance of texts; but if we except the temporary authority of the See of Arles, no church of Gaul could point to a permanent group of dependent sees. The canonical collections were fairly numerous, but none was generally accepted. The most widespread was the "Quesneliana", called after its editor (the Jansenist Paschase Quesnel), rich, but badly arranged, containing many Greek, Gallic, and other councils, also pontifical decretals. With the other collections it gave way to the "Hadriana", at the end of the eighth century.

(4) In Spain, on the contrary, at least after the conversion of the Visigoths, the Church was strongly centralized in the See of Toledo, and in close union with the royal power. Previous to this, we must note the collection of St. Martin of Braga, a kind of adaptation of conciliary canons, often incorrectly cited in the Middle Ages as the "Capitula Martini papae" (about 563). It was absorbed in the large and important collection of the Visigothic Church. The latter, begun as early as the council of 633 and increased by the canons of subsequent councils, is known as the "Hispana" or "Isidoriana", because in later times it was attributed (erroneously) to St. Isidore of Seville. It comprises two parts: the councils and the decretals; the councils are arranged in four sections: the East, Africa, Gaul, Spain, and chronological order is observed in each section; the decretals, 104 in number, range from Pope St. Damasus to St. Gregory (366-604). Its original elements consist of the Spanish councils from Elvira (about 300) to the Seventeenth Council of Toledo in 694. The influence of this collection, in the form it assumed about the middle of the ninth century, when the False Decretals were inserted into it, was very great.

(5) Of Great Britain and Ireland we need mention only the Irish collection of the beginning of the eighth century, from which several texts passed to the continent;

it is remarkable for including among its canons citations from the Scriptures and the Fathers.

(6) The collection of the False Decretals, or the Pseudo-Isidore (about 850), is the last and most complete of the "chronological" collections, and therefore the one most used by the authors of the subsequent "systematic" collections; it is the "Hispana" or Spanish collection together with apocryphal decretals attributed to the popes of the first centuries up to the time of St. Damasus, when the authentic decretals begin. It exerted a very great influence.

(7) To conclude the list of collections, where the later canonists were to garner their materials, we must mention the "Penitentials", the "Ordines" or ritual collections, the "Formularies", especially the "Liber Diurnus"; also compilations of laws either purely secular, or semi-ecclesiastical, like the "Capitularies" (q.v.). The name "capitula" or "capitularia" is given also to the episcopal ordinances quite common in the ninth century. It may be noted that the author of the False Decretals forged also false "Capitularies", under the name of Benedict the Deacon, and false episcopal "Capitula", under the name of Angilramnus, Bishop of Metz.

Canonical Collections to the Time of Gratian: The Latin Church was meanwhile moving towards closer unity; the local character of canonical discipline and laws gradually disappears, and the authors of canonical collections exhibit a more personal note, *i.e.* they pick out more or less advantageously the texts, which they borrow from the "chronological" compilations, though they display as yet no critical discernment, and include many apocryphal documents, while others continue to be attributed to the wrong sources.

They advance, nevertheless, especially when to the bare texts they add their own opinions and ideas. From the end of the ninth century to the middle of the twelfth these collections are very numerous; many of them are still unpublished, and some deservedly so. We can only mention the principal ones:

- A collection in twelve books, compiled in Northern Italy, and dedicated to an Archbishop Anselm, doubtless Anselm II of Milan (833-97), still unedited; it seems to have been widely used.
- The "Libri duo de synodalibus causis" of Regino, Abbot of Prüm (d. 915), a pastoral visitation manual of the bishop of the diocese, edited by Wasserschleben (1840).
- The voluminous compilation, in twenty books, of Burchard, Bishop of Worms, compiled between 1012 and 1022, entitled the "Collectarium", also "Decretum", a manual for the use of ecclesiastics in their ministry; the nineteenth book, "Corrector" or "Medicus", treats of the administration of the Sacrament of

Penance, and was often current as a distinct work. This widely circulated collection is in P.L., CXL. At the end of the eleventh century there appeared in Italy several collections favouring the reform of Gregory VII and supporting the Holy See in the in vestiture strife; some of the authors utilized for their works the Roman archives.

- The collection of Anselm, Bishop of Lucca (d. 1086), in thirteen books, still unedited, an influential work.
- The collection of Cardinal Deusdedit, dedicated to Pope Victor III (1087), it treats of the primacy of the pope, of the Roman clergy, ecclesiastical property, immunities, and was edited by Martinucci in 1869, more recently and better by Wolf von Glanvell (1905).
- The "Breviarium" of Cardinal Atto; edited by Mai, "Script. vet. nova collect.", VI, app. 1832.
- The collection of Bonizo, Bishop of Sutri in ten books, written after 1089, still unedited.
- The collection of Cardinal Gregory, called by him "Polycarpus", in eight books, written before 1120, yet unedited.
- In France we must mention the small collection of Abbo, Abbot of Fleury (d. 1004). in fifty-two chapters, in P. L., CXXXIX; and especially
- the collections of Ives, Bishop of Chartres (d. 1115 or 1117), *i.e.* the "Collectio trium partium", the "Decretum", es pecially the "Panormia", a short compilation in eight books, extracted from the preceding two works, and widely used. The "Decretum" and the "Panormia" are in P. L., CLXI.
- The unedited Spanish collection of Saragossa (Caesar-augustana) is based on these works of Ives of Chartres.
- Finally, the "De misericordia et justitia", in three books, composed before 1121 by Algerus of Liège, a general treatise on ecclesiastical discipline, in which is fore shadowed the scholastic method of Gratian, reprinted in P.L., CLXXX.

The "Decretum" of Gratian: the Decretists: The "Concordantia discordantium canonum", known later as "Decretum", which Gratian published at Bologna about 1148, is not, as we consider it today, a collection of canonical texts, but a general treatise, in which the texts cited are inserted to help in establishing the law. It is true that the work is very rich in texts and there is hardly a canon of any importance contained in the earlier collections (including the decisions of the Lateran Council of 1139 and recent papal decretals) that Gratian has not used.

His object, however, was to build up a juridical system from all these documents. Despite its imperfections, it must be admitted that the work of Gratian was as near perfection as was then possible. For that reason it was adopted at Bologna, and soon elsewhere, as the textbook for the study of canon law. (For an account of this collection see CORPUS JURIS CANONICI; CANONS.) We may here recall again that the "Decretum" of Gratian is not a codification, but a privately compiled treatise; further, that the building up of a general system of canon law was the work of the canonists, and not of the legislative authorities as such.

Quite as the professors at Bologna commented on Justinian's "Corpus juris civilis", so they began at once to comment on Gratian's work, the personal element as well as his texts. The first commentators are called the "Decretists". In their lectures (Latin *lecturae*, readings) they treated of the conclusions to be drawn from each part and solved the problems (*quaestiones*) arising therefrom. They synopsized their teaching in "glosses", interlinear at first, then marginal, or they composed separate treatises known as "Apparatus", "Summae", "Repetitiones", or else collected "casus", "questiones", "Margaritae", "Breviaria", etc. The principal decretists are:

- Paucapalea, perhaps the first disciple of Gratian, whence, it is said, the name "palea" given to the additions to the "Decretum" (his "Summa" was edited by Schulte in 1890);
- Roland Bandinelli, later Alexander III (his "Summa" was edited by Thaner in 1874);
- Omnibonus, 1185;
- John of Faenza (d. bishop of that city in 1190);
- Rufinus ("Summa" edited by Singer, 1902);
- Stephen of Tournai (d. 1203; "Summa" edited by Schulte, 1891);
- the great canonist Huguccio (d. 1910; "Summa" edited by M. Gillmann);
- Sicard of Cremona (d. 1215);
- John the Teuton, really Semeca or Zemcke (d. 1245);
- Guido de Baysio, the "archdeacon" (of Bologna, d. 1313); and especially
- Bartholomew of Brescia (d. 1258), author of the "gloss" on the "Decretum" in its last form.

Decretals and Decretalists: While lecturing on Gratian's work the canonists laboured to complete and elaborate the master's teaching; with that view they collected assiduously the decretals of the popes, and especially the canons of the Ecumenical councils of the Lateran (1179, 1215); but these compilations were not intended to form a complete code, they merely centred round and supplemented Gratian's "Decretum"; for that reason these Decretals are known as the "Extravagantes", *i.e.* outside of, or extraneous to, the official collections. The five collections thus made between 1190 and 1226, and which were to serve as the basis for the work of Gregory IX, mark a distinct step forward in the evolution of canon law: whereas Gratian had inserted the texts in his own treatise, and the canonists wrote their works without including the texts, we have now compilations of supplementary texts for the purpose of teaching, but which nevertheless remain quite distinct; in addition, we at last find the legislators taking part officially in editing the collections.

While the "Breviarium" of Bernard of Pavia, the first to exhibit the division into five books and into titles, which St. Raymund of Pennafort was later to adopt, is the work of a private individual, the "Compilatio tertia" of Innocent III in 1210, and the "Compilatio quinta" of Honourius III, in 1226, are official collections. Though the popes, doubtless, intended only to give the professors at Bologna correct and authentic texts, they nevertheless acted officially; these collections, however, are but supplements to Gratian.

This is also true of the great collection of "Decretals" of Gregory IX. The pope wished to collect in a more uniform and convenient manner the decretals scattered through so many different compilations; he entrusted this synopsis to his chaplain Raymund of Pennafort, and in 1234 sent it officially to the universities of Bologna and Paris. He did not wish to suppress or supplant the "Decretum" of Gratian, but this eventually occurred.

The "Decretals" of Gregory IX, though composed in great part of specific decisions, represented in fact a more advanced state of law; furthermore, the collection was sufficiently extensive to touch almost every matter, and could serve as a basis for a complete course of instruction. It soon gave rise to a series of commentaries, glosses, and works, as the "Decretum" of Gratian had done, only these were more important since they were based on more recent and actual legislation. The commentators of the Decretals were known as Decretalists. The author of the "gloss" was Bernard de Botone (d. 1263); the text was commented on by the most distinguished canonists; among the best known previous to the sixteenth century, we must mention:

- Bernard of Pavia ("Summa" edited by Laspeyres, 1860),
- Tancred, archdeacon of Bologna, d. 1230 ("Summa de Matrimonio", ed. Wunderlich, 1841);
- Godfrey of Trani (1245);
- Sinibaldo Fieschi, later Innocent IV (1254), whose "Apparatus in quinque libros decre taliurn" has been frequently reprinted since 1477;
- Henry of Susa, later Cardinal-Bishop of Ostia (d. 1271), hence "Hostiensis"; his "Summa Hostiensis", or "Summa aurea" was one of the best known canonical works, and was printed as early as 1473;
- Aegilius de Fuscarariis (d. 1289);

- William Durandus (d. 1296, Bishop of Mende), surnamed "Speculator", on account of his important treatise on procedure, the "Speculum judiciale", printed in 1473;
- Guido de Baysio, the "archdeacon", already mentioned;
- Nicolas de Tudeschis (d. 1453), also known as "Abbes siculus" or simply "Panormitanus" (or also "Abbas junior seu modernus") to distinguish him from the "Abbas antiques", whose name is unknown and who commented on the Decretals about 1275); Nicolas left a "Lecture" on the Decretals, the Liber Sextus, and the Clementines.

For some time longer, the same method of collecting was followed; not to speak of the private compilations, the popes continued to keep up to date the "Decretals" of Gregory IX; in 1245 Innocent IV sent a collection of forty-two decretals to the universities, ordering them to be inserted in their proper places; in 1253 he forwarded the "initia" or first words of the authentic decretals that were to be accepted. Later Gregory X and Nicholas III did likewise, but with little profit, and none of these brief supplementary collections survived.

The work was again undertaken by Boniface VIII, who had prepared and published an official collection to complete the five existing books; this was known as the "Sextus" (Liber Sextus). Clement V also had prepared a collection which, in addition to his own decretals, contained the decisions of the Council of Vienne (1311-12); it was published in 1317 by his successor John XXII and was called the "Clementina." This was the last of the medieval official collections. Two later compilations included in the "Corpus Juris" are private works, the "Extravagantes of John XXII", arranged in 1325 by Zenzelin de Cassanis, who glossed them, and the "Extra vagantes communes", a belated collection; it was only in the edition of the "Corpus Juris" by Jean Chappuis, in 1500, that these collections found a fixed form. The "Sextus" was glossed and commented by Joannes Andrae, called the "fons et tuba juris" (d. 1348), and by Cardinal Jean Le Moine (Joannes Monachus, d. 1313), whose works were often printed.

When authors speak of the "closing" of the "Corpus Juris", they do not mean an act of the popes for bidding canonists to collect new documents, much less forbidding themselves to add to the ancient collections. But the canonical movement, so active after Gratian's time, has ceased forever. External circumstances, it is true, the Western Schism, the troubles of the fifteenth century, the Reformation, were unfavourable to the compiling of new canonical collections; but there were more direct causes. The special object of the first collections of the decretals was to help settle the law, which the canonists of Bologna were trying to systematize; that is why they contain so many specific decisions, from which the authors gathered general principles; when these had been ascertained the specific decisions were of no use except for jurisprudence; and in fact the "Sextus", the "Clementinae", and the other collections contain texts only when they are the statement of a general law. Any changes deemed necessary could be made in teaching without the necessity of recasting and augmenting the already numerous and massive collections.

From the Decretals to the Present Time: After the fourteenth century, except for its contact with the collections we have just treated of, canon law loses its unity. The actual law is found in the works of the canonists rather than in any specific collection; each one gathers his texts where he can; there is no one general collection sufficient for the purpose. It is not a case of confusion, but of isolation and dispersion. The sources of law later than the "Corpus Juris" are:

- the decisions of councils, especially of the Council of Trent (1545-1563), which are so varied and important that by themselves they form a short code, though without much order;
- the constitutions of the popes, numerous but hitherto not officially collected, except the "Bullarium" of Benedict XIV (1747);
- the Rules of the Apostolic Chancery;
- the 1917 Code of Canon Law;
- lastly the decrees, decisions, and various acts of the Roman Congregations, jurisprudence rather than law properly so called.

For local law we have provincial councils and diocesan statutes. It is true there have been published collections of councils and Bullaria. Several Roman Congregations have also had their acts collected in official publications; but these are rather erudite compilations or repertories.

Codification

The method followed, both by private individuals and the popes, in drawing up canonical collections is generally rather that of a coordinated compilation or juxtaposition of documents than codification in the modern sense of the word, *i.e.* a redaction of the laws (all the laws) into an orderly series of short precise texts. It is true that antiquity, even the Roman law, did not offer any model different from that of the various collections, that method, however, long since ceased to be useful or possible in canon law. After the "closing" of the "Corpus Juris" two attempts were made; the first was of little use, not being official; the second, was official, but was not brought to a successful issue. In 1590 the jurisconsult Pierre Mathieu, of Lyons published under the title "Liber septimus" a supplement to the "Corpus Juris", divided according to the order of the books and titles of the Decretals. It includes a selection of papal constitutions, from Sixtus IV to Sixtus V (1471-1590), but not the decrees of the Council of Trent. This compilation was of some service, and in a certain number of editions of the "Corpus Juris" was included as an appendix. As soon as the official edition of the "Corpus Juris" was published in 1582, Gregory XIII appointed a commission to bring up to date and complete the venerable collection. Sixtus V hastened the work and at length Cardinal Pinelli presented to Clement VIII what was meant to be a "Liber septimus". For the purpose of further studies the pope had it printed in 1598: the pontifical constitutions and the decrees of the Council of Trent were inserted in it in the order of the Decretals. For several reasons Clement VIII refused to approve this work and the project was definitively abandoned. Had this collection been approved it would have been as little used today as the others, the situation continuing to grow worse.

Many times during the nineteenth century, especially at the time of the Vatican Council (Collectio Lacensis, VII, 826), the bishops had urged the Holy See to draw up a complete collection of the laws in force, adapted to the needs of the day. It is true, their requests were complied with in regard to certain matters; Pius X in his "Motu proprio" of 19 March, 1904, refers to the constitution "Apostolicae Sedis" limiting and cataloguing the censures "latae sententie", the Constitution "Officiorum", revising the laws of the Index; the Constitution "Conditre" on the religious congregations with simple vows. These and several other documents were, moreover, drawn up in short precise articles, to a certain extent a novelty, and the beginning of a codification. Pius later officially ordered a codification, in the modern sense of the word, for the whole canon law.

In the first year of his pontificate he issued the Tutu Proprio "Arduum", (De Ecclesiae legibus in unum redigendis); it treats of the complete codification and reformation of canon law. For this purpose the pope requested the entire episcopate, grouped in provinces, to make known to him the reforms they desired. At the same time he appointed a commission of consultors, on whom the initial work devolved, and a commission of cardinals, charged with the study and approval of the new texts, subject later to the sanction of the sovereign pontiff. The plans of the various titles were confided to canonists in every country. The general idea of the Code that followed includes (after the preliminary section) four main divisions: persons, things (with subdivisions for the sacraments, sacred places and objects, etc.). trials, crimes and penalties. It is practically the plan of the "Institutiones", or manuals of canon law. The articles were numbered consecutively. This great work was finished in 1917.

Ecclesiastical Law

The sources of canon law, and the canonical writers give us, it is true, rules of action, each with its specific object. We have now to consider all these laws in their common abstract element, in other words Ecclesiastical Law, its characteristics and its practice. According to the excellent definition of St. Thomas (I-II:90:1) a law is a reasonable ordinance for the common good promulgated by the head of the community.

Ecclesiastical law therefore has for its author the head of the Christian community over which he has jurisdiction strictly so called; its object is the common welfare of that community, although it may cause inconvenience to individuals; it is adapted to the obtaining of the common welfare, which implies that it is physically and morally possible for the majority of the community to observe it; the legislator must intend to bind his subjects and must make known that intention clearly; finally he must bring the law under the notice of the community. A law is thus distinguished from a counsel, which is optional not obligatory; from a precept, which is imposed not on the community but on individual members; and from a regulation or direction, which refers to accessory matters.

The object therefore of ecclesiastical law is all that is necessary or useful in order that the society may attain its end, whether there be question of its organization, its working, or the acts of its individual members; it extends also to temporal things, but only indirectly. With regard to acts, the law obliges the individual either to perform or to omit certain acts; hence the distinction into "affirmative or preceptive" laws and "negative or prohibitory" laws; at times it is forced to allow certain things to be done, and we have "permissive" laws or laws of forbearance; finally, the law in addition to forbidding a given act may render it, if performed, null and void; these are "irritant" laws. Laws in general, and irritant laws in particular, are not retroactive, unless such is expressly declared by the legislator to be the case.

The publication or promulgation of the law has a double aspect: law must be brought to the knowledge of the community in order that the latter may be able to observe it, and in this consists the publication. But there may be legal forms of publication, requisite and necessary, and in this consists the promulgation properly so called. Whatever may be said about the forms used in the past, today the promulgation of general ecclesiastical laws is effected exclusively by the insertion of the law in the official publication of the Holy See, the "Acta Apostolical Sedis", in compliance with the Constitution "Promulgandi", of Pius X, dated 29 September, 1908, except in certain specifically mentioned cases. The law takes effect and is binding on all members of the community as soon as it is promulgated, allowing for the time morally necessary for it to become known, unless the legislator has fixed a special time at which it is to come into force.

No one is presumed to be ignorant of the law; only ignorance of fact not ignorance of law, is excusable (Reg. 1:3 jur. in VI). Everyone subject to the legislator is bound in conscience to observe the law. A violation of the law, either by omission or by act, is punishable with a penalty (q.v.). These penalties may be settled beforehand by the legislator, or they may be left to the discretion of the judge who imposes them. A violation of the moral law or what one's conscience judges to be the moral law is a sin; a violation of the exterior penal law, in addition to the sin, renders one liable to a punishment or penalty; if the will of the legislator is only to oblige the offender to submit to the penalty, the law is said to be "purely penal"; such are some of the laws adopted by civil legislatures, and it is generally admitted that some ecclesiastical laws are of this kind.

As baptism is the gate of entrance to the ecclesiastical society, all those who are baptized, even non-Catholics, are in principle subject to the laws of the Church; in practice the question arises only when certain acts of heretics and schismatics come before Catholic tribunals; as a general rule an irritant law is enforced in such a case, unless the legislator has exempted them from its observance, for instance, for the form of marriage. General laws therefore, bind all Catholics wherever they may be. In the case of particular laws as one is subject to them in virtue of one's domicile, or even quasi-domicile, passing strangers are not subject to them, except in the case of acts performed within the territory.

The role of the legislator does not end with the promulgation of the law; it is his office to explain and interpret it (*declaratio, interpretatio legis*). The interpretation is "official" (*authentica*) or even "necessary", when it is given by the legislator or by some one authorized by him for that purpose; it is "customary", when it springs from usage or habit; it is "doctrinal", when it is based on the authority of the learned writers or the decisions of the tribunals. The official interpretation alone has the force of law.

According to the result, the interpretation is said to be "comprehensive, extensive, restrictive, corrective," expressions easily understood. The legislator, and in the case of particular laws the superior, remains master of the law; he can suppress it either totally (abrogation), or partially (derogation), or he can combine it with a new law which suppresses in the first law all that is incompatible with the second (abrogation). Laws co-exist as far as they are reconcilable; the more recent modifies the more ancient, but a particular law is not suppressed by a general law, unless the fact is stated expressly. A law can also cease when its purpose and end cease, or even when it is too difficult to be observed by the generality of the subjects; it then falls into desuetude.

In every society, but especially in a society so vast and varied as the Church, it is impossible for every law to be applicable always and in all cases. Without suppressing the law, the legislator can permanently exempt from it certain persons or certain groups, or certain matters, or even extend the rights of certain subjects; all these concessions are known as privileges. In the same manner the legislator can derogate from the law in special cases; this is called a dispensation. Indults or the powers that the bishops of the Catholic world receive from the Holy See, to regulate the various cases that may arise in the administration of their dioceses, belong to the category of privileges; together with the dispensations granted directly by the Holy See, they eliminate any excessive rigidity of the law, and ensure to ecclesiastical legislation a marvellous facility of application.

Without imperilling the rights and prerogatives of the legislator, but on the contrary strengthening them, indults impress more strongly on the law of the Church that humane, broad, merciful character, mindful of the welfare of souls, but also of human weakness, which likens it to the moral law and distinguishes it from civil legislation, which is much more external and inflexible.

The Principal Canonists

It is impossible to draw up a detailed and systematic catalogue of all the works of special value in the study of canon law; the most distinguished canonists are the subject of special articles in this Encyclopedia. Those we have mentioned as commentators of the ancient canonical collections are now of interest only from an historical point of view; but the authors who have written since the Council of Trent are still read with profit; it is in their great works that we find our practical canon law. Among the authors who have written on special chapters of the "Corpus Juris", we must mention (the date refers to the first edition of the works):

- Prospero Fagnani, the distinguished secretary of the Sacred Congregation of the Council, "Jus canonicum seu commentaria absolutissima in quinque libros Decretalium" (Rome, 1661),
- Manuel González Téllez (d. 1649), "Commentaria perpetua in singulos textus juris canonici" (Lyons, 16, 3);
- the Jesuit Paul Laymann, better known as a moral theologian, "Jus canonicum seu commentaria in libros Decretalium" (Dillingen, 1666);
- Ubaldo Giraldi, Clerk Regular of the Pious Schools, "Expositio juris pontificii juxta re centiorem Ecclesiae disciplinam" (Rome, 1769).

Among the canonists who have followed the order of the titles of the Decretals:

- the Benedictine Louis Engel, professor at Salzburg, "Universum jus canonicum secundum titulos libr. Decretalium" (Salzburg, 1671);
- the Jesuit Ehrenreich Pirhing, "Universum jus canonicum" etc. (Dillingen, 1645);
- the Franciscan Anaclet Reiffenstuel, "Jus canonicum universum" (Freising, 170O);
- the Jesuit James Wiestner, "Institutiones canonical" (Munich, 1705);

- the two brothers Francis and Benedict Schmier, both Benedictines and professors at Salzburg; Francis wrote "Jurisprudentia canonico-civilis" (Salzburg, 1716); Benedict: "Liber I Decretalium; Lib. II etc." (Salzburg, 1718);
- the Jesuit Francis Schmalzgrueber, "Jus ecclésiasticum universum" (Dillingen, 1717);
- Peter Leuren, also a Jesuit, "Forum ecclesiasticum" etc. (Mainz, 1717);
- Vitus Pichler, a Jesuit, the successor of Schmalzgrueber, "Summa jurisprudential sacrae" (Augsburg, 1723);
- Eusebius Amort, a Canon Regular, "Elementa juris canonici veteris et modern)" (Ulm, 1757);
- Amort wrote also among other works of a very personal character; "De origine, progressu... indulgentiarum" (Augsburg, 1735);
- Carlo Sebastiano Berardi, "Commentaria in jus canonicum universum" (Turin, 1766); also his "Institutiones" and his great work "Gratiani canonesgenuini ab apocryphis discreti", (Turin, 1752);
- James Anthony Zallinger, a Jesuit, "Institutiones juris ecclesiastici maxime privati" (Augsburg, 1791), not so well known as his "Institutionum juris naturalis et ecclesiastici publici libri quinque" (Augsburg, 1784).
- This same method was followed again in the nineteenth century by Canon Filippo de Angelis, "Praelectiones juris canonici", (Rome, 1877);
- by his colleague Francesco Santi, "Praelectiones", (Ratisbon, 1884; revised by Martin Leitner, 1903); and
- E. Grand claude, "Jus canonicum" (Paris, 1882).

The plan of the "Institutiones", in imitation of Lancelotti (Perugia, 1563), has been followed by very many canonists, among whom the principal are:

- the learned Antonio Agustin, Archbishop of Tarragona, "Epitome jurispontificu veteris" (Tarragona, 1587); his "De emendatione Gratiani dialogorum libri duo" (Tarragona, 1587), is worthy of mention;
- Claude Fleury, "Institution au droit ecclésiastique" (Paris, 1676);
- Zeger Bernard van Espen, "Jus ecclesiasticum universum" (Cologne, 1748);
- the Benedictine Dominic Schram, "Institutiones juris ecclesiastici" (Augsburg, 1774);
- Vincenzo Lupoli, "Juris ecclesiastici praelectiones" (Naples, 1777);
- Giovanni Devoti, titular Archbishop of Carthage, "Institutionum canonicarum libri quatuor" (Rome, 1785); his "Commentary on the Decretals" has only the first three books (Rome, 1803);

- Cardinal Soglia, "Institutiones juris privati et publici ecclesiastici" (Paris, 1859) and "Institutiones juris publici", (Loreto, 1843);
- D. Craisson, Vicar-General of Valence, "Manuale compendium totius juris canonici" (Poitiers, 1861).

School manuals in one or two volumes are very numerous and it is impossible to mention all.

- We may cite in Italy those of G.C. Ferrari (1847); Vecchiotti (Turin, 1867); De Camillis, (Rome, 1869); Sebastiano Sanguinetti, S.J. (Rome, 1884); Carlo Lombardi (Rome, 1898); Guglielmo Sebastianelli (Rome, 1898), etc.
- For German speaking countries, Ferdinand Walter (Bonn, 1822); F.M. Permaneder, 1846; Rosshirt, 1858; George Phillips (Ratisbon, 1859: in addition to his large work in eight volumes, 1845 sq.); J. Winckler, 1862 (specially for Switzerland); S. Aichner (Brixen, 1862) specially for Austria; J. F. Schulte (Geissen, 1863); F.H. Vering (Freiburg-im-B., 1874); Isidore Silbernagl (Ratisbon, 1879); H. Laemmer (Freiburg-im-B., 188fi); Phil. Hergenröther (Freiburg-im-B., 1888); T. Hollweck (Freiburg-im-B.. 1905); J. Laurentius (Freiburg-im-B., 1903); D. M. Prummer, 1907; J. B. Sägmüller (Freiburg-im-B., 1904).
- For France: H. Icard, Superior of Saint-Sulpice (Paris, 1867); M. Bargilliat (Paris, 1893); F. Deshayes, "Memento juris ecclesiastici" (Paris, 1897).
- In Belgium: De Braban dere (Bruges, 1903).
- For English-speaking countries: Smith (New York, 1890); Gignac (Quebec, 1901); Taunton (London, 1906). For Spain: Marian Aguilar (Santo Domingo de la Calzada, 1904); Gonzales Ibarra (Valladolid, 1904).

There are also canonists who have written at considerable length either on the whole canon law, or on special parts of it, in their own particular manner; it is difficult to give a complete list, but we will mention:

- Agostino Barbosa (d. 1639), whose works fill at least 30 volumes;
- J.B. Cardinal Luca (d. 1683), whose immense "Theatrum veritatis" and "Relatio curiae romance" are his most important works;
- Pignatelli, who has touched on all practical questions in his "Consultationes canoniccae", 11 folio volumes, Geneva, 1668;
- Prospero Lambertini (Pope Benedict XIV), perhaps the greatest canonist since the Council of Trent;
- in the nineteenth century we must mention the different writings of Dominique Bouix, 15 volumes, Paris, 1852 sq.;
- the "Kirchenrecht" of J. F. Schulte, 1856 and of Rudolf v. Scherer, 1886; and above all

- the great work of Franz Xavier Wernz, General of the Society of Jesus, "Jus decretalium" (Rome, 1898 sq.).

It is impossible to enumerate the special treatises. Among repertoires and dictionaries, it will suffice to cite the "Prompta Bibliotheca" of the Franciscan Ludovico Ferraris (Bologna, 1746); the "Dictionnaire de droit canonique" of Durand de Maillane (Avignon, 1761), continued later by Abbé Andre (Paris, 1847) etc.; finally the other encyclopedias of ecclesiastical sciences wherein canon law has been treated.

Modern cataloguing codes are actually sets of rules formulated according to certain principles for the creation and organisation of catalogue records. It is claimed that current cataloguing codes have been based on traditional principles developed over the past two centuries according to the limited technology of the time and that they are not geared to take full advantage of the electronic environment. At the time that cataloguing principles (mainly the principles internationally agreed upon at the International Conference on Cataloguing Principles, 1961, Paris) were adopted there was no perception of either the sophisticated electronic catalogue or the evolving online environment.

Review of the Related Literature

Little research has been done on the relevance (*i.e.* validity and adequacy) of existing cataloguing principles to the online environment. However, the literature shows a great deal of interest in this issue. It is often stated that the online catalogue provides new features and capabilities, such as enhanced content, sophisticated structure and more powerful search/retrieval/display facilities, that demand a new look at current cataloguing paradigms. While a number of writers claim that the current cataloguing principles are still valid, others support the idea that a new set of rules is needed. In this respect, the literature of descriptive cataloguing is controversial and, this controversy is evident in relation to some of the basic cataloguing principles.

One of the first to address the potential impact of electronic information systems upon the problems of cataloguing and the need for compatible cataloguing rules was C.D. Gull. In his working paper presented at the International Conference on Cataloguing Principles (ICCP) held in Paris in October 1961, Gull discussed the possible effects of an electronic environment on cataloguing rules and suggested that the issue should be taken into consideration in the design of relevant cataloguing rules (Gull, 1963). However, his ideas do not appear to have influenced the outcomes of that conference.

It should be mentioned that, in their discussions of the inconsistencies and implications of cataloguing principles and rules in relation to the online environment, most writers refer to the *Anglo-American Cataloguing Rules,* which conform to the

Paris Principles. As a standard and widely used set of rules, AACR2 has been much discussed by many cataloguing experts. It has been criticised on the grounds that it is based on manual systems and that a number of its rules are irrelevant in a developed online catalogue. Gorman (1978) points out that AACR2 could not fully take into consideration the effects of library automation because these had yet to be completely assessed and understood. Shinebourne (1979) is one of the first persons to criticise AACR2 severely for disregarding the possible influence of automation on cataloguing rules. Ayres (1980) discusses the incompatibility of the code to automated systems from the users' point of view and suggests the need for further research on the ways that users find, or fail to find, bibliographic information from the online catalogue. Fasana (1980: 100) states that: "We are implementing a cataloguing code that is inadequate to the needs of computerization."

Hagler points out that a key to understanding the implications of AACR2 in the online environment is that "... the second edition of AACR would have to be formulated in the context of the automated catalogue, but when it was being written between 1974 and 1977, what constituted an 'automated catalogue' was still far from clear" (Hagler, 1985: 12). He later (1989) discusses the need for rules relevant to bibliographic displays and formats in the online catalogue.

Maxwell (1989) criticises the code for being based on manual systems and for not contributing to the online catalogue. She believes that the code does not fulfil the requirements of bibliographic records in the online environment (Maxwell, 1989: 189). Rowley (1989: 8) states that the code is based on the concepts of card, microfiche and printed catalogues and points out that any revisions of the code should be in terms of the OPAC-oriented environment. Boll (1990: 6) agrees with Rowley and Maxwell and states that "Computers have now introduced a totally new environment, totally new potentials that, for the first time since 1908, really demand a new code."

Ayres (1990) states that the full use of the potential of automation requires a new look at cataloguing codes. He concludes that the rules which were essential in the card catalogue are no longer effective in an online environment. In an historical approach to the development of the Anglo-American cataloguing codes, Brunt (1992) challenges the compatibility of AACR2R to the new environment and suggests ways to change the current design of the code. Bourne (1993) believes that AACR2R cannot satisfy the information needs of online catalogue users.

According to Jeffreys (1993: 57), "The advent of the computerised catalogue, more particularly the online public access catalogue (OPAC), has radically changed both the physical appearance and the internal structure of library catalogues." He concludes that the online catalogue has yet to make any significant impact on the code and that cataloguing rules still have to catch up with users' needs and modern technology.

Taking an object-oriented approach to cataloguing, Heaney (1995) questions the validity of AACR2R in the new environment and states that cataloguing rules have not evolved in parallel with developments in technology. Taking the abstract 'work' as the basis for description and access, he proposes a fundamental shift away from the AACR2R philosophy of description of, plus access to, physical items (Ibid: 152).

The theme of papers presented at "AACR2000: Toward the Future of the Descriptive Cataloging Rules", the 1995 preconference sponsored by ALCTS (Association for Library Collections and Technical Services, a division of the American Library Association), dealt with some fundamental issues concerning the adaptation of cataloguing rules to online catalogues (ALA. ALCTS, 1995). For example, from a serials cataloguing perspective, Crystal Graham (1995) criticises AACR2 for being written for use in a card environment and for not addressing the problems posed by the online catalogue's handling and display of serial entries. She also criticises the code for lack of attention to bibliographic relationships at a time when online technology offers new ways to express such relationships, which are very important to the catalogue user.

Little has been written on the relevance of cataloguing codes other than AACR to the online environment. A non Anglo-American cataloguing code which has recently become a subject for revision in relation to the impact of the online catalogue is the German cataloguing code, RAK (*Regeln für die alphabetische Katalogisierung*). Several recent articles show that the code is being revised to make it relevant to the online environment (Münnich and Zillmann, 1994; Münnich, 1995). Some of the possible changes to RAK which challenge the Anglo-American tradition. Reference is also made to the Nippon Cataloging Rules (NCR), which have been in use in Japanese libraries since 1943. Although the 1977 edition of NCR adopted the concept of the no-main-entry principle, the code is not designed for an online environment. This concept in NCR has attracted the attention of a number of writers who believe that it can be adopted by other cataloguing codes as a step towards better compatibility to an online environment (Takawashi, Shihoto, and Oshiro, 1989; Shoham and Lazinger, 1991).

In conclusion, it should be mentioned that, despite the relative abundance of the literature on the inconsistencies and implications of the *Anglo-American Cataloguing Rules* in the online environment, together with a considerable emphasis on the need for a relevant set of cataloguing rules, the literature has been for the most part descriptive rather than research-based in nature. This may be why Svenonius, and the other contributors to the Conference on the Conceptual Foundations of Descriptive Cataloging, University of California, Los Angeles, 1987 (Svenonius, 1989), repeatedly call for further conceptual as well as empirical research on different aspects of bibliographic control, including descriptive cataloguing. Svenonius (1990: 43) later states that "Conceptual research is needed, particularly to address comprehensive questions such as the design of an optimal set of rules for organizing information in the online environment."

The Need for and the Purpose of the Study

The need for research on the relevance of cataloguing codes to the online environment has often been expressed in the literature. Many writers decry the lack of both conceptual and empirical research (Hill, 1988; Lambrecht, 1991; Svenonius, 1981, 1990). In its list of research topics requiring study the Policy and Research Committee of the Association for Library Collections and Technical Services of the American Library Association (ALA. ALCTS, 1992) identifies the concept of the relevance of cataloguing codes to the online environment as a major topic for research.

The aim of this thesis is to provide a re-assessment of current cataloguing principles in the light of the features and capabilities of the online environment. This research will explore the possible impacts of computerised catalogues and the online environment on major concepts and principles underlying the design of cataloguing codes; and it will attempt to see to what extent there are relationships between conceptual and technological considerations in descriptive cataloguing and how they might influence each other. In conducting this research the researcher has attempted to achieve the following purposes:

1. To address the basic differences between the online catalogue and the manual catalogue and to highlight those features and capabilities of the online catalogue which might influence principles for the creation of bibliographic records and the construction of catalogues.
2. To investigate and analyse the impact of the online environment on cataloguing concepts and principles and to study factors affecting the design of cataloguing codes for the creation, manipulation and organisation of bibliographic records in an online environment.
3. To study the impact of other bibliographic components of the online environment, such as the book trade, bibliographic databases and abstracting and indexing (A&I) services, on cataloguing principles and to see if such communities can use a single set of principles.

The study aims to examine the possibilities of, and to justify the need for, alternative principles and rules in certain typical or important cases, and to examine the implications of these proposed changes and omissions in these principles.

Significance of the Study

It is hoped that the findings will help identify the areas in which current cataloguing principles could undergo a thorough re-examination at an international level, particularly when the nature, structure and content of library catalogues are in a state of evolution, shifting from individual library catalogues to global, networked catalogues. In addition, a better understanding of the present implications and inconsistencies of current cataloguing rules, which make for critical access problems in the online catalogue, will be achieved. It is hoped that the results of the study will help with the future revisions/changes of a number of concepts, principles and rules and also assist with further development of cataloguing principles for the online environment.

Research Questions

In conducting this research the following questions are addressed:

1. How, and in what aspects, do online catalogues differ from manual catalogues? Are the differences so important that they may influence the way in which bibliographic records are created, manipulated, searched and displayed? How might the capabilities and/or limitations of online catalogues influence the effectiveness/functionality of catalogue records?
2. What critical access/retrieval problems are caused by current cataloguing principles and rules in an online environment? What access/retrieval problems in cataloguing principles and rules make them less effective in locating bibliographic information in that environment?
3. How might the capabilities and/or limitations of online catalogues influence the effectiveness of catalogue entries? In terms of searching, retrieval and display of bibliographic data (input, storage and output), do the features and capabilities of the online catalogue have any impact on traditional cataloguing principles and rules? For example, what might be the impact of the search/retrieval capabilities of the online catalogue on principles for the choice and form of access points?
4. How might conventions in current cataloguing codes clash with other bibliographical conventions to which the same end-users are now exposed? What are the possible effects of other components of the online environment such as the book trade, bibliographic databases and A&I services on cataloguing principles?

Methodology

This research consists of an historical study and an analytical study. From an historical perspective, the concepts and principles underlying the development of cataloguing codes over the last one hundred and fifty years will be explored. The main focus of this exploration will be on the demonstration of major concepts affecting the design and development of cataloguing codes. This involves a study of Anglo-American cataloguing codes, the Paris Principles adopted at the International Conference on

Cataloguing Principles (ICCP) and, to some extent, two non Anglo-American codes, *i.e.*, the German cataloguing rules (*Regeln für die alphabetische Katalogisierung* (RAK)) and the Japanese cataloguing rules (Nippon Cataloguing Rules (NCR)), to identify basic concepts underlying the design of cataloguing codes. Consideration will be given both to the historical rationale and the future importance of cataloguing principles in the creation and organisation of catalogue records. From another point of view, the historical study will deal with the possible influence of both physical form and the arrangement of the catalogue on the design of cataloguing codes. This will be followed by a comparison of the features and capabilities of online catalogues with those of manual catalogues to provide background for the analytical part of the study.

The analytical study will focus on the concepts and ideas underlying the principles for the construction of bibliographic records and catalogues in relation to the capabilities and requirements of an online environment. In this context, concepts and ideas will be reduced to individual elements, to study and evaluate the interrelationships between them and the factors which are involved in these processes. Major focus will be the basic concepts of cataloguing principles; the logic of their application and the relationship of these principles to the logic of the online catalogue; as well as an examination of the types of principles and rules that are likely to change when moving from a manual catalogue to an online catalogue.

A major source of information for this investigation is the published and unpublished literature. Attempts have been made to cover comprehensively the primary and secondary writings on the subject as well as results of contacts established with experts in the field. The arguments in the analytical part of the study will be accompanied by related discussions in the literature, concerning different aspects of the issue of cataloguing principles and rules in relation to both manual and online environments. Similarly, the findings of major catalogue use studies will be taken into account.

In terms of gathering sufficient material for discussion, the researcher has attempted to include and cite the ideas of many people, in particular those who are vitally involved in the implementation of cataloguing rules in an online environment. As a subscriber to the AUTOCAT list, the researcher has had the advantage of having access to communications from cataloguers who work in an online environment and whose postings reflect the problems of implementing cataloguing rules in this environment. A number of citations from the AUTOCAT, USMARC and PACS-L lists have been included in this thesis where they are necessary and relevant. A number of documents studied for this research were identified and acquired through different services and resources on the Internet, such as E-mail archives, ftp (file transfer protocol) sites and cataloguing Web pages.

In addition to a number of small search and retrieval experiments with local and remote online catalogues, an experiment was carried out, using hypertext, to construct a prototype catalogue of "super records" and to demonstrate the possible influence of new technologies on cataloguing principles.

It should be pointed out that, due to the nature of this research, several issues have been repeated in more than one chapter but always from different perspectives. Because discussions in different chapters are based on a number of basic cataloguing concepts, some repetition or rephrasing of those concepts is unavoidable in sketching the context of topics raised in other chapters.

Limitations Placed on Coverage

The concept of the relevance of cataloguing codes to the online environment involves many different aspects. This study deals mainly with the possible influence of current technological developments, such as various search/retrieval/display capabilities of online catalogues, on cataloguing principles and rules. It also takes into consideration the potential influence of the networked environment on cataloguing concepts.

Almost all major and widely-used cataloguing codes are today based on the same set of principles, *i.e.*, the Paris Principles. Taking one of the most internationally used codes, *i.e.*, the Anglo-American Cataloguing Rules, is an appropriate approach by which to explore the relevance of cataloguing principles and rules to the online environment. The literature about other cataloguing codes which might be useful to this study was in languages other than English and there was little or nothing about them in English; thus, only the German and the Japanese codes have been dealt with.

The main thrust of this research is on the examination of cataloguing principles and rules for the handling of print materials. The issue of new forms of materials, such as electronic files and the cataloguing of Internet resources, is outside the scope of this study and would require another piece of research. It is simplistic to believe that print and other forms of linear communication will be utterly abolished by electronic technology. Books will not disappear with the advent of electronic texts, at least in the foreseeable future. Books and printed matter are still the most widely used carriers of knowledge and information. Despite early prediction, it seems likely that electronic documents will not become either the predominant form of communication or a major part of library materials in the foreseeable future (Gorman, 1994: 41; Crawford and Gorman, 1995). Gorman (1994: 41) states that: "Experience is showing us already that electronic publications are supplementing, not replacing, print publications in most instances." We are still in a transitional period from the Automated Library (paper and other tangible documents controlled by electronic records) to the Electronic Library (electronic documents controlled by electronic means) as put forward by Buckland (1992), who suggests that this transitional period will last for a long time.

This research does not deal with standards as technical specifications for communication within an automated information processing environment or between online systems. Issues such as ISBD, MARC, the Z39.50 standard and A&I services will be discussed only to the extent that they are relevant to this research.

Also specifically excluded are the economic and political/institutional factors behind the design and introduction of cataloguing codes, as this research will mainly be a conceptual study of cataloguing principles.

The Organisation of Chapters

Through an historical approach to the development of catalogues and cataloguing codes, serves as background for the discussions in the other chapters and will review some of the major concepts and principles in modern descriptive cataloguing codes of the last two centuries. The major characteristics and capabilities of online catalogues which might influence cataloguing principles and rules. Investigate a basic question: whether the conceptual foundations of cataloguing codes might be influenced by the capabilities of online catalogues.

In this context, deals with a conceptual analysis of the bibliographic universe, *i.e.*, bibliographic entities, their attributes and relationships that should be described in bibliographic records. Thread and analyses the bibliographic record in terms of the data elements which are used to describe and provide access to bibliographic entities and construct catalogues. A conceptual analysis of cataloguing principles in the light of the features and capabilities of online catalogues forms the content of, in an attempt to see how far the current cataloguing principles will remain valid in the new environment.

Some of the current and future issues underlying the development of cataloguing principles for the online environment. It will also propose solutions to some of the searching, retrieval and display problems that result from the treatment and/or inadequacy of current cataloguing principles in the online environment. An overall conclusion and will propose relevant approaches concerning the further development of cataloguing principles for the online environment.

Online Catalogues and Card Catalogues

Introduction

In any comparison between the online catalogue and the manual catalogue, it seems appropriate to choose the card catalogue among the other forms of catalogues (book catalogues, computer-produced book catalogues, and computer-output microform (COM) catalogues) as an appropriate approach, because: 1) the card catalogue has been and still is one of the most important manual systems in use for more than a century, 2) it is the basis from which the present cataloguing standards (cataloguing codes, ISBDs, and MARC formats) have been developed, and 3) it is the basis on which the structure and contents of online catalogues have been developed, *i.e.*, online catalogues are the logical successors to card catalogues.

It is not the intention of this chapter to reject the merits of the card catalogue. A realistic approach in comparing the online catalogue with the card catalogue should reveal advantages and disadvantages in both catalogues. Although there is overall support among librarians for online catalogues, most librarians consider having knowledge about the card catalogue to be very useful for an understanding of the origins of the present online system, particularly the structure of the MARC format and how individual records fit into the idea of a catalogue system. This was clearly the case in the general discussions about the card catalogue on the AUTOCAT list, 20 November 1994 to 3 December 1994, commenting on the need to teach the card catalogue in library schools.

In fact, an understanding of the origins and underlying concepts from which the present environment has evolved will help us develop catalogue systems based on substantive assumptions. In short, this understanding and comparison of the two environments will help us to reassess, refine and redesign our standards for the construction of catalogues. According to John Hickey : "Even if nobody still uses catalogue cards, more of our professional assumptions that we recognize are based upon unit cards & card displays; it helps to have some acquaintance with the previous technology."

It should be noted that online catalogues and card catalogues can be compared from different perspectives and according to different criteria. However, this study will compare them with regard to the processes by which bibliographic records and files are created, manipulated and organised on the one hand and searched, retrieved and displayed on the other. The differences between the online catalogue and the card catalogue will be explored in terms of the input, manipulation and output processes of bibliographic data.

Online Catalogues: What They are?

Online catalogues are a norm today; they are not static; they have developed rapidly and will continue to evolve further. By utilising the various capabilities of computers and telecommunications, online catalogues are adding new features that make them totally different from traditional catalogues. Online catalogues are now gateways to larger information systems or, as Hopkins (1993: 127) says, they are the 'one-stop information store'.

The online environment is an environment encompassing a wide range of information tools, both bibliographic (such as library catalogues, abstracting and indexing services and book trade databases) and non-bibliographic (such as numeric databases, directory databases, and full text databases). Library catalogues are now a small but very important component of the evolving online environment and are accessible through different tools in the networked environment, the public access computer system (PACS). The global network is the Internet including various PACS components such as Gopher, WAIS (Wide Area Information Servers), Netscape and Mosaic and other access modes such as Archie and FTP (File Transfer Protocol) tools. The Webpages created by libraries and other information providers are becoming very pervasive and are often used both by librarians and endusers as linking sources for library information. The same workstation serves as a means of navigating the whole world of the Internet. In the online environment not only are the information tools different from the traditional tools but also the whole concept of access to bibliographic information has changed. Time and location are irrelevant in searching the online environment.

Developments and Directions of Online Catalogues: As a result of a significant growth in scientific and technological information after the second world war and a resulting expansion in library collections, manual systems could no longer respond effectively to the ever-growing information needs of society. In terms of fast and effective retrieval of bibliographic information, the card catalogue had many disadvantages. Its large size, complexity and high costs of maintenance made it more and more difficult for libraries to maintain as an up to date searching tool (Freedman, 1979a; Guilford, 1979; Matthews, 1985; Reynolds, 1985). It became obvious that a more flexible tool was needed to cope with the new conditions of libraries. It was thus necessary to think of alternative ways of constructing library catalogues that could be cost-effective, manageable and easy to use. Following on the application of computers in other fields, librarians became assured that the computer's theoretical capability to control library operations constituted adequate grounds for embracing a mechanised approach (Hazen, 1981: 30).

As Weihs and Howarth (1988: 41) point out, "It was necessary to investigate the computer as a relatively cost-effective tool to provide library catalogs." Computer applications, however, first occurred in library activities other than the provision of public access to the catalogue. Computers were used in libraries mainly for housekeeping types of activities such as circulation control, acquisitions and serial control. This did not directly affect patrons' access to the library catalogue (Matthews, 1985: 3). Library automation began in the early 1960s with the rationale that "If a job could be done by computer, then the number of staff required to work at a defined level of expertise could be reduced" (Montague, 1978: 313).

Although some evidence of automation of library operations other than cataloguing is reported from the 1950s and 1960s (Reynolds, 1985), it is the MARC (Machine-Readable Cataloging) project that has been considered as one of the most important factors in the development of automated catalogues (Weihs and Howarth, 1988: 41). With the beginning of the MARC Distribution Service in 1969, large libraries began to utilise MARC magnetic tapes mainly for automated cataloguing in the standard form provided by the Library of Congress. The usefulness of MARC services in cataloguing, along with the increasing availability of computer technology in the late 1960s, led to more developments in automated catalogues.

In response to the needs of small and medium-sized libraries without access to a mainframe computer, centralised cataloguing services gave way to the establishment of bibliographic utilities in the early 1970s. The Online Computer Library Centre (OCLC, formerly the Ohio College Library Centre), established in 1971, has been considered to be a significant factor in the development of automated catalogues. With the standard cataloguing services of such bibliographic utilities, libraries were able to utilise the power of computer technology in a cost-effective way (De Gennaro, 1983: 631; Reynolds, 1985: 55). The proliferation of MARC-based cataloguing led to the realisation of the importance of uniform, standardised bibliographic description as the nucleus of bibliographic services at national and international levels. The growth of bibliographic utilities in the early 1980s as well as developments in telecommunication technology accelerated the move toward centralised MARC-based cataloguing and the need for standardised descriptive cataloguing (Reynolds, 1985: 55, 56).

A significant factor further affecting the development of online catalogues was that some libraries began to use MARC bibliographic information for their circulation systems in an online mode. Using short bibliographic records rather than full MARC records for circulation operations, a number of libraries tried to help their patrons in checking whether an item was on loan, on order, or at binding. This was a form of public enquiry module, which later developed into the online public access catalogue (OPAC). However, as Seal (1984b: 9) pointed out "The public enquiry module will often replicate the structure of a card or COM [Computer Output Microform] catalogue."

Another major factor leading to the rapid development of online public access catalogues was the contribution, by some library system vendors, of designing and developing public access modules as an important part of their turnkey systems. These vendors tried to incorporate a more sophisticated structure for the public enquiry module with more searching facilities. It should be noted that the early public enquiry systems were not integrated with other library modules, such as acquisitions and serials control.

Due to both the relative success and acceptability of online public enquiry modules, and pressures from patrons and librarians, libraries began to consider developing online public access catalogues (OPACs) with more bibliographic information, *i.e.*, full MARC records and more searching capabilities, such as keyword access and Boolean searching (Seal, 1984b: 9). The possibility of utilising MARC records as the foundation of bibliographic databases led to the development of the concept of the Integrated Online Library Systems (IOLS) in which "The information that was input at the acquisitions stage would form a basis for the catalogue record which, in turn, would support all library functions. Thus, a number of integrated systems, such as GEAC, ULISYS, ATLAS, DOBIS, NOTIS and VTLS, were established incorporating this modular design (Weihs and Howarth, 1988: 43-44).

The overall factors relating to the growing interest in online catalogues have been numerous. It is generally agreed that the most important factors that led to the rapid proliferation and development of online catalogues in the early 1980s were those related to their search, retrieval and display capabilities. Moreover, the opportunity of feedback from librarians and library patrons has provided a continuing momentum for upgrading the structure, contents and capabilities of online catalogues.

Tracing the historical development of online public access catalogues, Hildreth (1984, 1989) and Matthews (1991) identify three generations of OPACs. This categorisation is based on the features and capabilities of online catalogues in the processes of input, storage and output of bibliographic information. Matthews (1991: 7) claims that most of the existing online catalogues are still in the first or second generations and only a few systems have moved beyond first-generation. Added to the three generations identified by Hildreth and Matthews, recent advances in OPACs using graphical user interfaces (GUIs) have introduced a fourth generation to online catalogues.

First-generation Online Catalogues

Derived from circulation or cataloguing systems, first-generation online catalogues were in fact computerised card catalogues with almost the same traditional features. In contrast to the patrons' expectations from their use of computerised database systems, these new library catalogues provided limited author, title and controlled vocabulary subject heading access points. For this reason, first-generation online catalogues have been criticised as having no advantages over the card catalogue (Hildreth, 1984: 39; 1987: 650).

Searching in first-generation online catalogues was essentially based upon pre-coordinated information retrieval principles and was possible only through inputting the exact form of words or phrases. In contrast to searching in card catalogues, the patron had great difficulties as he/she had to input something into the system so that it could respond to his/her query. As this was possible only through inputting the exact form of words or phrases, which was difficult to remember, searching was not as successful as the searcher expected. Keyword access was not available and refining a search by further limiting it to elements such as date of publication, language or country of publication was not possible.

The interfaces, which were usually menu-driven, replicated traditional catalogues in their form of access by providing mainly phrase access to separate subject headings, title, and author indexes (Mitev, 1989: 144). Output and display of search results generally had a single format.

Second-generation Online Catalogues

With further developments in information technology, it was possible to provide a more sophisticated system for input, storage and output of bibliographic information. Second-generation online catalogues are a departure from traditional card catalogues and incorporate many new features for the provision of effective access. In contrast to the limited input, storage and output capabilities of first-generation online catalogues, second-generation online catalogues are characterised as being powerful tools for the searching of bibliographic information. Keyword search, Boolean keyword search, cross index search and increasing or reducing of search results are among the features of second-generation online catalogues (Matthews, 1991: 11). Hildreth (1987: 650-651) writes:

> *Today's second-generation online catalogs represent a marriage of the library catalogue and conventional online information retrieval (IR) systems familiar*

to librarians who search online abstracting and indexing databases via DIALOG, BRS, ORBIT, MEDLINE, etc. Improved card catalogue-like searching and browsing (via headings and cross references) capabilities have been joined with the conventional IR keyword and Boolean searching approaches. Many online catalogs support the ability to restrict searches to specified record fields, to perform character masking and/or right-hand truncation, and to limit the results by date, language, place of publication, etc. Also, bibliographic records may be viewed and printed in a number of different display formats.

However, it should be noted that there are a number of major differences between online catalogues and these IR systems that make second-generation online catalogues easier searching tools (Ibid: 651). With a combination of different search methods, the user is offered possibilities that were not available in first generation online catalogues. Due to improvements in the design of database management softwares, the structure and content of bibliographic records in second-generation online catalogues may be enhanced by incorporating full records augmented by information such as tables of contents, summaries, content notes, abstracts and links to full electronic texts. Considerable increase in the length of fields was another improvement in second-generation systems.

Interfaces are usually in two modes, menu-driven and command-driven; this makes the interaction between the user and the catalogue more flexible. In terms of user assistance, these catalogues provide more options including, for example, help screens, error messages and suggestive prompts. Ease of use and user-friendliness are two major features of today's second-generation online catalogues.

Third-generation Online Catalogues

As mentioned earlier, only a few systems have moved beyond second-generation online catalogues into third-generation online catalogues with enhanced or more sophisticated features. Due to the growing sophistication and availability of technology, new capabilities are being added to online catalogues making them more adaptive to the needs of library patrons. Free text search, enriched database search and simultaneous journal citation searching are among the retrieval capabilities in third generation online catalogues. Furthermore, the mode of interaction has been developed to the point of conversational, adaptive dialogue and the bibliographic format can be tailored according to user preference. Operational assistance such as automatic, context-based correction is also available (Matthews, 1991: 8).

Fourth-generation Online Catalogues

Beginning from the late 1980s, a most recent development in online public access catalogues has been achieved in providing easy access to bibliographic information by using graphical user interfaces (GUIs) such as Windows. These systems, which can be considered as fourth-generation catalogues, have moved away from the traditional menu-type interfaces and are more associated with client server and graphical user interface. They use WIMP (windows, icons, mouse and pointers) interfaces to speed and simplify searching. With the Windows-style user interface available through PCs (personal computers, *i.e.*, intelligent, and not dumb terminals), there is much more functionality. In these systems the user has the flexibility to click on various buttons, each of which carries a special function. Nevertheless, these systems do not eliminate but augment the keystroke access. There is also the possibility of using function keys for different purposes when keyboards are involved. In general, access is via mouse or keyboard or a combination of both.

Searching capabilities in the Windows version of OPACs are greater than those found in other generations of online catalogues. Pointer capabilities allow the searcher to select exactly the term he/she is looking for, while pull-down menus provide additional options to make searching even more useful. By using scroll bars and pull-down menus, browsing in different indexes is very simple. With the capability of post-Boolean searching, the search software also attempts to interpret users' search requests in order to present matches of greater or lesser interest to the user. This is called relevance ranking of the search terms. Similar to second and third generation online catalogues, these systems search for terms through using an implicit Boolean 'AND'. Other Boolean operators such as 'OR' and 'NOT' can also be used to narrow down search results or such search strings can be constructed using the mouse alone. In addition, access has been enhanced by text retrieval qualifiers such as 'language', 'date' and 'form' of the text. With this feature, it is possible to include new data elements that help in the better identification of the sought item. Integral or add-on text retrieval modules to provide range searching, related term searching, wild card features, adjacency and proximity are supplied by some systems.

As will be discussed in section 2.3.2, one of the recent additional advanced features of fourth-generation OPACs is the 'hypertext' function. Through this function, any word that the user selects or highlights can be used to search all the fields and subfields in all the records in the database for any occurrence of that word. This dynamic feature helps the searcher to navigate the database to find more relevant sources of information.

Online Catalogues: How They Differ from Manual Catalogues?

There have been some general attempts in the literature of the past decade (for example by Cochrane, 1985: 256, and Matthews, 1985: 6) to briefly compare different types of library catalogues. However, these comparisons have not been concerned with the concepts that underlie the nature and structure of the catalogue. In the following sections, the two types of catalogue will be compared in terms of the creation, manipulation and search/retrieval/display of bibliographic records.

Creation and Manipulation of Bibliographic Records—Structure and Content of Bibliographic Records: By 'structure of the record' is meant the bibliographic description consisting of data elements arranged and presented in a given order, such as card catalogue formats and MARC formats (Svenonius, 1989: 129). It is generally understood that the medium, via which bibliographic records are created, manipulated and made accessible to the searcher, influences their structure and content.

The computer has made possible the enriching of the structure and contents of bibliographic records. While the space limitations of 3" x 5" cards generally restrict the level of data elements to be entered in a record, the content of a bibliographic record in an online catalogue makes it possible and desirable to include more data elements such as those fixed-length data elements indexed in field 008 in the USMARC bibliographic format and even data such as summaries, tables of content, and full texts. This issue has been of major interest to librarians and system designers during the past decade and there have been some proposals in this regard. User studies of the early 1980s showed that most users of online catalogues would like to have access to tables of contents, back-of-the-book indexes and summaries (Matthews, Lawrence, and Ferguson, 1983: 134). Other suggestions have included the titles of essays in collected works or festschriften, book introductions, book jacket material, and the assignment of more subject headings (Markey, 1984: 85).

With the advent and further development of online catalogues it has become possible to assign a larger number of access points to bibliographic records. In comparison to the conventional main and added entries in the card catalogue, any data element in a bibliographic record may be designated as an access point.

MARC Format and Categorisation of Data Elements: As a set of standards for the identifying, storing and communicating of cataloguing information, MARC has significantly contributed to the growth of library automation and to the development of online catalogues. Although the MARC record was conceived as an automated version of the catalogue card, the structure is flexible enough to store bibliographic information in more detailed fields and subfields due to the requirements of automated systems for separate identification of data elements. While the medium for the card catalogue is the 3" x 5 " card with a fixed, less flexible format, most online catalogues use MARC as a communication format for the exchange of bibliographic information. In this regard, MARC communicates bibliographic information with more flexibility than the card catalogue. With the machine-readable format, in which the bibliographic information on a record has been broken down into fields and subfields, it is possible to separately identify each data element. This approach also allows for inclusion or exclusion of data elements for output as desired.

Based on the MARC format, bibliographic records can be created and tailored according to the specific needs of the library without either discarding standardisation or diminishing the quality of cataloguing. In the card environment, cataloguing depends on a longer process of manual checking against other catalogues (such as NUC, the National Union Catalogue), the ordering of card sets and receiving and interfiling them in the catalogue. This process in online catalogues is done more comprehensively and easily by subscribing to bibliographic utilities or by purchasing MARC products and downloading the needed records into the library's automated system.

MARC records permit a fuller level of description; more data elements to be included in the description and many more data elements to be assigned as access points for retrieval. A MARC record also includes other data, including non-bibliographic data that are used for catalogue maintenance. There is now a trend toward preserving detailed bibliographic records in machine-readable form. According to Reynolds (1985: 285):

> *The amount and type of information that constitute a 'full bibliographic record' is certainly open to debate, but since the late 1960s the accepted standard has been the MARC format.... The data that can be contained in a MARC record include the entire spectrum of information normally presented on catalogue cards plus a great deal of other potentially valuable categorizing information that can be encoded in fixed elements and elsewhere on record.*

However, MARC format has been criticised for being an electronic version of the catalogue card and for its limited accommodation of hierarchically structured information (Gaynor, 1996: p. C). There are also some problems with the MARC tagging and indexing of data elements that influence retrieval in online databases. Systems may differ from one another in the indexing of fields and it is often difficult to find out what fields are indexed by a given system. This results in retrieval and display problems, leading to user confusion.

Bibliographic Standardisation: In comparison to manual systems, the online environment gives much more emphasis to the concept of standardisation. Although the idea of standardised bibliographic description seems to have first appeared with derived cataloguing and the sale of Library of Congress cards in 1898 and later with the introduction of the National Union Catalogue (NUC), it was not until the 1970s that the application of computers to library operations and the advent of online catalogues gave to standardisation a much more significant role. With regard to the description, choice and form of data elements to be included in a bibliographic record, conformity to standards, *e.g.*, cataloguing codes, ISBDs and MARC formats, are vital to online catalogues. Unlike libraries of two decades ago with their independent card catalogues, libraries of today often create their own catalogue records according to national and/or international standards for the purposes of easy communication of and access to bibliographic information. Now, it is common for libraries of any size to participate in networks. One result of this, as Wajenberg (1992: 105) points out, is an ever-increasing pressure to conform to national and international standards.

Uniformity and consistency are basic requirements for effective bibliographical control. The rapid growth of shared cataloguing systems, developments in bibliographic utilities and the need for bibliographic exchange between databases in the last decade has led to a stronger reaffirmation of the value of standardisation in bibliographic records. Standardisation helps bibliographic records to be uniformly created, manipulated, exchanged and retrieved. According to Weihs and Howarth (1988: 78-79):

> *As the cataloguing community moves closer to making the ideal of universal bibliographic control a reality through local, regional, provincial, national, continental and international networks, all libraries assume the responsibility of maintaining standards requisite to maintaining the network. Integration and standardization are the keywords in the increasing movements towards, and promotion of, interconnected telecommunicating automated systems.*

Despite this emphasis on the significance of standardisation in the online catalogue, this concept has been considered only in the inputting of data elements in bibliographic description and not in the output and display, whereas in the card catalogue both input and output are standardised. For example, both the card catalogue and the online catalogue conform to the ISBD standard for the input format, *i.e.*, the order of areas, punctuation and levels of description. However, in online catalogues the output format is not fixed as in card catalogues and may be flexible. As Gorman and associates (1990: 32) state, the standardisation and formalisation of description and access points is crucial to the online environment and to the effective exchange of bibliographic records. As an important concept that has developed over the last hundred years to meet the changing forms of the catalogue and the needs of the profession, standardisation will continue in the future and as Wajenberg (1990: 497) points out, at an accelerated pace.

Input Inconsistencies and Level of Tolerance: A major difference between a manual and an automated catalogue lies in the fact that the creation of bibliographic records for online catalogues demands more precision and logic in terms of typography, spelling, punctuation, spacing, coding of fields and subfields. This is a critical requirement for computerised systems, since such errors can result in a serious separation or an improper sequencing of entries and therefore can lead to the irretrievability of records. In other words, any errors, even if very small, for instance a faulty keystroke, will be magnified in the online catalogue (Knutson, 1990: 24). However, in a manual system, when filing catalogue cards or when retrieving information, the human brain can often ignore such minor errors and treat them as if they are correct and file them in the right place.

Errors and inconsistencies can be corrected in the process of filing cards, whereas in the automated catalogue there is a lower level of tolerance towards such errors as variations in format, filing and indexing, and literal and logical inconsistencies within the catalogue. In general, the online catalogue is far less forgiving of cataloguing and typographical errors than is the card catalogue.

Construction and Maintenance of the Catalogue—Structure and Content of the Catalogue: By 'structure of the catalogue' is meant how the catalogue is built up, the kinds and content of files and indexes constituting it and the relationships of these files and indexes to one another. For example, a card catalogue, whether in dictionary or divided form, may include different files such as authors (personal; and corporate); references; titles (including other title information and series titles); subject headings (including references) and shelflists.

The advent of the online catalogue has given new dimensions to the catalogue's structure. It is generally maintained that the online catalogue can support a more complex yet more dynamic structure than that of the card catalogue. The online file may be independent and self-contained, it may be related to files of similar scope and structure or it may be integrated with other files such as holdings, circulations, acquisitions and authority files. The online catalogue provides services that were not part of the traditional library catalogue. Access to circulation information, status information, holding information, indexing of special collections, serials and so on have become possible through the development of the contents and structure of the catalogue (Potter, 1991: 77).

While the structure of the card catalogue is based on the concept of several discrete entries for a single item, the online catalogue maintains a single-entry structure for a single item (*i.e.*, in a master file), but with several indexes as access points to records in the master file. Emphasising what constitutes the structure of an online catalogue, Svenonius (1989: 129) states that:

> *In its general sense* structure *refers to an aggregate of elements related, or arranged with respect, to each other.... The structure of a catalogue or catalogue database consists of bibliographic, authority, and holdings records arranged in a given order and referencing one another through a variety of syndetic relationships. Thus, filing rules, together with ordering devices, such as the*

main entry and see and see also references, define a catalogue structure.... The structure of bibliographic descriptions consists of data elements arranged and presented in a given order. Thus, card catalogue formats and MARC format represent different but related bibliographic structures, the former intended for display and the latter for communication.

In terms of addition to the contents of the catalogue, the online catalogue has a growing ability to enlarge its own scope. Results of a nationwide survey on the use of online catalogues in the United States (Matthews, Lawrence, and Ferguson, 1983) revealed that respondents were enthusiastic about accessing journal articles, newspaper articles, encyclopaedias, dissertations, films and government documents through online catalogues. Other studies showed that users wanted the catalogue to be expanded to include journal titles, government publications and dissertations (Markey, 1984: 86), and journal citations, indexes to collections, content services, abstracts and book reviews (Burke, 1991: 41). Thus, it can be concluded that the contents of the online catalogue will be expanded in parallel with developments in the technology of catalogue construction.

Integration of the Catalogue: Integration has been considered as an important feature of the recent online catalogue in the sense that different parts of the library automated system are integrated through the use and manipulation of the same record as the basis for different library operations. In such an integration, a single master bibliographic record is tagged and can be manipulated for different library operations, such as acquisitions, cataloguing and circulation. A consequence of integration of the online catalogue, as pointed out by Buckland (1992: 34), is that bibliographic information in different parts of a library system, as well as other useful information, can be accessible to users and to other libraries. Such a concept indicates the importance of uniformity and standardisation of bibliographic records in the online environment.

Another interpretation of integration in the online environment is related to various methods of access to bibliographic information (Hagler, 1989: 205). In such an integration, different files and databases can be accessible via the same terminal. This concept has opened up a new era in bibliographic services and is considered as a significant factor in the enhancement of the catalogue. There are increasing attempts to build information systems with integrated access to different types of information services. The trend toward the integration of book trade bibliographic databases and A&I services with the online public access catalogue is an approach which makes the library catalogue a window to the whole bibliographic apparatus, a concept not feasible in the manual catalogue. These different kinds of integration have implications for cataloguing principles.

Authority Control: Authority control ensures the consistent use of names, series and subjects. No bibliographic record can be entered into the system until all assigned headings under which it can be searched are verifiable against the approved authority file (Hagler, 1985: 15). In a manual system, it is a time-consuming and costly operation and requires the services of skilled staff. There are many advantages to authority control in an online catalogue: in terms of maintaining cataloguing operations, it is particularly advantageous when major revisions to name and subject headings have to be done. In terms of searching, the actual search that the user does is via an authority control file. What the user inputs to the system is automatically switched through the index (authority file) to the correct form. In the online environment, the authority records are usually linked with bibliographic records.

There are a number of reasons for the resurgent interest in authority control in the online environment. The various difficulties that users have had with searching names and, as Potter (1986: 128) points out, the inconsistencies and errors in the records used to build the databases for online catalogues have led to new attention being given to the concept of authority control. For example, the ability to search personal names in either direct order or through initials has led to the enhancement of the scope and structure of authority files. Another major difference in the process of authority control between a manual system and an automated system is that correction or change of any heading in the card catalogue is a time consuming operation, whereas this task in some automated systems is to a great extent facilitated through a 'global change' which automatically generates a correction or change in all relevant records (Reynolds, 1985: 73; Weihs and Howarth 1988: 71; Tillett, 1989a: 158).

Although authority control in the online environment is at an early stage of development and, at present, only a few systems have operational authority control modules, the online catalogue's features and capabilities have given a new dimension to the notion of authority control. According to Seal (1984b: 14), "Much work needs to be done into the need for authority control in online catalogues; access by name will decrease and the concept of name references will change (a reference being in fact little more than an added entry) and the need for authority files in the traditional sense may become less important." In making the concept of authority control in the online environment clearer, Gorman (1990: 70) points out that:

It is evident that traditional reference structure was designed for premachine catalogues. The ideas that underlie references have been taken over in machine systems and incorporated into the notion of authority files. An authority file consists, very simply, of the approved form of access point for a person, body, or title, together with the references to that approved form and links to other related authority records (the latter being the computer equivalent of a see also reference). We have already seen that, in the computer catalogue environment, the distinction between a main and added entry access point no longer has meaning. The authority record takes this progress a step further. It, in effect, abolishes the distinction between an access point and a reference.... In other words, two of the basic assumptions of traditional catalogue codes—the main entry and the distinction between a heading and a reference—have survived.

Filing Rules and Problems: In any library catalogue, access points are usually filed according to alphanumeric order, which is a conventional arrangement applicable to most information systems accessed by human beings (Hagler, 1991: 263). However, filing is different in the manual catalogue and the automated catalogue.

The arrangement of access points has always been of particular interest to librarians and there have been a number of specific filing rules published to date. The *ALA Filing Rules,* The *Library of Congress Filing Rules* developed by John Rather, and the rules developed by the British Library Filing Committee are among the most important. Although developments in filing rules have been strongly in the direction of commonsense and are oriented toward the intelligent user (Rather, 1972), users actually have major problems in identifying the exact location of a heading in the sequential order of a large card catalogue.

In a manual system, filing is flexible and can be executed according to the order which seems desirable to the catalogue user, whereas, in a computer catalogue, it must follow the logic of the computer. Filing in a manual system follows the principle of *file as if*: that is, the form and order in which access points are arranged is according to the interpretation of the librarian with the supposition that the arrangement would be the most desirable to the user. For instance, the number *3* can be filed as if it were the word *three*. The use of the computer has influenced filing practices and it is generally agreed that the principle of *file as is,* which is necessitated by the introduction of computer filing, has more validity in the computer environment (Byrum and Hinton, 1979: 180; Gorman, 1979: 135; Malinconico, 1980: 33). This principle states that characters or words should be filed as they are and not as if they were something else; for example, the number '3' as *3,* and 'three' as *three.*

This realisation of the logical as well as the practical differences between filing in a manual catalogue and a computer catalogue came with the earliest attempts in the application of computers to bibliographical work. Current filing rules, which were developed for manual systems, proved not to be effective in a computer environment (Lubetzky, 1979: 154; Hagler, 1991: 272).

Users of online catalogues can encounter many problems when searching for bibliographic information. Due to different software specifications, computer-based filing has not been entirely standardised and the burden of thinking, for example, about the exact form of access points and the way punctuation and non alphabetic symbols are treated is left to the user (Hagler, 1991: 274-275). In manual filing it is possible, by a simple convention, to ignore stop words such as 'the', 'and', 'of', 'a', 'an', etc. at the beginning of titles whereas, in the computer catalogue, this issue demands special programmeming and in some cases they are difficult to handle (for example, if the stop word is a necessary part of the title and is not to be ignored). The treatment of punctuation poses another problem for the computer catalogue; while symbols, such as commas, apostrophes, periods and hyphens, may cause problems in the manual catalogue, they are considered as characters and are located in their 'logical' places by the computer unless software is created to overcome these difficulties. While the presence or absence of punctuation may be important in access points, they may or may not be important for online display. Diacritics and extended character sets to accommodate non-roman scripts are other important issues in computer filing of entries.

In sum, the logical arrangement of data elements in the computer has implications for the form of access points in the online catalogue. As an example, see the treatment of "Sir," which comes before forenames and thus interferes with filing. This can be seen in the change of some rules for the form of headings in the second edition of the Anglo-American Cataloging Rules (AACR2, 1978, and AACR2R, 1988). In fact, the incorporation/modification of some rules in AACR2 concerning the filing of data elements has arisen in response to the requirements of filing in the computer catalogue. For example, the inclusion of given names in parentheses in cases where the initials are not adequate for identification of authors with identical surnames (*e.g.*, Johnson, A. H. (Allison Heartz) and Johnson, A. H. (Arthur Henry)) is to respond to computer filing (rule 22.18). In terms of conference headings the form and order of the number, the date and the location of a conference in parentheses is an illustration of filing relevant to a computer (rules 24.7B1-B4). The place of numeric identifying elements in music uniform titles, *e.g.*, "Pianos (2)" rather than "2 Pianos", is another example of this issue (rules 25.30-34).

Searching, Retrieval, and Display of Bibliographic Records—User Interfaces: A significant difference between the online catalogue and the card catalogue comes at the stage in which the user interacts with the catalogue, *i.e.*, bibliographic records can be searched, retrieved and displayed. Online catalogues are here considered to be a great departure from card catalogues and it seems that there will be more developments in this regard in the near future. While the card catalogue is a self-evident medium with a clear physical existence, the online catalogue is not revealed to the users and is not easy to grasp in their first interactions with it.

In an online environment, the user cannot immediately understand the catalogue or its structure, coverage and searching mechanisms unless he/she interacts with the system and tries different options for searching and displaying of bibliographic information. Despite these limitations of the online catalogue, users show a high degree of satisfaction with the variety of features and capabilities it has at the output stage. Graphical user interfaces (GUIs), as indicated earlier in section 1.2, have made interaction with and use of online systems easier and more desirable. It seems likely that, in the near future, new generations of online catalogues will incorporate intelligent interfaces and sophisticated search/retrieval/display facilities.

Interactivity

Online catalogues have often been defined in the literature as 'interactive' catalogues (Cochrane and Markey, 1983; Fayen, 1983; Matthews, 1985; Bradriff and Lynch, 1985; Hildreth, 1989; Mitev, 1989). In the *Dictionary of Information Technology* (Collin, 1987), *'interactivity'* is defined as "system or piece of software that allows communication between the user and the computer in a conversational mode." Interactivity is considered as a major advantage of online catalogues over card catalogues. "It is this interaction between the user and the computer system that really sets apart the online catalogue from the other types of library catalogs" (Matthews, 1985: 13) Unlike in the card environment, if the user does not input a query in the system, the system will not respond to him/her. This process, namely the action of inputting a query by the user and responding by the computer, occurs quickly in real time and in a dynamic and progressive way (Fayen, 1983: 3). In sum, the concept of interactivity in the online catalogue is well defined by Seal (1984b: 3):

> *...online catalogues can be reactive and able to respond to the user in an intelligent way. This can be used to indicate what searching options are available, to correct operational errors, to suggest alternative items which might particularly match the search criteria and to guide the user through a long search. The reader can then be given help and feedback from the system itself, without needing to consult library staff. This approach is impossible in a card or a COM catalogue.*

With the introduction of the online interactive catalogue, it has also become possible to record how users interact with the system and search the catalogue. In this way, *i.e.*, through 'transaction log' analysis, librarians are able to check how users approach the catalogue and how frequently search terms appear, as well as to examine other aspects of search/retrieval problems, *e.g.*, users' errors and unsuccessful searches. Many catalogue use studies have been and are being done using transaction logs as a means of data collection.

User's Input Errors and the Catalogue's Level of Tolerance

As pointed out earlier, online catalogues are less forgiving than card catalogues in terms of any kind of error, either in the input stage by the cataloguer, or in the searching stage by the user. A general problem with computers is that they are usually unforgiving of errors; if the user makes the smallest of mistakes, they will not necessarily recognise it as a mistake, and even if they do they will often not offer help in correcting the mistake (Seal, 1984c: 55). However, there are systems being developed that recognise errors, display the type of error, and offer help to the searcher.

User Assistance

In comparison to card catalogues, online catalogues have the ability to provide user assistance in a variety of ways and at different levels. Mitev (1989: 145-6) classifies such aids in four categories as 'retrieval aids', 'linguistic aids', 'navigational aids', and 'semantic aids'. This is a major advantage over the card catalogue in that the system can respond to the user's problems and help him/her as to what the next move to achieve the result would be. Online catalogues have developed, over the past decade, different devices for providing help to their users in the different stages of searching the system (Lewis, 1987: 156).

Most online catalogues have the ability to customise help messages, screen displays and system prompts according to the needs of the user. Online assistance enables the user to influence the dialogue at all times in a clear way. This is not possible in manual systems.

User Satisfaction

It is generally stated that there is a higher level of satisfaction with online catalogues than with card catalogues and that users prefer this new form of the catalogue to the traditional card catalogue. According to Matthews, Lawrence, and Ferguson (1983: 152), over 90% of users like the online catalogue and almost 75% of users rate the online catalogue as being better than the card, book or microform catalogue. It is also interesting to note that this high level of satisfaction is consistent across all types of libraries (Matthews, Lawrence and Ferguson, 1983: 152). Lewis (1987), in reporting the results of different user studies, states that: "Users have a strong preference for online catalogs over card catalogs, and they very much want the new technology to succeed". Balaam (1993) and Burton and Hawkins (1993) report user satisfaction with OPACs despite their shortcomings.

A reason for preference of the online catalogue, even in its primitive form, to the card catalogue is related to its search and retrieval capabilities. It is also safe to assume that, as online catalogues continue to mature in terms of user interface, enhanced content and access, the level of satisfaction will be even greater. Another point worth mentioning is that the result of different online use studies show that use of the catalogue and use of the collection have increased with the introduction of online interactive catalogues (Matthews, Lawrence and Ferguson, 1983: 171). This, in turn, leads to higher user satisfaction as he/she becomes able to fulfil his/her information needs in easier, faster and more effective ways.

A major group of OPAC users are librarians themselves who are among the strong supporters of such systems. In a series of discussions in the electronic mail discussion group PACS-L@UHUPVM1.UH.EDU, 7-20 April 1994 and in response to Nicholson Baker's "Annals of Scholarship: Discards" published in the *New Yorker*, 4 April 1994, concerning the closing or storing of card catalogues, most librarians supported online catalogues as being superior to card catalogues. Charles Hildreth considers Baker's article to be a nostalgic approach to the historical value of card catalogues. For Hildreth card catalogues represent a dead-end technology and their maintaining would be very expensive.

Instead, online catalogues are open-ended, with a pure potentiality that will never reach its 'final' form. Walt Crawford asserts that online catalogues are ever-evolving systems that, when reasonably well designed, offer substantially better access and, unlike card catalogues, can be maintained as well as improved. Robin Alston supports online catalogues for their advantages over card catalogues in many ways and states that a major advantage is that most of the key elements on a record in an online catalogue are searchable, while massive amount of information on catalogue cards are not retrievable. Although there are deficiencies in OPACs, as Baker (1994) expresses very well from the point of view of a scholar, online catalogues will keep improving, while card catalogues have not any potential for improvement.

Searching and Retrieval Capabilities: With regard to searching capabilities, the online catalogue is a significant departure from traditional library catalogues. One of its most interesting features and a major advantage over the card catalogue, is the ability of the user to search for the needed item in a variety of ways that are not available in the manual catalogue. Online catalogues are able to generate both a greater number of access points as well as new searching capabilities that enable the user to search the catalogue with little information to hand. In addition to controlled-vocabulary searches by author, title and subject headings, for which relevant indexes have been created and maintained in the online catalogue, it is possible to search bibliographic records through access points such as other title information, series, standard numbers and any other significant data through keyword searching. In general, although there are still shortcomings in the searching capabilities of online catalogues, particularly in subject searching (Markey, 1984; Crawford, 1987a; Klugman, 1989; Lancaster, 1991; Larson, 1991), the findings of various studies indicate that users show much enthusiasm in online catalogues' searching capabilities (Hildreth, 1991: 17; Kalin, 1991: 132; Lipow, 1991: 105).

The following types of searches in the online catalogue are not available in the manual catalogue and can help the user to execute a greater variety of searches:

Keyword Searching

Keyword access is a very powerful search tool and can create much greater flexibility for the user to search item(s) of which he/she has not exact information. This is extremely difficult in the card catalogue. Keywords, *i.e.*, every indexed word in the bibliographic description, mainly headings, titles, other title information, contents notes and subjects, are appropriate alternatives for the catalogue user who cannot match the exact bibliographic information in the catalogue. When searching the catalogue, it is not necessary for the user to enter the exact form and order of words; while keyword searching is an alternative to controlled-vocabulary searching, it can also act as a complement to it. The potential value of keyword searching has often been highlighted in the literature. For example, reporting the result of a transaction log analysis of the Colorado University Library OPAC, Wallace (1993) found that 53% of searches were keyword searches.

In many online catalogues, there are options for limiting keyword searching to fields such as author, title, subject, or cross index. Among these options, title keyword searching provides a useful tool both as a substitute for subject access and for specific items when the exact or full title is not known. Some online catalogues provide keyword searching of abstracts and a number of systems extend this capability to the entire text of a document (*i.e.*, full-text searching), a trend that is becoming common in many online search services. It is extremely difficult to search authors under their forenames in manual catalogues, whereas in online catalogues with keyword access it has become possible to execute such searches. The same capability is available in the online catalogue for searching compound words of which the exact, full form is not known. However, keyword searching has its disadvantages: in some cases too many records may be retrieved and some records may be irrelevant to the searcher's need.

Boolean Searching

Influenced by A&I (Abstracting and Indexing) services, many online catalogues have the ability to run Boolean searches. With the use of Boolean operators, such as AND, OR, NOT, it is possible to define subsets of the desired subject or concept when two or more sets are combined. Specificity is what Boolean searching offers: the user can combine two or more terms (from the same index or different indexes) in a search statement and narrow or broaden the parameters of the subject of his/her interest.

Matthews (1985: 63) points out that: "In most OPACs, a Boolean 'and' is assumed when two or more terms are entered in a search statement, especially if the search is conducted on a single field or type of information, such as author, title, or subject."

Truncation

As in A&I services, some online catalogues permit the user to broaden the set of records to be retrieved by shortening the search word through entering a special truncation symbol immediately after the shortened search word (right-hand truncation), or before it (left-hand truncation), or within the word (mid truncation). Most online catalogues perform right-hand truncation implicitly rather than explicitly. This feature of online catalogues provides greater flexibility for the user to broaden access to the necessary information when character-by-character exact match does not help. It should be noted, however, that users have difficulty in understanding and using this type of searching in online catalogues (Crawford, 1987: 136). In some cases, truncation also results in either too many hits or irrelevant records.

Browse Searching

When the search aim is not specific, the desired results are not precisely known in advance or the correct terms for representing the user's query are not known at the outset, "browse searching is the most useful and preferred approach" (Hildreth, 1991: 26). Browsing, which is a good feature of the card catalogue, is becoming available in the form of browsable indexes in more and more online catalogues (Cherry et al, 1994: 180). The natural searchability that browsing offers satisfies users. In this type of searching, lists of index terms are usually presented in alphabetical order and the searcher can navigate the database by going forward or backward through the desired index until he/she finds the index term(s) which may lead him/her to relevant records.

A novel interface for browsing, which can improve access and the effectiveness of end-user searching, has been developed very recently. Using a GUI (graphical user interface), some advanced online systems (*e.g.*, Hibrowse for Europe) offer improved searching functionality by providing a multi-windowed view of data stored on a relational database management system (Pollitt, Ellis and Smith, 1994: 413). This novel interface can help the user to search bibliographic databases in a multi-windowed environment, each of which represents an index of the catalogue with scrollable windows. This approach has the advantage that the user can browse different indexes on the same screen to filter their content and find the most relevant items. Among the indexes are: author, title, publication date, document type, language and subject headings. It would be possible, therefore, to match different indexes and find related documents which have the same values, *i.e.*, identical data elements. This facility helps the user in appreciating the actual contents of the database through its different indexes and removes the problem of search specification using values that are not present (Ibid: 423).

Hypertext Searching

A most recent addition to searching capabilities in information retrieval systems, including advanced online catalogues, is hypertext searching or 'hypersearch'. Non linear, associative hypertext systems offer a search approach that attempts to more closely mimic human thought processes (Dimitrioff and Wolfran, 1995: 22). It is stated that hypertext, when used with bibliographic records, could overcome the static nature of existing catalogues (Bjorkland, Olander and Smith, 1989).

The hypersearch facility, such as that one offered by GoPAC from Data trek, can simply be applied by highlighting a term or clicking on a highlighted term in the record. The system will search for any occurrences of the highlighted term in all fields and subfields or all authority-controlled fields in all records in the database. The number of postings associated with the term will be indicated or the system will show a brief display of those related records which contain the same term. The term is highlighted in the retrieved records so that the searcher can see in which field it is located and can decide on the relevance of the record to his/her information need. During the display of related records, the possibility exists for the user to shift his/her focus and to continue a hypertext search on new and more relevant data elements. In this way, the hypertext facility helps users to navigate throughout the catalogue to find possible related works.

Author-title Search

In most online catalogues, there is an option for searching a known item through the author's surname combined with any keyword from the title. This is the clearest way to execute known-item searches (Crawford, 1987: 176). However, in those systems which restrict the search to author surname and the first word of the title, this type of search has the disadvantage of retrieving too many records when the author's surname is a common name, such as 'Smith', 'Johnson', and so on, or the title of the item begins with common words, such as 'Introduction', 'History', and so on. Another disadvantage is that, in most cases, users do not remember the first word of titles and thus fail to use this type of search in online catalogues. Nevertheless, it is very useful, for example, for searching titles on reading lists and it emphasises the importance of surname field.

ID Numbers

Another type of search in some online catalogues is possible through ID numbers. Among possible ID numbers are: call number; International Standard Book Number

(ISBN); International Standard Serial Number (ISSN); document number; computer system number, *e.g.*, OCLC (Online Computer Library Centre), RLIN (Research Libraries Information Network) or WLN (Western Library Network); local system number, *e.g.*, accession number; These types of search are usually performed by library staff (Matthews, 1985:59).

Other Searching Capabilities

Other types of searches in online catalogues include full-text searching, proximity searching, adjacency searching which are available only in a few online catalogues.

As mentioned earlier, these new searching capabilities in the online catalogue have revolutionised the way in which users search the library catalogue. The results of different use studies (for example, by Markey, 1983; Cochrane and Markey, 1983) indicate that the searching patterns of users in online catalogues have changed. In other words, the online catalogue has affected the ways in which users search for bibliographic information in library catalogues.

Output and Display: Display of bibliographic information is another major aspect in which the online catalogue departs greatly from the card catalogue. Surveying OPACs in a number of Canadian academic libraries, Cherry et al. (1994) report that screen display is the best developed area in online catalogues. The last step at the catalogue, viewing a search result through the display of the bibliographic record(s), is what the user actually gains from the system. The quality of such a display affects the overall usefulness of the catalogue (Crawford, 1987: 192). While the form and content of bibliographic records in the input/output format in the card catalogue (even when computer-produced) are fixed, the online catalogue permits a flexible format, with the possibility of displaying bibliographic information in a variety of ways and at different levels. The ways in which bibliographic information is presented in the online catalogue in response to searches vary from system to system. Each system has its own techniques for manipulation of a search result. This is impossible in the card technology where space limitations and the fixed form of bibliographic description do not permit any flexibility or manipulation of search results.

The level of bibliographic description is usually flexible and can be designed according to the user's needs. On the other hand and from a system perspective, as Boll (1990: 20) points out, there is a range of display formats suitable for a computer screen or a page printout rather than a three by five inch card. Online display formats usually include: 1) 'brief-listing display' which shows, on one or more screens, the overall results of a search through 'author', 'title' and 'date' of publication, 2) 'medium-level display' containing the standard bibliographic description, access points and status and location information, and 3) 'full bibliographic display' which shows full description with all access points, including added entries, and may contain summary and/or table of contents of the item.

Another major difference between the online catalogue and the card catalogue is the way in which data elements in a record make up and represent a bibliographic record. Reynolds (1985: 501) points out three functions in this regard: the labelling of data elements, the sequence in which data elements appear and the spacing between them. The online catalogue can include identifying labels before data elements for distinguishing the bibliographic text in a record. Labels may be highlighted, or displayed in uppercase characters or in a different colour. In relation to the sequence of data elements appearing in a bibliographic record, there is a fairly high degree of uniformity among online catalogues (Reynolds, 1985: 501). As in the card catalogue, the arrangement usually follows the numerical sequence of MARC tags or the ISBD order. Some online catalogues do not incorporate ISBD punctuation on the basis that users do not comprehend such 'secret punctuation' (Crawford, 1987: 196).

However, it should be noted that a number of problems may arise from the differences in the input and output formats in the online catalogue. A problem which would be difficult for the user to understand is that the relationships of headings (*i.e.*, access points) to bibliographic data may not be clear to him/her. For example, the role (*i.e.*, the responsibility) of persons associated with the work or manifestations of a work may not be distinguished in the way these names are displayed on the screen in conjunction with the title of the work. Therefore, the user may miss what he/she is seeking. In short, output in online catalogues is not controlled by cataloguing standards, a concept which will be discussed.

Limiting Search Results

Limiting or restricting the search results is a good feature of online catalogues and seems to have been copied from A&I services. According to Crawford (1987: 164), this capability of online catalogues should be offered or performed only when the search yields a large result. Matthews (1985: 55) points out that assisting the searcher in refining or expanding a search shows the powerful capability of the online information retrieval system over the card or COM catalogue.

In terms of refining the search results, the online catalogue has a great advantage over the card catalogue. When many records are retrieved in response to a search, the user may want to restrict them to certain aspects that might seem more relevant to his/her need. This is not possible in the card catalogue whereas, in most online catalogues, due to the assigning of some subfields in the MARC format as active and searchable, the user has the opportunity of further restricting, reducing or narrowing the search results (Matthews, 1985: 69; Hildreth, 1987: 651; Cherry et al., 1994: 180).

For example, the searcher can limit all the search results to works in a particular language, in a particular type of material or all the works published prior to, during or after a given date, or even works of a certain level of difficulty. This is done by specifying certain control fields and other MARC elements that can be used for limiting search results.

With further developments in online catalogues it is expected that the limiting of search results will become more sophisticated and more flexible for the user. In addition to the usual access points available in the card catalogue, more data elements are being indexed and more indexes are likely to be created in the online catalogue.

Sorting Search Results

Another feature of online catalogues is the opportunity offered to the user to sort the search results in the way that will best fulfil his/her need. Most online catalogues can sort the retrieved records according to such data elements as the author, the title and the date. This sorting capability requires that, in addition to usual access points, more data elements be indexed in MARC records in the database.

Some systems, such as OKAPI (Online Keyword Access to Public Information, the experimental OPAC developed at the Polytechnic of Central London), SMART, the US National Library of Medicine catalogue CITE (Current Information Transfer in English), STATUS/IQ, CANSEARCH, PLEXUS (Hartley et al., 1990: 356-357), provide ranked output and relevance feedback. They sort and display results of a search in order of highest occurrence of keywords. Given the searcher's judgments of retrieved items as either relevant or irrelevant, some of these systems can be asked to perform another search modified automatically by relevance feedback to provide a new ranked output list.

Status, Holdings and Location Information

A major feature of the online catalogue is its ability to link circulation information to bibliographic and holdings information and to show to the searcher the status and location of the sought item(s). The user of the online catalogue is able to see the status of any volume and/or copy of the item and whether the item he/she is looking for is available on the shelf or it is on loan, on order, at binding, missing or is not for loan. The status information also displays the 'date due' of an item on loan. The online catalogue can also show the location of the item in the library, *e.g.*, on which level and/or in which section it is located. All such information is useful also for stock taking and check-in purposes. These features help the patron, particularly the remote user, saving his/her time in knowing the status and location of the needed item(s).

Access and Availability: Unlike in a manual system, the user of the online catalogue has access to bibliographic, circulation, acquisition, holdings and location information at the same terminal, whether within the library or in other libraries through remote access. Again, this capability may be an indication of the need for uniformity and standardisation of data elements and also the importance of integrity in the structure of different files in the system.

In contrast to the possibilities for online consultation, card technology is a strictly localised medium with many physical restrictions to its use (Wilson, 1989, Svenonius, 1989, Buckland, 1988, 1992). Almost all libraries have a single set of catalogue cards for a document. To some extent a book catalogue or a COM catalogue might help in making the library catalogue available in different locations but these catalogues are costly to update at regular intervals, particularly when the collection is very large.

Unlike the card catalogue, the online catalogue is accessible through terminals located in different places in the library and outside the library via local area networks (LANs) and wide area networks (WANs). In the online environment it is possible for different users, whether inside the library building or outside it, to use the catalogue online and to even search the same record simultaneously. In terms of access to library catalogues, distance has now become irrelevant. Technology has enabled us to have decentralised access to bibliographic information (Buckland, 1988: 301, 1992: 75; Svenonius, 1989: 2; Wilson, 1989: 6, 7).

Interconnectivity is one of the most important goals of libraries today and can take different forms. Many library catalogues are now accessible through the different tools in the Internet such as Netscape, Gopher, Mosaic and Telnet. This is a great advantage over the manual system and will continue to expand with further developments in telecommunication allied to a decrease in telecommunication costs.

There is also more flexibility with interconnectivity for the searcher to go from one catalogue to another. This is done through the same catalogue or other catalogues which have a WWW forms-based interface. These developments, have brought with them new concepts such as globalisation of catalogues and the 'library without walls'.

With the availability of different types of OPAC systems to remote users over networks, for example, over the Internet, libraries need to conform to a new standard known as Z39.50. This standard is a protocol for information search and retrieval in a client-server environment, and is now moving from a standard to an operational reality. Z39.50 is used by libraries to access and search remote databases.

The WAIS system has implemented the standard to provide a consistent environment with consistent user interface, search and retrieval services. In environments supporting Z39.50 connectivity, the user sees remote catalogues as though they were additional databases available from the local system (Tomer, 1992: 567).

The standard is also being used in different library operations such as technical services, acquisitions and interlibrary loans. In this context, Z39.50 encompasses bibliographic databases, full-text documents, even numeric databases. For example, for bibliographic databases, a list of fields needed to exchange information and support those functions has been developed.

With advances in telecommunications and the rapid development of different facilities in the Internet it is now also possible to have access to electronic texts and files stored anywhere in the world. As we move to the end of the twentieth century, more full text services will become accessible through remote databases.

Summary and Conclusions

With regard to all the differences between the card catalogue (as a representative of the manual system) and the online catalogue (as a representative of the online environment), it can be concluded that the interactive online catalogue has many advantages in terms of content, structure and search/retrieval/display capabilities. Today's online catalogues provide more effective access to bibliographic information through capabilities that were not possible in the manual catalogue. These capabilities have affected the ways in which users use the library catalogue and it seems that, with further developments in information technology, there will be more opportunities for enhancing, extending and expanding the online catalogue.

Similarly, access to remote library catalogues and other bibliographical tools has been significantly improved through the demonstrated superior performance and effectiveness of computers and telecommunication technology. The online catalogue is now evolving into one of several components of a larger, integrated information system. Thus, remote access places OPACs in a potentially key position in relation to information systems generally.

In the 90s, the computer is now an integral part of modern society and has caused fundamental changes in many aspects of our life, most basically in the ways we organise information for fast and effective retrieval. However, unlike in the manual environment, cataloguers do not have control over the whole processes of record creation and catalogue construction as manipulation and output of bibliographic data are less controlled by cataloguing codes. From a comparison of the online catalogue and the card catalogue it can also be concluded that the cataloguing standards which are based on the concept of the traditional catalogue need to be reassessed and redesigned in terms of their relevance to the new electronic environment. A critical question here is whether cataloguing principles and rules need to be reconstructed and developed on a basis parallel to the development of the environment in which they are used. To answer this question, it seems appropriate to commence with a study of the basic concepts underlying the bibliographic universe, an issue which forms the content.

A Conceptual Analysis of the Bibliographic Universe

An understanding, in abstract terms, of the components that make up the bibliographic universe and the relationships that exist between them will help to grasp the nature of bibliographic entities and their place in the hierarchy of the bibliographic universe.

The major aim of the present chapter is to identify what constitutes the bibliographic universe and also the value and role of attributes of entities viewed as data elements in bibliographic records. Another aim is to see in what ways the online environment may influence the treatment of bibliographic entities and their attributes as well as the relationships that exist between entities, between entities and attributes, and among attributes in bibliographic databases. Since this chapter deals with the conceptual analysis of the bibliographic universe, it aims also to see to what extent cataloguing concepts are inherent in the bibliographic universe and whether they are independent of the environment in which bibliographic entities are described, *i.e.*, from the technology of catalogue construction.

A conceptual approach will be used to explore the bibliographic universe. The conceptual models employed in this study, as will be discussed in section 0.3, represent those elements of real world information (here, bibliographic entities, their attributes and the types of association that exist among entities). The advantage of such conceptual models is that they describe the inherent properties of data, which are independent of the hardware or software used; *i.e.*, conceptual modelling is not affected by the constraints of a particular database system.

Regarding conceptualisation as a way of interpretation, the conceptual approach in this chapter also provides a framework for the discussions concerning the functional analysis of the bibliographic record: which functions are carried out by which data elements and how data elements represent bibliographic entities and their relationships.

Some Definitions: It is appropriate to define briefly a few basic concepts which are important to the introductory section of this chapter; these definitions are treated in detail in their corresponding sections.

Bibliographic Entity. A general term for a work or any manifestation or part of a work which contains the intellectual or artistic creation and which is an object of interest to catalogue users and an object of description in bibliographic databases. In this thesis the term "entity" has been repeatedly used to express works at any hierarchical level. Entity also encompasses persons, corporate bodies and subjects.

Bibliographic Universe. The totality of bibliographic entities and their relationships. In a sense, the bibliographic universe consists of all types of intellectual or physical objects in any format which contain works of imagination as well as information.

Attribute. A property or characteristic that is common to some or all of the instances of an entity. It is piece of information associated with an entity or a relationship. For example, 'title', 'language' and 'readership level' are some of the attributes of the entity 'work'. Entities are described and identified through their attributes.

Bibliographic Relationship. An association between or among bibliographic entities that have common characteristics, such as the relationship between a person and a work or between a work and an item. The concept also applies to relationships between entities and their attributes and between attributes.

The Entity-relationship Model: Over the past three decades of library automation, librarians have had the chance to become familiar with the basic elements of database management systems and their logic. Most database management systems are conceptually based on the entity-relationship model.

The E-R model allows us to capture and preserve some of the important aspects of the semantics of the real world. Like most models in database management systems, this model is based on the concepts of 'entity', 'relationships' and 'attributes'. Applicable also to bibliographic databases, the E-R approach is an attractive means for conceptual modelling within the bibliographic universe and has been applied by a number of librarians.

No other conceptual models have been used to illustrate bibliographic entities. Tillett (1989a) applied the E-R model in her study of bibliographic structures and relationships. The IFLA Study Group on Functional Requirements of Bibliographic Records has used the same approach to delineate the different functions performed by the bibliographic record (drafts 1993, 1994, 1995, 1996). Emphasising the primacy of the object, or entity, over its relationships, Heaney (1995) uses this approach (but under the term 'object-oriented modelling') for studying the possible re-structuring of cataloguing rules and standards, namely AACR2 and MARC, in relation to computerised catalogues. In this chapter the E-R approach will serve as the foundation for later discussions about the identification of entities, their attributes and the relationships that exist among them.

Problems and Complexities of Designing a Common Conceptual Model: The question of whether or not to generalise a given model often confronts anyone trying to use E-R models as an analysis tool. This is partly due to the fact that the bibliographic universe itself is a complex environment encompassing various entities at different aggregate levels. Furthermore, each category of library materials (*i.e.*, bibliographic items) is different in terms of its nature and attributes. For example, monographs differ from serials in that certain types of relationship (*e.g.*, equivalence, derivative, and whole-part) are more common to them than to serials. Since the nature of each material type is different from the other, the types of attributes and relationships in each category of library material are different and, therefore, demand different treatments.

Another problem is the wide variation in definitions and inconsistent application of terminology which will be discussed in the following section.

Bibliographic Entities

A clear identification of entities is a first step in the conceptual analysis of the bibliographic universe. If we are going to identify various attributes of, and relationships between, bibliographic entities at different stages and create bibliographic records in a way that could be functional in a multitude of environments—*i.e.*, from the creator to the publisher to the printer to the distributor to the library and in a local, national, or global catalogue—the first step is to define different constituents of the bibliographic universe such as 'works', 'expressions', 'manifestations', 'items', 'persons', 'corporate bodies', etc. It will then be possible to design a conceptual framework for bibliographic entities to be described in any environment.

There is no definite terminology for entities at different bibliographic levels. Furthermore, the bibliographic vocabulary used by each community (*e.g.*, library, book trade and A&I services) is somewhat different from that of other communities. In the library context terms have been, and are being, used interchangeably. Various definitions have been provided by different people, for example, by O'Neill and Vizine-Goetz (1989), Svenonius (1992), and by the IFLA Study Group on Functional Requirements of Bibliographic Records (drafts 1993, 1994, 1995 and 1996). Even in the context of book-like materials there is a dearth of consensus on the definitions of various entity types, *i.e.*, different manifestations of works.

There are at least four justifications for arriving at a consensus on the definition of bibliographic entities:

1) Conceptual modelling of bibliographic entities would become easier and more understandable,
2) The increasing possibility that the same work may be produced in different manifestations and formats,
3) The proliferation of shared cataloguing systems and union databases that create and exchange bibliographic records, and

4) The trend toward cooperative creation and use of bibliographic records by publishers, library suppliers and libraries which demands definitions that are simple and understandable to all.

In this study the categories of bibliographic entities include 'work', 'expression', 'manifestation', 'item', 'copy', 'reproduction', 'person', and 'corporate body'. While referring to different definitions in the literature, this study uses the IFLA's (Draft 1996) definitions to set the framework for later discussions about attributes and bibliographic relationships. This would make the context of this research more consistent with IFLA's ongoing study on the Functional Requirements of Bibliographic Records.

Work. There is no universally accepted definition of 'work'. The term 'work' has frequently been used inconsistently in the literature of descriptive cataloguing and often without a clear definition. According to Yee (1994a: 9), a definition of work has never been included in the glossary of any Anglo-American code.

Ranganathan (1955: 26) defines 'work' as 'expressed thought'. Lubetzky (1979: 7) considers the work as an abstract entity which is the object of readers' interest but which is contained in the book. Lubetzky's definition is a book-oriented definition, of course. Tillett (1987: 22) defines a 'work' as the abstract intellectual content embodied in an item. O'Neill and Vizine-Goetz (1989: 167) clearly differentiate between a 'work' and a 'book': the former is the intellectual creation of an author and the latter is a material object or medium used to convey the intellectual work. They point out that: "Because the material book embodies and represents the intellectual work, the two have come to be confused, and the terms are synonymously used not only by the layman but also by the cataloguer himself." Pointing out that there is no straightforward definition that applies to all sorts of work, Wilson (1989: 10) provides a definition which is very different from Lubetzky's: definition. To him, 'work' is an abstract entity in the form of a text consisting a string of ordered array of symbols. He claims that the text of a work is the work. His definition applies to any type of product, even the electronic documents which may be open-ended texts. The IFLA Study Group on Functional Requirements of Bibliographic Records (Draft 1996: 11) defines work as an abstract entity. In general, it is the abstract 'work' that is the basis for later expressions and manifestations.

Expression. Conceptually, 'expression' indicates the next level in the bibliographic hierarchy and provides a linkage between a 'work' and any 'manifestation' based on that work. It is a specific presentation of the abstract work in the form of text (*i.e.*, sequence of symbols, words, sentences) and/or illustrations, etc. IFLA (Draft 1996: 12) defines expression as "the specific intellectual or artistic form that a work takes each time it is 'realized.'" Expressions include entities such as editions, adaptations, changes of genre, dramatisations, novelisations, and translations.

In the context of 'expressions', the term 'edition' should be defined clearly because it is a term very much used in dealing with the bibliographic universe. Defining what constitutes an 'edition' is one of the most important requirements for any conceptual model of the bibliographic universe and also in cataloguing practice; there is no general consensus on such a definition. Terms like 'edition', 'reprint', 'reissue', 'issue' and so on have always been problematic to cataloguers, especially in shared cataloguing systems. In practice, deciding on whether or not to create a new bibliographic record for the item being catalogued depends on the delineation of 'edition'. A new edition can be defined as any significant change in the intellectual or artistic content or form and/or layout of a work which makes it different from another edition of that work. Modifications, revisions and translations are therefore new editions of the same work.

Manifestation. Conceptually, 'manifestation' shows the transition from the abstract entity to the physical entity: any expression can potentially be embodied in different physical formats. Thus manifestation is a general term representing any kind of physical embodiment of an expression of a work. Yee (1994c: 227; 1994d: 356) defines 'manifestation' as a version or edition of a work with significant difference from another version of the same work. However, her definition does not identify physical form as a characteristic of manifestation. IFLA (Draft 1996: 14) defines 'manifestation' as the physical embodiment of the 'expression' of a work.

It should be noted here that the term 'version' has been used in the literature interchangeably for both the intellectual and physical forms in which an edition is produced and represented for use. For example, the same expression of a work can be represented in different physical formats, such as print and electronic formats, or the same work may be produced in several literary forms, *e.g.*, a version of the 'Arabian Nights' for young readers. The problem of 'multiple versions' refers to the description of different physical formats of (the same) work in a catalogue. In this study, the term manifestation encompasses the term 'version'.

Item. The term 'item' is frequently used in the literature and in practice and has a more concrete meaning than the term 'work.' While 'work' is an abstract entity, 'item' represents the physical object. IFLA (Draft 1996: 15) defines 'item' as a single exemplar of a manifestation. In the context of monographs, the terms 'book' and 'document' are often used interchangeably with the term 'item'. This is not a desirable approach in cataloguing because the term 'item' is broader than 'book' or 'document' and applies to different material types.

Copy. One physical unit identical to other units produced from a single type image, *e.g.*, a single example of a book. Thus 'copy' is an instance of the item and has a content identical to other copies of the same item. However, a copy may be specific in that it contains new characteristics not common to other copies of the same edition. For example, a copy may include handwritten notes by author, or annotations added after production of the copy, or may have some parts missing, or may be in a special binding.

Reproduction. An imitation of a copy of an item in another physical form without any change to the text and content. For example, a photocopy, a facsimile or a microform reproduction has exactly the same content as the original item.

Person. An individual related to a work either as responsible for the intellectual/artistic creation of the work or as the subject of the work. IFLA (Draft 1996: 16) provides a similar definition: person is an individual. Persons are important entities in the bibliographic universe and in the conceptual models illustrating that universe.

Corporate Body. A group of persons or organisations with corporate responsibility, action, etc. From a bibliographic perspective, corporate bodies act like persons; they are either responsible for a work or are the subject of a work. They may be of permanent or contemporary nature. AACR2R defines corporate body as an organisation or a group of persons that is identified by a particular name and that acts, or may act, as an entity. IFLA (Draft 1996: 16) defines 'corporate body' as an organization or group of individuals and/or organizations acting as a unit." Corporate bodies are important components of the bibliographic universe.

In addition to these levels, the following definition should be considered when dealing with the identification of bibliographic entities:

Superwork. Superwork is not an entity by itself. It is a concept which may be applied to the totality of a work, *i.e.*, its different expressions and manifestations and other related works. Svenonius (1992: 6) defines superwork as: "The set of all manifestations of an original work and all manifestations derived from it." Superworks also encompass new works, such as reviews, criticisms, indexes and bibliographies, which are based on the same work. In this context, many bibliographies (for example, of writers, philosophers, etc.) have a superwork approach in bringing together all expressions and manifestations of a work and also other related works.

In general, what libraries actually collect and describe through records are entities at a lower level in the hierarchy of the bibliographic universe; that is copies of items that embody expressions of works. The catalogue or the bibliographic database should clearly demonstrate the hierarchy and the place of each entity in that hierarchy.

The following conceptual models represent a partial picture for some of the entity types in the bibliographic universe. In these models, square boxes represent entities, circles represent attributes and lines represent relationships. Illustrates the concept of superwork as a set of related works and any expression, manifestation, and item derived from a work. IFLA (Draft 1993) represents a similar model for superworks. Figures show the place of each entity in the hierarchy of the bibliographic universe, *i.e.*, in its relationship to higher-level and lower-level entities. In general, conceptual models illustrate four levels of 'work', 'expression', 'manifestation', and 'item' in the bibliographic hierarchy. But, the present models are extended to two more levels ('Copy and 'Reproduction') to show all possible entity types in the hierarchy. Illustrates different manifestations derived from one particular expression of a work. A different approach, in that it shows different manifestations derived from different expressions of a work. Illustrates the bi-directional relationships that exist between entities in the bibliographic hierarchy.

Attributes of Bibliographic Entities

Entities and relationships are qualified by attributes representing their descriptive properties. Each entity has a set of attributes. Attributes can be viewed as data elements associated with bibliographic entities to describe and identify them clearly during the processes of creation, publication, production and cataloguing. For example, the title of a work is an attribute that makes the work known to readers. To identify an entity uniquely, a combination of attributes such as the author's name, the title, the edition and the date of publication can be used. Even this combination might need further clarification, such as format (*e.g.*, is it the paper or microfiche version?). A major concern of cataloguing codes has been, and still is, how to identify and record the least number of attributes that are necessary for adequate identification of, and access to, bibliographic entities in a catalogue. By 'adequate identification' is meant sufficient information, such as content, readership level, document type, publication information and imprint, that help users to decide on one particular item over another and confirm that the item described is the one for which they are looking in the catalogue.

Possible attributes of bibliographic entities at different levels: 'work', 'expression', 'manifestation', and 'item'. As can be seen, new attributes are added to entities at the lower level of the hierarchy (*i.e.*, at the manifestation and item levels). Attributes such as 'name of the publisher', 'place of publication', 'date of publication', 'series title', 'series number', 'standard numbers', 'physical format', and 'price' normally belong to manifestations. Nevertheless, attributes, such as 'title of the work', 'name of the author(s), 'content', 'genre', and 'language' which belong to entities at the work level are usually more useful for maintaining bibliographic relationships and for accessing entities.

Attributes can also be identified in terms of cardinalities (*i.e.*, of primary importance) and optional/mandatory factors. In Matrix 4.1 optional attributes, which are not as essential to the major functions of the record as mandatory attributes, have been marked with an asterisk ("*").

Matrix 4.1 (on the next page) represents a clearer and more comprehensive idea of the common attributes of different entity types (including persons and corporate bodies). Some attributes, such as 'title', are common to entities at different levels while others apply to entities at a certain level. Each entity can also be identified by a combination of two or more attributes, that is, a *composite identifier*. For example, the composite attribute 'Imprint' actually denotes a group of attributes: the place of publication, the name of the publisher and the date of publication. Potentially, any attribute or combination of attributes of a bibliographic entity may serve as an entry element, that is access point, to bibliographic record in a the catalogue. In traditional descriptive cataloguing, identifying and accessing bibliographic entities have in general been restricted to a few key attributes such as author, title and subject headings, those headings that have closer and more meaningful associations with their related entities.

Attributes of Bibliographic Entities in an Online Environment: It should be noted here that many of the following attributes have been used, at one time or another, as entry points in some manual catalogues. The concept of the machine-readable record, however, has made possible the inclusion of new attributes and/or new ways to make old attributes more easily retrievable. These attributes can be useful in an electronic environment and help to identify, retrieve, organise and display records according to users' needs. The language of the item, readership level (*i.e.*, target audience), genre/form, document type or category of material, physical format, geographic area code, standard numbers and record number are attributes which, due to the constraints of the manual catalogue, were either not included in bibliographic records or were not usually search/retrieval elements.

Bibliographic Relationships

Entities do not usually exist in isolation but are associated with one another through different types of relationships. In its simplest definition, *bibliographic relationships* are the associations between two or more entities in the hierarchy of the bibliographic universe. Any study of the bibliographic record must take into account relationships that exist between entities in the bibliographic universe and in the catalogue that is a partial representative of that universe. The end results of these relationships and the object of bibliographic records is access to adequate and precise information, to entities that satisfy information needs. The objectives and functions of the catalogue can be completely met through bibliographic relationships and linking devices. The study of bibliographic relationships is central to an understanding of the nature and structure of the bibliographic record, the catalogue, and ultimately, to the study of cataloguing principles.

Types of Relationship: In a broad sense, bibliographic relationships can be categorised into two types: those that hold between the entity and its attributes and among attributes (*i.e.*, internal associations); and those that hold between or among entities (*i.e.*, external relationships). Cataloguing principles and rules are concerned with both types of relationships.

Internal Relationships: In the first type of relationship, when a work is created by the creator (*e.g.*, the author), relationships are established between the creator and the work. Associations in the data, such as 'an author has written a book', are called relationships. In this case, the relationship between the entity 'author' and the entity 'book' is 'has written'. This type of bibliographic relationship forms the structure of the record and is an integral part of the bibliographic record. No attributes can be included in a record without its having associations to the entity itself. This is a simple yet very important type of relationship in the bibliographic universe and one to which cataloguing codes devote considerable attention.

Some types of internal connections are themselves presented in the record in the way that data elements are displayed in relation to each other; for example, the relationship between the author and the title is directly maintained by displaying the author's name near to the title, either as the 'main entry heading' on top of the title or by repeating it with relating words, such as 'by', 'written by', 'editor:', etc., as the 'statement of responsibility' following the title. Similarly, on the title page or the chief source of information, the name of the author usually appears near to the title. Even if it does not, the cataloguer seeks to establish this relationship on the record.

More attributes are added when the abstract 'work' is embodied in an 'item'. At this stage, attributes, such as the place(s) of publication, the name of the publisher(s), the date of publication, the extent and size of the item and the International Standard Book Number (ISBN) are introduced. The cataloguer's task is to identify various types of relationships and to create bibliographic records based on a certain structure for the display of the relationships between the entity and its attributes and among attributes, that is, data elements.

External Relationships: Another important type of relationship, which is established at the early stage but frequently not indicated clearly by the creator, is the relationship between entities. This is the type of relationship which the cataloguer attempts to distinguish and describe according to the rules provided for in cataloguing codes. The relationship between a newly created work and works by other authors that have been used as sources for the creation of the work is usually not defined except by indicating a general note such as: 'Includes bibliographical references'.

External relationships are considered very important and are a very complex element in the bibliographic universe (and hence in the catalogue). In order to identify this type of bibliographic relationship, different categorisations have been offered by different writers, for example, by Goossens and Mazur-Rzesos (1982), Hagler (1991) and Tillett (1987, 1992c). Goossens and Mazur-Rzesos (1982: 14) identify three general categories of bibliographic relationships: 1) the hierarchical relationships: the linking of the whole to its parts and of the parts to a whole, 2) the chronological relationships: the linking in time between the succeeding issues of an item, and 3) the horizontal relationships: the linking of versions of an item. Hagler (1991: 47) identifies five types of relationships between entities: 1) editions of the same work, 2) sequels, continuations, etc., 3) items both physically and bibliographically separate from one another but issued and intended to be used together, 4) important separately identifiable works contained within one publication and 5) items in the same series. Tillett (1987, 1992c) has developed one of the most comprehensive taxonomies in this area. She categorises bibliographic relationships into seven types: Equivalence, Derivative, Descriptive, Whole-part, Accompanying, Sequential, and Shared relationships. One more type of bibliographic relationship was added to Tillett's taxonomy by the IFLA Study Group On Functional Requirements of Bibliographic Records: 'work relationships', that hold between abstract works and their physical manifestations (IFLA Study Group on Functional Requirements of Bibliographic Records, Draft, August, 1993: 8, 10; Draft July 31, 1995). In the 1996 draft of the *Functional Requirements of Bibliographic Records,* the IFLA Study Group has modified Tillett's categories to 1) Work-to-work relationships, 2) Expression-to-expression relationships, 3) Expression-to-work relationships, 4) Manifestation-to-manifestation relationships, 5) Manifestation-to-item relationships, and 6) Item-to-item relationships. This study uses the IFLA's new categorisation as the framework for discussions about relationships.

Devices for Relating Bibliographic Entities: From a general perspective, linking devices refer to devices to connect bibliographic entities. In other words, bibliographic relationships are maintained through some attributes working as linking devices. Tillett (1992b: 23) defines linking devices as "...those specific devices within the catalogue that connect or link bibliographic records for related items."

A review of modern cataloguing codes shows that the devices for establishing bibliographic relationships have varied over the years and have been influenced by the form of the catalogue, that is, the technology to construct library catalogues (Tillett, 1987: 26, 196; 1989a: 151; 1992b: 23; 1992c: 163). The emergence of the concept of main entries, added entries, uniform titles and cross references, together with the abandonment of 'dash entries' are common examples of this dependency of linking devices on type of catalogue. In Matrix 4.3 various attributes working as linking devices are matched with the types of bibliographic relationship they support.

Bibliographic Relationships in an Online Environment

Bibliographic relationships are inherent in the bibliographic universe, and consequently in catalogues, and are not dependent on the medium by which and the environment in which records are created, manipulated and made accessible for searching. The new technology has made it possible for bibliographic relationships to be maintained and displayed more effectively and more flexibly in the online catalogue than was possible in the card catalogue. There has been a rebirth of interest in bibliographic relationships over the past decade and this may be as a result of the impact of the online environment on the structure of library catalogues, bibliographic files and indexes within the catalogue. To Tillett (1991a: 151), the demand for a new look at this concept has come from two factors: the development of online catalogues and the implementation of the second edition of AACR. There are at least two other factors: an increase in the types of media being catalogued and the growth of shared cataloguing systems and union databases. When we move to a shared online environment such as shared cataloguing systems, union catalogues and national or international networks the need for expressing bibliographic relationships and the types of associations has become more important, since it is most likely that, with an increase in the number of participant libraries and library collections, the number of manifestations and editions of a work will increase.

In such an environment it is important for the user to identify the relationship of entities to one another and to distinguish the place of entities in the bibliographic hierarchy. For example, a problem for the user appears when relating holdings to works or items which may be catalogued as collections or as separate parts (*e.g.*, identical item catalogued as part of a series to which it belongs, or as a monograph in its own right). In regard to the advent of computer catalogues, however, there has been little evolution in the concept of linking devices; many of the traditional devices have been embodied in online catalogues (Tillett, 1987: 196; 1992b: 23). As mentioned earlier, the provisions in current cataloguing codes for linking bibliographic entities are not adequate in terms of displaying all types of relationships explicitly and in a uniform approach. According to Attig (1989: 142):

> *The traditional technique used to link records is to rely on the data in the records to establish the relationships. In virtually all access points, the content of the heading field may be used to establish the relationship of the record to other records with identical heading.... In current systems, data from linking fields are rarely used to establish a direct link between records. Instead, the searcher is expected to use the information about related items as the basis for further searching. However, the format does support more direct linkage, and the possibilities deserve exploration.*

In an online environment each type of relationship (*i.e.*, bibliographic, name, subject and access points) can be established in accordance with the structure, content and search retrieval capabilities of the computerised catalogue. Online catalogues have the potential to provide displays of related bibliographic records, clustered according to the type of bibliographic relationships. What has been retrieved can direct the user in further searching.

In terms of maintaining bibliographic relationships as well as the types and forms of linking devices, the question arises as to whether the rules in current cataloguing codes are relevant to an online environment: do they give instructions on how to provide the most appropriate devices for linking related records? Since the technology of catalogue construction determines the types of linking devices (either abandoning some, *e.g.*, the dash entry, or introducing some, *e.g.*, standard numbers), should cataloguing codes provide separate rules for bibliographic relationships and linking devices to take best advantage of the online environment? Another question that seems relevant here is: which types of linking device to secure all types of bibliographic relationships are appropriate for an online environment? For example, the variety of linking devices for expressing the whole-part relationships may be a critical problem for the online catalogue. Is it possible and relevant to reduce this diversity in the treatment of relationships in an online environment? Is it possible to make one record for both the whole and its parts, or to make multiple records, *i.e.*, each part to have a separate record citing the whole? This is an important question in a network environment since library policies may differ from each other in describing the parts of a whole. These are some of the considerations concerning the principles and rules for bibliographic relationships in an online environment.

The general approach for bibliographic records constructed under current cataloguing codes and MARC formats is not capable of properly maintaining and displaying different types of relationships. There is no clear and uniform approach towards the treatment of different types of relationships. In many cases, as noted earlier, different devices are used to demonstrate the same type of relationship. For example, the equivalence relationship can be displayed by different linking devices, such as dash entries; notes to acknowledge equivalent copy; notes to acknowledge the original; shared uniform titles and holdings statements for copies. This divergence in the treatment of bibliographic relationships through different linking devices, as also highlighted in Matrix 4.4, is not suitable to online shared environments, where uniformity in access to related entities is crucial to the exchange and understanding of bibliographic records. Regarding the treatment of bibliographic relationships and linking devices in cataloguing codes, Tillett (1991b: 398) states that:

With regard to bibliographic relationships, history has shown no rationale and little consistency in how we relate bibliographic entities. A review of cataloging rules since 1841 reveals differing methods and devices used over the years to show bibliographic relationships, but also reveals a lack of any theoretical rationale for the [linking] devices.

New Ways of Linking Bibliographic Records: This researcher believes that online catalogues and future computerised systems may provide new and more effective linking devices to help the searcher to navigate a catalogue. The logic of database systems makes it possible to establish a more flexible linkage between data elements than exists in manual systems. It is possible to link two or more fields or subfields in machine-readable records in such a way as to better identify bibliographic relationships. For example, the computerised catalogue can match the value of the field 'uniform title' with the value of the subfield 'Language' or 'Part' or 'Date' in all records so as to retrieve and cluster those records that have these data elements in common. It is also possible to provide different structures for the retrieval and display of different types of relationships. This depends, to a large extent, on both the structure of machine-readable records and the software to design strings of fields and/ or subfields so that the computer can retrieve and display all related records in a user-oriented manner.

The current approach in establishing bibliographic relationships in the online catalogue is through the incorporation of linking tags; in most MARC formats blocks 76X-79X in the USMARC formats (particularly formats for books and serials) are for linking entries. These linking entry fields are designed to display a note in the record in which the linking entry field appears and to provide machine linkage between two related records (USMARC Bibliographic Format, 1990: 76X-79X, p. 2). The linking fields (block 4XX) that are incorporated in UNIMARC for a limited number of types of bibliographic relationships could be expanded for other types, using new means for this purpose. More coded linking devices are needed in MARC formats. For example, devices for providing links to other expressions of the same work or other manifestations of the same expressions and so on. Another example is to assign 'edition' as a coded link to provide access from an edition to any other edition of the same work. This is a pre-coordinated approach, as can be seen in examples of super records in the Prototype Catalogue developed. Nevertheless, in the MARC format all such devices need to be incorporated in a consistent way.

In online catalogues, there is the possibility of assigning more data elements as linking devices to establish relationships. Standard numbers, such as LCCN, ISBN, ISSN, OCLC record number and other similar numbers are one of the most useful elements for linking related records to one another. However, as Attig (1989: 143) has noted, these numbers do not always uniquely identify a single bibliographic entity and are not good candidates for the display of bibliographic relationships.

With regard to online catalogues, the question arises as to whether it is possible to have a special block in the Notes Area to include relationship information in a way in which related records can be retrieved and displayed. Tillett (1989a: 161) proposes that the types of relationships be tagged and reflected through notes. This will avoid the need for a redundant tracing in a machine-readable record. To achieve this, as Tillett (1989a: 161) points out, "We would need to slightly modify some of the MARC tags and indicators for notes which incorporate links to another bibliographic record."

Using hypertext techniques for linking related records is another promising method in bibliographic databases. This technique can be developed through pre-coordination, in that the cataloguer consciously creates links between related records in user-oriented ways in order to maintain different kinds of relationships. A prototype of such a catalogue has been developed, for maintaining relationships between related works/items. It is also possible that a hypertext technique could enable linking which is not pre-coordinated.

Summary and Conclusions

A thorough understanding of bibliographic entities, their attributes and relationships is essential to capture the concept of the bibliographic universe and to construct useful catalogues, as tools to navigate that universe. Descriptive cataloguing is in fact an attempt to describe and provide access to bibliographic entities in the most effective way. From a conceptual analysis of the bibliographic universe we can arrive at the following conclusions:

The bibliographic universe encompasses a variety of entities at different levels with different types of relationships to one another. Entities may evolve into new entities and maintain complex relationships with their original entities. For an exhaustive description of bibliographic entities in catalogues and databases, we need to understand the nature of each entity type and the expressions in which entities at different levels are to be manifested and/or presented in databases.

The Bibliographic Record in the Online Environment

Introduction

Its main aim is to explore the content and functions of bibliographic records as a whole and with respect to the online environment's possible impact on them. Through an analytical approach and a matching technique, the study will help to identify and examine the elements necessary for each function of the record and how this is influenced by the capabilities and characteristics of the online environment.

Functional analysis will be concerned here with a review of the relevance of individual data elements in relation to the processes for functional areas: searching, retrieval, browsing and display of bibliographic records. In this context, the chapter is prerequisite, in that the re-examination of cataloguing principles and rules needs to be carried out with respect to the different functions of the bibliographic record and the various data elements within it. Part two will demonstrate the need for a greater uniformity in the indexing of data elements for online retrieval which may significantly influence the functionality of the catalogue record.

Based on the recommendations of the Seminar on Bibliographic Records, held in Stockholm in 1990, the IFLA Study Group on Functional Requirements of Bibliographic Records has undertaken to define the functional requirements of bibliographic records in relation to both the variety of user needs and media (Bourne, 1992: 145). The purpose of the Study, an ongoing work in this area, is "to delineate in clearly defined terms the functions performed by the bibliographic record with respect to various media, various applications, and various needs" (IFLA Study Group on the Functional Requirements of Bibliographic Records, 1992: 1). The Study attempts to encompass all major types of library materials. From the approach of the IFLA Study Group, it can be implied that it was driven partly by the idea of the size of the bibliographic record—minimum requirements for national bibliographies—as well as by the economies which can be made in its creation. To recommend a basic level of functionality that relates specifically to entities was an additional charge given to the Study Group.,

This chapter attempts to complement IFLA's work, in that it will consider the influence of the new technologies (*e.g.*, the indexing of cataloguing data and the search/ retrieval/display capabilities of online systems as well as networking) on the functionality of individual data elements in the bibliographic record. For example, in terms of the functional requirements of data elements used for searching and retrieval of remote databases, the attributes defined in the Z39.50 standard will be taken into consideration. By discussing the need for individual data elements in different communities, this chapter will attempt to justify the need for a fuller level of description in bibliographic records functioning in an online environment. The chapter will also attempt to categorise data elements according to their various functions and provide the necessary background for the discussions on how the functions of the bibliographic record should be taken into consideration in any re-examination of cataloguing principles.

Identification of the Content

This part deals with the content and functional analysis of bibliographic records with respect to the needs of different communities in general and the library community in particular. Functional analysis is the analysis required for identification of the types of data elements, their various uses and the requirements associated with a particular function.

Before examining the functions of the bibliographic record in different contexts and to determine which data elements perform which functions, it is appropriate to commence with a brief study of trends in the cooperative creation and use of bibliographic records by different communities such as publishers, booksellers and librarians.

The Bibliographic Record in the Bibliographic Chain: As electronic access to bibliographic files is becoming increasingly commonplace, there is a parallel awareness of the advantages of cooperative creation and use of bibliographic information by different communities. Almost everyone involved in the book world in the developed countries produces, exchanges, edits and accesses bibliographic data. Thus the bibliographic record in the online environment reflects a wide spectrum of objectives, interests and uses. The identification and functional analysis of data elements used at each stage of the bibliographic chain can help provide a more comprehensive approach toward the rationale and requirements of bibliographic records.

A major concern for bibliographic control in different communities relates to the duplication of effort and resulting expense in the creation of bibliographic information. In fact, the chain is the sequence of bibliographic activities by different interested parties which have some elements in common. These elements should not be duplicated where it is feasible to avoid duplication. Ideally, a bibliographic record for each publication should be created only once and thereafter used and built upon by all persons involved in the bibliographic chain. Libraries, being more dependent on bibliographic records, would benefit more than others. A record created by publishers at the first stage would be useful to both librarians and library patrons. Descriptive and, particularly, subject description elements such as abstracts, pages of contents, back-of-book indexes and identification of the target audience, are very useful to libraries. In reality, the special needs of different users as well as economic, technological and administrative factors would influence the achievement of this concept. In terms of this ideal, Hagler (1991: 107) asks:

Who should create the model record? Who should be responsible for transmitting it to its potential user(s)? What is the best method of communicating it? Who should pay the costs involved? How can quality control be administered if responsibility for record creation is dispersed among different agencies? What priority should be assigned in pursuing the ideal in areas where it conflicts with local service and administrative considerations? None of these questions admits of any single or any permanently valid answer.

A number of national and international meetings have been held over recent years focusing largely on the creation and use of bibliographic information in a variety of environments and also on the need for a re-examination of the concept of the bibliographic record. The Newbury Seminar on Bibliographic Records in the Book World (November 1987), which was one of the first attempts in this area, aimed to identify real requirements for bibliographic records by various users such as librarians, booksellers and readers (Greenwood, 1988). The Seminar on Bibliographic Records, Stockholm, 1990, sponsored by the IFLA Universal Bibliographic Control and International MARC Programmeme (UBCIM) and the IFLA Division of Bibliographic Control is one of the most recent attempts in this field (Bourne, 1992). The Seminar was basically concerned with the possibility of introducing a common approach towards the creation of bibliographic records at a national level through the coordination of the different operations in the bibliographic chain.

The Book Industry Communication (BIC), set up in the UK and sponsored by the Publishers Association, the Booksellers Association, the [British] Library Association and the British Library has as its major objective the development and promotion of standards for electronic communication of information within the book industry (Book Industry Communication, 1992: 8). To achieve this objective, the BIC has developed guidelines and standards for the construction of publishers' bibliographic databases (Ibid: 3). One of these guidelines provides publishers with the identification of those data elements which should be included in the bibliographic database. As is seen, there are signs of a demand for extra descriptive information in bibliographic records. Most data elements used in the book world have relevant fields in

What are the Functions of the Bibliographic Record?

As noted earlier, the bibliographic record is the principal means for bibliographic control. In a cataloguing context, the major functions of the bibliographic record are:

1) to describe the physical item at a self-sufficient level,
2) to identify the intellectual/artistic nature, content and scope of the work and to uniquely distinguish bibliographic entities,
3) to provide links to related works/items,
4) to provide common information for citation purposes, and
5) to locate the item for physical access.

The cataloguing community is attempting to achieve a thorough examination of all the functions of the bibliographic record to meet users' needs. The functions of the bibliographic record as a whole have been elaborated on by the IFLA Study Group on Functional Requirements of Bibliographic Records (1995: 7) as follows:

1. to identify bibliographic items uniquely,
2. to relate, that is, to indicate related bibliographic entities (*e.g.*, through various linking devices as well as collocation in displays of records),
3. to assist in the choice of a particular bibliographic entity (*e.g.*, through annotation, summary, etc.),
4. to assist in the delivery or retrieval of bibliographic entities themselves (*e.g.*, through call number, physical location, text retrieval, etc.), and
5. to provide information about itself for database maintenance (*i.e.*, to housekeep).

Computer technology has influenced the functions of the bibliographic record in many different ways:

1) it has made it possible both to integrate all separate functions and procedures and to make a single bibliographic record that is applicable to various operations in the library database management system. Integrated systems support more operations based on the same multi-functional, electronic record. It is, therefore, essential that the bibliographic record should satisfy the needs of cataloguers, reference librarians, interlibrary lending librarians, acquisitions librarians and, most importantly, the needs of endusers.
2) it has made possible the formatting and reformatting of records for different purposes in different environments.

3) it has facilitated record enhancement for better identification of and access to bibliographic entities through the addition of tables of contents, summaries, back of the book indexes and full texts.
4) it has facilitated the communication of bibliographic records between systems and within systems.
5) it has made bibliographic control possible in a more precise way not feasible in the manual environment. This is done through providing multiple access points, both customary and new.

The various functions of the bibliographic record are carried out through a set of data elements (*i.e.*, attributes of entities) structured in a defined order. These data elements are derived from the entity at different levels of the bibliographic hierarchy. A thorough identification and functional analysis of data elements and data types helps to identify how the bibliographic record fulfils its functions in a database management system.

Data Elements in the Bibliographic Record: Identification and Functional Analysis: Few studies have been done so far on the identification and functional analysis of data elements in bibliographic records. According to Bregzis (1970), in the early 1960's there did not even exist a systematic listing of all data elements that could function as structural components of the bibliographic record. Three major studies on this issue are: first, a study carried out by Curran and Avram (1967). In this study, done for the Sectional Committee on Library Work and Documentation (Z-39) of the United States of America Standard Institute, they emphasised the importance of and need for separate identification of all possible data elements for the structural formulation of the bibliographic record. The study served as the basis for the formulation of the MARC II format by both the Library of Congress and the British National Bibliography.

The second, which has been one of the most notable studies concerning the identification of major data elements in bibliographic records, was a research project carried out by Seal, Bryant and Hall (1982) for the University of Bath Centre for Bibliographic Management. By creating a parallel catalogue of short entries, a major aim of the study was to identify which data elements were most used by catalogue users, mainly university students, in order to find and locate items. The study, however, has been seriously criticised for a lack of external validity, in that it was carried out with a limited sample representing only library patrons needs and excluded librarians working in different operations (Svenonius, 1990: 40; 1992: 4). The third study, as indicated earlier, is being carried out by the IFLA Study Group on Functional Requirements of Bibliographic Records.

To achieve the major aim of this chapter, *i.e.*, to identify the content and functions of the bibliographic record, it is necessary to analyse all the areas of bibliographic description as well as some other data fields that have been added to the record in its machine-readable form.

In the following section, a minimum set of data elements will be introduced according to the sequence in which they appear in a machine-readable format. The reason for this approach, as a starting point for the identification and functional analysis of data elements, is that database systems impose a record structure that is different from that of manual systems, *i.e.*, a structure that is broken into fields, subfields and further data elements. This structure and the separate identification and tagging of data elements allow for their inclusion or exclusion as well as their organisation, formatting and reformatting. This is also a requirement for integrated systems, in which a single record forms the basis for different operations.

For the purposes of this chapter, the USMARC bibliographic format has been selected, not as a framework to predetermine data elements but to illustrate the concept of separate identification, categorisation and coding of data elements. The reason for the choice of USMARC (and not, for example, UNIMARC) is that USMARC follows, to a large extent, a specific cataloguing code, *i.e.*, the Anglo-American Cataloguing Rules. This is in line with the general aim of this study which deals with the relevance of cataloguing principles and rules to the online environment. Moreover, almost all discussions in the AUTOCAT list concerning problems in indexing of fields and subfields refer to USMARC. This latter issue will be dealt with in Part 2 of this chapter. Reference will also be made to relevant values in the Z39.50 standard (for a list of attributes in this standard, see Appendix 2) to accomplish the study of the content and functions of bibliographic records in relation to searching and retrieval in an interconnected environment. The Z39.50 standard has identified and coded a list of data elements necessary for searching and retrieval of bibliographic information in remote databases and files.

In the following section, a field-by-field approach to the bibliographic record will be taken to identify data elements deemed to be most important for different functions within the library context and to analyse them from both conceptual and database perspectives. Thus the list of data elements is not intended to be exhaustive. It correspond more closely to the AACR and the required fields in the MARC format. For the purposes of this section, with some modifications to the name of fields in the USMARC bibliographic format, major fields which will be examined here are:

Fixed-length data elements

Standard numbers and codes

Language of the item

Main entry headings (personal names)
Title and statement of responsibility
Edition statement
Publication, Distribution, etc.
Physical Description Area
Series Statements

Fixed-length Data Elements (Control field)

The USMARC field 008 contains coded information about the record as a whole and about the nature of the item being catalogued. The coded data elements in the field 008 are potentially useful for retrieval and data management purposes (USMARC Bibliographic Format, 1989: 008, p. 3). For all formats, some of the information is: /06 Type of date/Publication status; /07-10 Date 1/Beginning date of publication; /011-14 Date 2/Ending date of publication;/15-17 Place of publication, production, or execution; /35-37 Language. Values 52-61 in Z39.50 are considered essential for similar functions when searching remote databases.

This field also has different meanings depending on the type of material. For books, it contains different values such as: Illustrations; Target audience; Form of item; Nature of content; Government publication; Conference Publication; Festschrift; Index; Fiction; Biography. Such values, which express the nature of works, are important for the user. However, most of them are now redundant since the same information is in a variable field. While the information is not in everyday use, some automation systems (*e.g.*, MELVYL) use the information in the 008, most notably the date, language and country codes, for limiting searches and provide, for example, a listing of all the items published in a certain country in a particular type of publication in a particular year. The same information is also much used for database management (housekeeping) purposes, such as record de-duping.

Publication type (*e.g.*, government publication, technical report, patent, conference publication, festschrift, fiction, biography, dissertation) is an attribute reflecting the nature of the entity. Such information is becoming more important to different users, *i.e.*, librarians, publishers, library suppliers and library patrons. It is a data element that helps the searcher to choose one type of publication over others. Whilst indicating this element in the manual environment was partially done by the addition of the type of publication as a subdivision to subject headings, in the machine-readable record it is also specified in a specific field (008), which is broken up into separate fixed fields, enabling the system to restrict the search to the type of publication specified by the searcher. The type of publication code can be used to select records to print a bibliography of, for example, dissertations.

Standard Numbers and Codes

Standard numbers are among the attributes that are usually added to most bibliographic entities at the publishing stage (*i.e.*, the manifestation level) and at the cataloguing stage (the item level). These numbers are nationally and/or internationally agreed upon and are intended to identify books and serials uniquely. The International Standard Book Number (ISBN), field 020 in USMARC and value 7 in Z39.50 and the International Standard Serial Number (ISSN), field 022 in USMARC and value 8 in Z39.50, are two widely used data elements in the bibliographic chain and are assigned to entities by related international bodies. Publishers, booksellers and library suppliers, as well as librarians, frequently use these numbers in different operations to identify and refer to 'specific' publications. In addition to ISBN and ISSN, different control and classification numbers are considered in both USMARC and Z39.50 for identification, finding and locating functions but such numbers are mostly related to a particular database or library.

Some systems allow searching through standard numbers. Since such numbers are controlled codes, retrieval based on them is straightforward (Rowley, 1989: 11). However, it is difficult for library patrons to identify items through such numbers since they are rarely familiar with them. These data elements are also not the type of attributes associated with the entity at the work level. Although they are assigned to items at the item level, they usually do not appear on the front cover or title page where the reader normally looks for key data elements. According to Lancaster and Smith (1983: 43), there are a number of disadvantages with the standard number as a searching element: 1) not all documents have ISBNs (or ISSNs), 2) very few present catalogues allow access via the ISBN, and 3) it is rather unlikely that the end-user of a library catalogue will know the ISBN for a sought item. Since few standard numbers turn out to be sufficiently 'well-behaved', they do not always uniquely identify a single bibliographic entity (Attig, 1989: 143).

In terms of the use of the MARC area for standard numbers as linking devices, Hagler (1991: 232) points out that, although not intended so in theory, the area is sometimes used in practice for recording standard numbers for related items, such as a paperback version or an edition distributed by a different publisher. In the case of serials with variant titles, the ISSN can function as a collocating device. For example, in some cases, standard numbers can be used to link successive titles of serials and create a cluster record to include the separate records for the different titles (Alan, 1993). Another problem with standard numbers is that they cannot normally be combined, for searching, with other key data elements such as the author heading or title or subject headings. There is no logical link between standard numbers and key data elements such as the author, title, or uniform title.

Language of the Item

Language is an important attribute of a work and an essential data element in bibliographical control that serves for the identification of items as well as for restricting search results. It can show the differences between versions of the same entity or different languages in a work. Most publishers and library suppliers include language in their data bases. Some online catalogues and most bibliographic databases, particularly journal article databases, allow combination of 'language' with other data elements to narrow search results and to find more specific items. For the same reason, language is one of the attributes defined in the Z39.50 standard as a potential element when searching remote bibliographic databases. Language Code (field 041) is used for works containing more than one language or in the case where the language of the text is different from the language of table of contents, summary or abstract. There are also other cases, such as texts in two or more languages, in which more than one language has to be coded in a record to identify an item better. In short, with the coding of language in 008/35-37 (Control field-language), 041 (Language Code), 500 (General Note) and 546 (Language Note) the usefulness of this element has added to the functionality of bibliographic records.

While language is being treated as more important in electronic data bases, current cataloguing codes have a traditional approach toward it; except in the case of uniform titles and notes, language as a data element does not usually appear on the catalogue record in traditional cataloguing.

Main Entry Heading (personal name)

Although the block 1XX in USMARC is defined as main entries (personal name, corporate name and meeting name), this section focuses on personal names as a primary and common data element associated with entities and used in different environments.

As an identifying element, the name of the author is one of the most important and widely used data elements in trade lists, catalogues, bibliographies and citations, in that where there is an author's name associated with the work or the item, it forms an integral part of the bibliographic record. As a finding device, the author heading is considered to be an essential element for providing access to the desired item in a catalogue, whether it is manual or online. If the searcher cannot recall the exact title, the name of the author would be a useful search key. From the result of their studies, Meador and Wittig (1991) conclude that 65% of searches in the field of chemistry and 86.66% of searches in the field of economics are done through the author's name. Hufford (1991: 58) reports that 22.9% searches by reference staff were author searches. Reporting the findings of her study of the OCLC bibliographic records, Arlene Taylor (1992: 227) notes that only 5.6% of a random sample of records do not have any personal or corporate names. Name access is an integral part of the bibliographic record.

As a collocating device, the author heading provides access to all works by a given author, so far as it is subject to authority control. In this sense, it is a data element which serves the needs of different users such as the book trade, librarians and library patrons. As an organising device, the name of the author is a key element in alphabetical catalogues and lists. In this context, it has been one of the most important elements for constructing catalogues, bibliographies, citations and trade lists in the Western tradition. In a computerised system, however, the role of the author's name as an organising element is limited only to name browsable indexes and brief displays in which the search result can be sorted according to author heading, as in the following title search:

In almost all online catalogues that maintain a brief display, the author heading is an essential element in the display of bibliographic information. Since a title may vary from edition to edition, or the titles of two or more different items may coincidentally be identical, the exclusion of the principal author heading from the brief display (author, title, and date) would obscure the relationship of the retrieved items between themselves and would fail in the finding and identification of the sought item(s). A search under the title 'History of civilization' in large databases would retrieve many records (for example, it resulted in 17 items in the University of New South Wales OPAC). As can be seen, the author heading is needed to differentiate between publications in alphabetical lists and its exclusion from the display would obscure one important element in the further identification of entities.

Names of secondary authors and of other persons associated with the work may be important to different users. In library cataloguing, only the name of the principal author (*i.e.*, the person considered to have primary intellectual/artistic responsibility) is entered in field 100 and the names of other persons are entered in the statement of responsibility (subfield $c) and repeated in access point form in block 7XX (added entries). In other communities, such as publishers and booksellers, the names of all authors and principal contributors are usually treated equally and are entered in one place. This is an area in which the scope of the function of this data field differs between library cataloguing and publishers' practices. Another difference can be seen in the attributes of the author, such as dates of birth and death and his/her affiliation. Library cataloguing considers dates associated with an author to be important, whereas publishers are less concerned with such information.

In short, the name of the persons responsible for the intellectual/artistic content of items is needed for the following purposes: 1) to find works by a given person,

2) to collocate entries for the same person, 3) to organise entries and to differentiate between publications in alphabetical lists such as card catalogues, printed bibliographies, browse indexes for persons and brief displays in online catalogues, 4) to differentiate between items with identical titles, and 5) to identify items for ordering, circulation and interlibrary loan.

Title Information and Statement of Responsibility

As can be seen in the USMARC format and also from the values assigned to the title, the title is one of the most important identifying and finding attributes of a work and is usually determined at the first stage when a work is created and made ready for publication. While author, subject or any other data element alone does not represent the bibliographic entity (the work or the item), the title is usually a useful data element for expressing an entity. In titling a publication, however, different persons, such as the author, the editor and the publisher are involved or may influence the process. That is one reason why a title may change at different entity levels or additional titles (*e.g.*, cover title, spine title and abbreviated title) may be assigned to the publication. In general, the title of an item may not be the same as the title of the work of which the item is a representation.

The title is one of the most important and widely used data elements in the bibliographic chain and in bibliographic control. Publishers, library suppliers, acquisition librarians, circulation librarians, reference librarians, document delivery librarians and cataloguers use the title for different operations. For example, from his study of three ARL libraries, Hufford (1991: 58) found that 53.1% of searches by reference staff members were title searches. The title also forms one of the most important indexes in national bibliographies and trade lists. In an alphabetical catalogue, the title is an important and useful access point, as an identifier of publications and, usually, as a summary of the content of documents.

While the title has considerable potential in retrieval, it is not, in some cases, a reliable identifier of publications such as in the case of documents with identical titles. For example, as illustrated, there are many books with titles such as *History of Civilization*. In some cases, even a title and an author's name together will not help the searcher to identify and locate the exact document unless a third element, such as an edition or a date of publication or a name of a publisher, is displayed. It would be better if the user used a combination of the title with other bibliographic data elements to specifically search for what is needed.

Another problem with the title is that it may vary in later edition(s), version(s), translation(s), etc. The searcher cannot rely on the words of the title to retrieve all editions or versions of a given work. Variations in the title have been a cause for concern throughout the history of descriptive cataloguing. While a slight change of title may be considered insignificant, it may have implications for online catalogues, possibly resulting in a 'no hit' situation. The provision of notes such as 'Title varies slightly' would not help the searcher find the item under variant titles.

The title is a useful element for keyword searching. With keyword access to titles it is possible to retrieve a title when the exact form is not known to the user. Another advantage of title keyword searching is that, in some disciplines such as science and technology, titles usually describe the subject content of publications and so can be used for subject searching. This approach, which has already been applied in manual indexing techniques such as KWIC (keyword in context) and KWOC (keyword out of context), has also been promoted in online catalogues through keyword searching. In stating that titles can form a useful basis for subject searching, Rowley (1989: 11) asks whether AACR2R should have made recommendations concerning the enrichment or expansion of titles.

The title is usually a key element in the arrangement of entries. In online catalogues maintaining a browsable title index, titles should be arranged in their right place with a certain degree of predictability for retrieval. In this context, 'various title information', such as uniform title, other title information, alternative title, parallel title, cover title, spine title, former title, abbreviated title, collective title and expanded title (fields 130, 21X-24X, 440, 490, 730, 740, 830, 840, subfield t in 400, 410, 411, 505, 600, 610, 611, 700, 710, 711, 800, 810; and 811; values 34-44 in Z39.50) can be included in the browsable title index to help the searcher find his/her item of interest.

As a linking device, the title, when indexed as an added entry and as long as it does not change, serves to link related entities. In those cases where a title does not change in the different editions of a work, it can automatically link related works and items.

For example, in books such as reference sources and textbooks edited and published at short intervals, a title collocates all the editions prepared by different editors or published by different publishers. In those cases where the title changes in different editions, an added access point for the original title will serve as a means to link different editions. There are other linked title fields (*e.g.*, 78X) and notes to linked titles (*e.g.*, 501) that provide linkage between related titles.

A useful construct in the context of title information is the name of the work or 'uniform title' (fields 130, 240 and 730; value 6 in Z39.50) which is used as a device for bringing together different editions and manifestations of a work and also as a filing element in alphabetical catalogues. As a cataloguing principle that needs to be re-examined in relation to the online environment. As a data element whose inclusion in the bibliographic record enhances retrieval functions, the uniform title has been one of the most important constructs devised in library catalogues. It should be noted that the term 'uniform title' actually encompasses many kinds of titles: including form headings, filing titles, unique titles for serials, collective titles and standard titles (Tillett, 1987:??). While the emphasis on uniform titles was introduced by Lubetzky in the 1960s, some forms (*e.g.*, Bible, Laws) have been in use for a long time.

As a search key, uniform title alone does not make sense in online catalogues any more than it does in large manual catalogues. The difference is, of course, that the next step towards differentiating between entries online is not as immediate as in card or book catalogues where the rest of each entry is immediately viewable. A search in large catalogues under 'Hamlet' will retrieve too many records, for different editions and manifestations, works about Hamlet, as well as works with the title 'Hamlet' written by other writers. The problem will be increased when the user searches in a large shared catalogue, such as a national union catalogue, in which there will be a greater number of editions and translations or manifestations of a work held by different libraries.

Although uniform titles are considered important in library cataloguing and a considerable portion of the rules are devoted to them, publishers and booksellers are less concerned about them in their bibliographic work. Now that many of them are constructing and using online/on disk bibliographic databases, providing this data element, particularly for works in literature, music, and law, can be useful in terms of providing more control in identifying and collocating related items and works.

Not only do all the four functions of the title (as a document identifier, a content descriptor, a linking device and an element for the arrangement of entries) remain valid in computer catalogues, but they also perform a more significant role in an online environment. Various title information related to an item can also be useful elements both for representing an entity and as useful points for accessing an item. However, system capabilities/limitations influence their effectiveness.

Statement of Responsibility

Based on the ISBD standard and AACR2, the name of author(s) and other contributors responsible for the intellectual or artistic content of the work should be transcribed (according to the title page information) after the title statement. Although in many current MARC formats the statement of responsibility is not indexed and therefore is not searchable in online catalogues, its major function is to display the link between name(s) and the title in the bibliographic record and thus to further identify and characterise the work. This function of the 'statement of responsibility' element is very important in enabling the catalogue user to appreciate the role of different contributors to the creation of the work, especially in cases of shared and mixed responsibility. The names of other contributors to a work, which appear as added entries, are not usually displayed, particularly in brief and medium displays. The lack of an explicit treatment of this data element in online displays, can obscure the description of the entity or even lead to confusion on the part of the user, thus reducing the identifying function of the record.

Another problem with the lack of a proper treatment of all the names in the 'statement of responsibility' area is that, if only the first statement is compulsory in cataloguing and recording of the names of other collaborators is optional, the catalogue would then lose the potential of being able to be searched under added access points. This is in conflict with one of the most important objectives of the catalogue: to show what the library has by a given author. Rules, such as 'rule of three' which limit the number of authors to maximum three, are not relevant to an online environment where there are much more storage and retrieval capabilities. There are certainly more benefits for users if we provide additional author/contributor access under statement of responsibility.

A reason for considering as mandatory the transcribing of the name of the author in the 'statement of responsibility' field according to the form in which it appears on the chief source of information (*e.g.*, title page) is in its potential use for free text searching in computerised catalogues. This is particularly useful when the form of name is different from the author heading. In the case of other contributors to a work, free text searching also makes it possible to search on names if they are not indexed as added access points in block 7XX. The 'statement of responsibility' could then be an alternative means for searching and retrieval of items.

It should be noted, however, that the name transcribed in the statement of responsibility may be in a form different from the name on the title page of other publications by the same person. Thus the name in subfield $c in the 245 field cannot be used to collocate all the works/items by a particular author. Neither can it be an organising element for the arrangement of records retrieved in response to a query. For this reason, the name of persons also appear in controlled headings (main and/ or added entries) to allow the arranging and collocating functions of the bibliographic record.

Edition Information

The 'edition' area includes the edition statement and any statement of responsibility associated with it. Since information in a work may differ from edition to edition, it is essential that this change be shown to the user. The 'edition statement' usually denotes intellectual rather than physical change of the item being described from other items of similar origin. It is also important in that it is an element for the further identification and characterisation of documents, and is important to various creators and users of the bibliographic record: to publishers, booksellers, acquisitions librarians, cataloguers, reference librarians and, most importantly, end users, in that it expresses the currency of a work. The proper description of the edition information will also prevent duplication of records and will help the searcher to identify the needed item properly. This is crucial for cooperative cataloguing systems and union catalogues that merge the catalogues of many libraries into one database.

In the context of the 250 field, there is little opportunity for the development of linkages between two editions of the same work. It is very important to include edition information in its right place in bibliographic records and display it for the better identification of entities. The treatment of edition information needs a new approach in the online catalogue, in that cataloguing principles and rules should address this issue both how to include such information in the record and how to display it. In anticipating the bringing together of different linking devices for the same information, all edition information and its linkages could be incorporated into a single block with tags capable of establishing linkage between related items exactly, as is possible in database systems. According to Laurel Jizba, "Maybe the place to locate all edition information is in the note area, coded in a new field next to the 533 note, or maybe the reproduction information needs to move up closer to the 250."

Publication, Distribution, etc. (Imprint)

Information concerning the place(s) of publication, the names of publisher(s) and the date(s) of publication constitutes the 'imprint.' This kind of information is usually attributed to documents at the item level, when an edition of a work is produced and published. The potential uses of imprint data add to the value and functionality of the bibliographic record for both libraries and publishers/booksellers. As identifiers, the data elements in the imprint area are usually more significant to publishers, booksellers, acquisition librarians, cataloguers and reference librarians than to end-users. In many cases the place of publication, the name of publisher, and the date of publication reflect the value, quality and orientation of the document. According to Hagler (1991: 40), "Publication information, like most other bibliographic data, is of value in identifying both the content (the work) and the document." In a sense, the publication information helps the catalogue to fulfil one of its functions perceived by Cutter: to assist in the choice of a book.

The publication information in cataloguing codes has been traditionally devised for description and not for access. In current cataloguing codes and MARC formats, the data elements in the imprint area are not prescribed to be used as access points, organising elements or linking devices. Although in the taxonomy developed by Tillett (1991a), such data elements demonstrate 'shared characteristic relationships' (*e.g.*, common publisher, date of publication and country of publication), the traditional catalogue cannot use them to display bibliographic relationships. In a broad sense, these data elements can be used to search items published in a given place or by a given publisher or in a given time.

However, since such a search can result in too many records, this approach is usually not advisable. Instead, each of the data elements in the imprint area can be used in conjunction with other key data elements, such as the author's name and title, to narrow down the results of a search. It should be added, however, that in some cases the publication information is the only clue for users to search for items they are looking for. These data elements have also been used to limit search results in A&I services and some online catalogues: for example, the date of publication has already proved to be an effective element for restricting or sorting search results in A&I services (for example, see Siegfried, Bates and Wilde, 1993: 283). Most online catalogues provide the same facility.

With a separate identification of each data element in the 260 field (and also the 'date of publication' in 008/07-10, 260$c, 046 and 533$d; and 'place of publication' in 008/15-17) it is possible to index these elements for later manipulation in bibliographic databases in the finding, identifying and housekeeping functions. For example, with keyword access it is possible to do further searching on the name of the publisher and find other works by the same publisher. However, recording names such as 'Aust. Govt. Pub. Service' does not help in that regard. In the case of a need to identify publications by a publisher, some systems allow searching on subfield $b in 260.

A problem that may arise from different approaches in the recording of publication information is that a document with more than one place of publication or more than one publisher may result in duplicate records in shared environments since each cataloguing agency follows its own priorities. This problem will not only result in duplicate records in a shared environment but will also mislead the catalogue user "into thinking there are two editions which differ in some significant respect" (Hagler, 1991: 41). Similarly, a lack of uniformity in the recording of the form of names of places of publication and the names of publishers, particularly of government bodies, may lead to the same problem unless suitable matching algorithms exist. Uniformity of names in the Imprint area is important, especially to publishers and booksellers, who do not provide additional points of access to such names as some cataloguing systems do in the field 710. Of the data elements in the Imprint Area, only 'Date of publication' (value 31) and 'place of publication' (value 59) have been considered in the Z39.50 standard. There is no value for the name of publisher.

Physical Description Area

The data elements recorded in this area include the extent of the item and other physical details and dimensions. These allow for the physical description of the item and can help in its further identification, in that they are indicative of the nature of documents. Although such elements are transcribed according to the physical item produced by the publisher and the manufacturer at the item level, they may have roots at the 'work level' and may indicate the nature of the work; for example, the extent of an item and its type of illustrations may be considered as an indication of the depth of treatment of content.

In this respect, they are important to the different users of bibliographic records: publishers, booksellers, library suppliers, librarians and sometimes to end users. In some cases, the information recorded in the physical description area assists both the librarian and the reader in their choice of relevant items, thereby fulfilling the 'choice function' of the catalogue. For non-book materials in particular the physical description area is very important to identify the carrier/container (007), which will be important to some users. In general, these data elements are not used in searching and have no finding or collocating function. There is no value attributed to 'physical data elements' in Z39.50.

Series Information

'Series' are defined in AACR2R (1988: 622) as: "A group of separate items related to one another by the fact that each item bears, in addition to its own title proper, a collective title applying to the group as a whole." As the sixth area of ISBD(G), the series area includes the series statement and the statement of responsibility and number(s) associated with it.

Series statements are the type of data elements that are usually attributed to the bibliographic entity at the publishing stage, *i.e.*, at the item level. Series information has a three-fold function: 1) it further characterises the item and indicates the orientation of the work by showing a specific subject area or the interest of its publisher, 2) it collocates items in the same series whether by the publisher or the author or the topical area, and 3) it can be used in the searching and identification of items. It is equally important bibliographic information for publishers, booksellers, and librarians and end users. In the library context, the information in a series statement is useful to acquisitions librarians, cataloguers and reference librarians as well as to library patrons for the identification and assembling of items in a group, *i.e.*, whole/part relationships.

As a linking device, series statements maintain the whole/part relationships. The approach is especially useful in searching publications of corporate bodies, because the name of a body usually expresses its field of activities and its mission-oriented responsibilities. However, a problem with series information is that, in some cases, the degree of topical connection among items is not bibliographically relevant (Hagler, 1991: 53). This implies that, in some cases, the series title is not to be considered as an access point and need not be indexed. For example, some publishers' series which bear only the name of the publisher, without any indication of the content of the items in the series, are not useful elements.

In a manual environment, the information in series statements is searchable only through added entries under the exact form of the series title and also through name/ title cross-references provided for them. In a computerised catalogue, series information can be searched not only through added access points (field 800 for personal name, 810 for corporate name, 811 for meeting name, 830 for uniform title), but also through keywords both in series statements and series added entries. Since it is difficult for the user to remember the exact wording of series statements, keyword searching can help retrieve such information.

The wording and order of the series title, followed by the related number within the series, followed by the title of any subseries and, finally, the related number should be treated in a uniform manner so as to permit easy collocation of items in the same series. Series information, particularly for online catalogues, should be subject to authority control in such a way as for it to be searchable. In terms of searching and retrieval of series information in remote databases, the Z39.50 standard requires value 5 for series title.

Notes: (5XX in USMARC; values 62 and 63 in Z39.50)

Notes are additional bibliographic information (*e.g.*, extended physical description, relationship to other works or contents) that are recorded for different purposes. Sometimes notes are regarded as indispensable; they included as justification for added entries. Some notes are included because the cataloguer considers them important for further identification of the item or for displaying its relationships to another work.

Over the past two centuries, the notes area has embodied various as well as more types of information. A comparison of the type and amount of notes information on a catalogue card with different fields in the 5XX block in the USMARC format shows the variety of notes (more than 50 different coded notes) that perform different functions, especially the identifying and relating functions: 'general note' (field 500), 'with note' (field 501), 'dissertation note' (field 502), 'bibliography note' (field 504), 'formatted content notes' (field 505), 'summary, abstract', 'annotation and scope notes' (field 520), 'target audience note' (field 521), 'reproduction information note' (field 533) and 'local note' (field 59X) are some important kinds of notes in the USMARC format. Only the value 62 for 'Abstract' and the value 63 for 'note' have been assigned to notes information in the Z39.50 standard. Not only do notes provide better description and better ways for users to identify the contents of items but they can also facilitate the fulfilment of the catalogue's objectives, especially in a network environment in which the searcher has no direct access to the physical item. In general, there is overall support among cataloguers for adding more extensive notes to bibliographic records. However, library administrators more typically want to eliminate notes, for example, those that are included merely to justify an added entry or are redundant with other information or access fields.

Notes include both relationship and non-relationship information. Notes containing relationship information are of various types: for example, notes about title variation and earlier edition(s), notes related to an immediately preceding or succeeding title, notes to acknowledge an equivalent copy, notes to acknowledge the 'original', notes about the described item on the analytical entry and notes of minor accompanying matter. In a sense, notes more than any other data elements demonstrate different types of relationships. Descriptive relationships, which hold between a work and a description, criticism, evaluation or review of that work, can only be found in the '500' general notes. Reporting the results of her study of the catalogue of the Library of Congress, Tillett (1992c: 182) found that 70% of the records with '500' notes were records with relationship information. Her study also revealed that every category of relationship, except the shared characteristic relationship, is represented in the general notes.

In their present structure, notes do not maintain a practical or automatic linkage between related records. According to Tillett (Ibid: 183), some types of relationships, such as sequential and whole-part relationships, are more likely to be shown by explicitly coded fields while other types, such as equivalence, derivative, descriptive and accompanying relationships, are more likely to be embedded in a general note. This disparity is also apparent in the MARC format. This is a case in which the structure of the MARC format inhibits the effective retrieval of the full content of bibliographic records. Many links to related records may be coded in a more explicit and structured format in the notes area. Tillett (1989a: 161) proposes that types of relationships be tagged and reflected through notes. This will avoid the need for a redundant tracing in a machine-readable record. To achieve this, Tillett (Ibid: 161) points out: "We would need to slightly modify some of the MARC tags and indicators for notes which incorporate links to another bibliographic record."

In a traditional sense, notes created according to current rules are mainly descriptive and are not structured for effective computer retrieval. It is not possible to search notes information via controlled access, unless they have been provided as added entries in blocks 7XX and 8XX. Even in formal notes in which an invariable introductory word or phrase or a standard form of words is presented (AACR2R rule 1.7A3), the aim is primarily for further description and not for access. If notes are to be searched as a part of the bibliographic record, they should be described and coded in a way that will allow the system to retrieve them. Duke (1989: 123) points out that:

However, if the contents note is also a point of analytical access to the record, transcribing the names of authors and complete titles as they appear on the publication would enhance the potential for retrieval. The USMARC format allows for specific subfielding of the 505 content notes, but many libraries consider this unnecessary and laborious.

Since the information in the Notes Area can be retrieved through keyword searching, the transcription of some data elements, such as titles and personal names, requires a high degree of uniformity and fullness. Whether the forms of names as they appear on the title page (or the chief source of information) are sufficient for effective searching and retrieval, or whether they need to be subject to authority control is a question that needs to be dealt with in a uniform approach. Whether there also needs to be a standard approach to the number of authors that should be named and whether subtitles should be included in tables of contents is a matter of local versus network preferences. This problem has significant implications for the design of the MARC format as well as for cataloguing codes. In relation to the content of notes for potential retrieval, Duke (1989: 123) also states that:

As long as the contents note was used only in a display as a block paragraph on the catalogue record, there was no need to precisely delineate its elements; however, to assist the computer in manipulating contents information in retrieval a formal structure of tags and subfields is necessary. In terms of the requirements of the bibliographic record in an online catalogue and with regard to potential keyword access to notes information, it is desirable that notes be provided in such a form and language that their content can be retrieved and accessed effectively. In terms of providing access to and collocation of related works or items, different types of notes require different treatments. There would be a need to have relevant rules about how to make notes and to provide relationship information (*i.e.*, links) in machine-readable records. This is one of the most important areas cataloguing codes and MARC formats could contribute to the effective fulfilment of the collocating function of the catalogue.

In summary: notes are considered necessary both for further description and for better identification of an item and also for a more explicit demonstration of bibliographic relationships. Although some librarians believe that bibliographic records should be briefer than they are now and that notes, in particular, if not displayed effectively, should be reduced in number, notes are at present considered to be more important than they were in the past and will probably have a more significant role in the future structure of records. With the capability of online systems to maintain large amounts of data on a record and with various search/retrieval/display capabilities, it is possible to input more data elements as notes to a record. Notes can perform more functions in an online environment where the remote user has no physical access to the items.

Functional Categorisation of Data Elements

Based on the discussions in the preceding section and according to their roles in fulfilling various functions in different environments, data elements in the bibliographic record can be categorised into the following five groups as follows::

1) 'finding' data elements: attributes that are necessary for searching and retrieval of known items. They provide access to the text of records. Such data elements include author headings, titles proper, other title information and standard/ control numbers such as ISBN, ISSN and LC control numbers..
2) 'identifying' data elements: those that help in the further characterisation of the work/item so that the searcher can distinguish a particular edition/ manifestation over other editions/manifestations of the same work. These elements are: author headings, title information, edition information, series information, language, readership level, summary/abstract, type of publication, genre/form, place of publication, name of publishers, dates of publication and country of publication.
3) 'organising' data elements: these elements are restricted to attributes that help in the arrangement of records, file indexes and in the sorting and limiting of the search results when more than one record is retrieved. Author headings, titles proper, dates of publication, call numbers and record numbers are among the most important organising data elements.
4) 'relating' elements: those attributes that show the relationship of the work/ item to other related works/items. These elements may include author headings, uniform titles, edition statements, series information, and some kinds of the notes information.
5) 'locating/accessing' data elements: attributes that provide physical access to copies of the item. Call numbers, location numbers, the names of library(ies), in case of union catalogues, are major accessing elements.

Data elements may perform other functions that are very important in computerised systems. In addition to housekeeping functions (for database management such as detecting duplicate records), some data elements can be used in narrowing the scope of a search. For example, date of publication, language of the work, readership level, country of publication, genre/form and document type are very much used by different users to make searching more specific. This is an area that should be taken into consideration in any analysis of the functions of data elements in bibliographic records and, consequently, in the re-examination of the catalogue's functions.

Matrix 5.2 and Figure demonstrate a categorisation of data elements according to the above types of function. The bibliographic record as a combination of data elements structured according to standards for different operations is the basis for carrying out the required functions.

As can be seen in Matrix 5.2, each data element may perform more than one type of function; indeed, one single type of function may be carried out through different data elements. Almost any data element serves to fulfil the identifying function more than other functions. The least function being fulfilled is the locating function which can be carried out only through the call number. It is interesting to note here that current cataloguing rules are less concerned about the locating function. Control fields, as can be seen, have identifying and organising functions only and are usually used by librarians. Notes are not used for finding purposes. They can be used mostly for further identification of entities and in some cases for displaying the relationship of the item to other items.

The MARC area for standard numbers such as ISBN and ISSN is sometimes used as a linking device to relate, for example, paperback version or an edition distributed by a different publisher. In case of serials with variant titles, the ISSN can be used to link successive titles of serials and link separate records for different titles.

In general, while descriptive data elements are more common to different users in the book world and in libraries, organising elements may differ in the two environments as a result of different objectives and functions. Nevertheless, in a variety of environments, encompassing different material types and varying degrees of focus on data elements, it is difficult to develop a categorisation that is both totally exhaustive and mutually exclusive.

That data elements can be grouped in three major categories: 1) control fields including data elements such as standard numbers, language, type of publications and country of publication, 2) description including descriptive data elements such as those recorded in the ISBD description, and 3) headings or controlled access points including name headings, uniform titles, and subject headings. The lines which link these categories or packages show that there is a close relationship between them, in that they constitute the structure of the bibliographic record in an automated system.

The reason for such a categorisation for a record structure is that the data elements in each box are prescribed and controlled according to different standards. The first category is prescribed and formulated by the MARC format. The second category is recorded according to the ISBD standards and the third category is controlled according to name and subject authority lists. As can be seen, the three categories or packages of data elements perform almost similar functions. However, with respect to the treatment of data elements there are some inconsistencies and overlaps between cataloguing rules, ISBDs and MARC formats. This is a source of problem in the proper functioning of the bibliographic record. Any inconsistency or overlap between cataloguing standards influences the different functions of the bibliographic record. As an example, the inconsistency in the indexing of cataloguing data will be discussed in the next part of this chapter.

A Uniform Approach towards the Indexing

The way in which data elements are correctly stored and manipulated is very important for the various functions of the bibliographic record and to the objectives of the catalogue, especially in a global online environment. In relation to the requirements of the bibliographic record for searching, retrieval and display, agreement needs to be reached nationally and internationally regarding the coding of certain data elements to allow for their indexing. This is a necessary requirement and a principle for large catalogues and for databases in shared environments. The treatment of some fields and subfields for indexing and display does not, at present, follow a uniform approach.

Part of the trouble lies in the fact that, unlike cataloguers in the manual catalogue environment, cataloguers now have less control over some of the cataloguing processes, such as the manipulation and display of cataloguing data. There is no guidance in current cataloguing codes for the handling of cataloguing data in online systems, such as the consistent indexing of fields and subfields for their searching, retrieval, display and sorting. Another reason is that database vendors provide record formats which may not be flexible in terms of indexing of cataloguing data. Gildemeister notes that online systems are designed by vendors for what people "want", *i.e.*, not necessarily what cataloguing standards require.

In this part some of the problems concerning lack of consistency in indexing of cataloguing data will be explored in relation to the uniform title, title proper, series information and notes information as examples of indexing problems in online catalogues. Such problems have often been a cause for discussion among cataloguers working in automated environments. A review of postings to AUTOCAT and USMARC lists indicates that a considerable amount of discussion is concerned with problems associated with the indexing of fields and subfields.

Indexing of Uniform Titles: As an example, a problem of some automated catalogues inhibiting access to records through uniform title as main entry is that, in systems where each field in the machine-readable format is indexed in a separate file, it is difficult for the catalogue user to distinguish which index, *e.g.*, author, title, etc., should be consulted for that particular access point. The discussions by different cataloguers in AUTOCAT (9 June to 11 August 1994 and also 8-9 September 1995) concerning different aspects of uniform titles in USMARC and their implications in online catalogues illustrated how different automated systems have different approaches to this problem. In some systems, uniform titles (*e.g.*, fields 130, 240) are not indexed as titles but are indexed as added entries (*e.g.*, 730, added entry—uniform title). On the other hand, some systems never duplicate the 130 or 245 (title statement) in 730. Coral (1992: 30) points out that:

The fact that the first uniform title for a bibliographic record is carried in a separate, but unlinked, field in many MARC formats, while all subsequent uniform titles are carried in linked fields, presents indexing problems for most computer systems. In a USMARC record the first uniform title is carried in the 240 field and its related author in the 1XX field. These two fields are not linked to one another. All subsequent uniform titles with authors are carried in 7XX fields with the author in the subfield a and the title in the subfield t. Thus the author and title are linked together. Most systems do not find it easy to keep the 1XX and 240 linked together in their indexing for some reasons.

In the context of some automated systems uniform titles are indexed as authors. For example, while one would expect *'Bible'* or *'Arabian Nights'* to be treated as if they were titles and to find them in the title index (due to the related fields in the USMARC format, for example, fields 130, main entry—uniform title and 240, uniform title), these titles are indexed as authors. Studying the problems of uniform title as author, Sanders (1987: 236, 237) states that treating uniform title main entries as author does still occur and inhibits access in some automated systems.

All these problems indicate that there is no consistent approach toward the indexing of uniform titles in online catalogues and that this divergence makes the input of accurate uniform titles into shared databases, and consequently, online retrieval and display difficult and, in some cases, impossible. As a possible solution to such an indexing inconsistency, Z39.50 assigns 'value 6' as the single field for uniform titles. In all systems using this standard the searching and retrieval of uniform titles will be carried out in a consistent way.

Indexing of Titles Proper: It is very important in a network or shared environment that a uniform approach be taken to the coding and indexing of various elements of title information. For example, due to different software specifications and varying approaches towards the indexing of 'title proper' ($a) and 'other title information' ($b), the same document may be retrieved in separate indexes in different systems. Some systems index both the $a and $b. They break the title at the earliest possible break and allow searchers to retrieve it under either 'title proper' or 'other title information'. Other systems index only titles proper ($a) and do not provide access to other title information. The treatment of 'other title information' as added entries and indexing them in 730 may cause further problems in online catalogues. If only some libraries index subtitles, the user will assume that they are the only ones that own those titles. If only titles proper are indexed, they may not be distinguishable from similar titles in the resultant brief display format.

Another problem in online retrieval of titles in large databases is that, in some systems, the default index for searching titles is the keyword index. This would result in too many hits. For example, a search (carried out on 12/10/1995) in the RLG (Research Libraries Group)'s database under the title of 'History of Civilization' resulted in 5790 hits of which only a small number of records had the title proper of 'History of Civilization'. The search was, in fact, a default title keyword search.

The Z39.50 standard assigns separate values for different title information: 'value 4' for title proper, 'value 5' for series title, 'value 35' for the title proper in another language and/or script, 'value 39' for the running title, 'value 40' for the spine title, 'value 41' for a variation from the title page title appearing elsewhere in the item, 'value 42' for former title, 'value 43' for shortened form of title, and 'value 44' for an expanded (or augmented) title.

Indexing of Series Information: As in the case of titles proper and uniform titles, a difficulty in searching 'series information' in an online catalogue is that the searcher may not have a clear understanding of the index that should be searched for this information. The problem is that there is more than one type of series statement: subject series, commercial publisher series, corporate body series and author series, each of which requires a different solution. In addition, there may be a combination of two types of series; for example, publisher and subject. This has caused the treatment of series information in machine-readable records to be problematic, leading in some cases to catalogue user confusion.

Indexing of Notes Information: The treatment of the field 505 (formatted content notes) is another example of the problem in indexing for searching or display: some systems are not set up to handle the indexing of subfields such as subfield t in the 505 field, which allows the system to limit keyword searches to titles only and subfield r to authors only. In relation to the indexing problems of 505 Cynthia Watters wrote:

> *We are redoing our keyword indexing table, and the question comes up, do we want to index the 505 $t in the keyword title index or, as has previously been*

done with the 505 $a, index it in the keyword notes index. If we want to index it in the title, what do we want to do with the $a? Or, put another way, if we index the 505 $t as title, it means two areas to specify to retrieve all titles in 505 fields—both the title fields and the note fields. Along with the question of title is the question of author. Do we want to index the new 505 $r in the keyword author index or the keyword notes index? Author seems potentially more tricky because, unlike the "regular" author fields, the 505 $r will have the name in direct order. Thus if we index it as an author, the searcher may have to specify something like: Doe John or John Doe (our system treats strings as strings; you could say John and Doe, but if you say John Doe it will look for them in that order; you can specify proximity, but this all gets more sophisticated than most users).

The relationship between 505$t and 740s is also important for the efficient indexing of titles. At present, it is a function of how the system indexes. While the coding of titles in 505 as $t is done in some systems to allow their indexing, the addition of 740s may result in double hits in retrieval. Some systems (*e.g.*, MultiLIS) index the 505 up to the / in the title index, so making the 740 redundant. In other systems, for example, Geac Advance, the 505 field can be indexed into a notes searchable category which is separate from the 'title' searchable index. It is said that this approach "makes it easier to distinguish between a title coming from a 245/246/740 and a title from a 505". In summary, as the discussions about the issue on the AUTOCAT (22-29 May and 1 December 1995) indicate, there is at present no consistent approach in the indexing of 505$t and added title entries in the 740s.

A similar problem can be seen in the different approaches by different cataloguing agencies of the indexing of 'Dissertations' or 'Theses' information. Since access to such information in academic libraries is important to many users, in that they want to limit searches to theses or there may be a need to print out a list of theses available in a collection, many libraries provide additional access to theses. However, as different postings to AUTOCAT on the question of 'Theses' (20-26 February 1996) show, this type of data is indexed differently by cataloguers in various fields (such as fields 500, 502, 533, 610, 650, 655, 690, 710 and 830) with a lot of redundancy.

Z39.50 assigns a single field (value 63) for different note information, such as extended physical description, relationship to other works, or contents. As can be seen, this approach cannot fully respond to the indexing, and consequently, to the searching and retrieval of different types of information in the Notes area.

A Possible Solution: As a promising solution to the present inconsistencies in the indexing of data elements in online catalogues, the approach in the Z39.50 standard can be followed by automated systems. This is particularly important because of the increasing use of WWW front-ends to library catalogues and other information systems. The Z39.50 standard standardises the indexing of different attributes. Each attribute has a given value so that any system using the standard can index the cataloguing data in a consistent way.

The user can use the local system to search the local catalogue, local CD-ROM databases of MARC records and also other library catalogues. The Z39.50 standard allows the user to search other catalogues as if he/she is searching the local catalogue with familiar search techniques. In essence, Z39.50 provides a consistent search interface to bibliographic databases.

Conclusion: In terms of networks and shared environments, the tagging of fields and subfields for improved indexing should follow a more uniform approach so that retrieval and display would be more efficient. What a local system is set up to do may not be in line with the requirements for searching and retrieval by remote users. Existing systems may not actually be capable of such indexing but the potential exists. MARC formats should take advantage of enhanced indexing and create records that not only meet today's system needs and present software but also will meet future enhancements and be portable to other softwares. The Z39.50 standard is a promising approach towards a consistent handling of data elements for searching and retrieval in networked environments. It can help to remove problems possibly arising from the indexing differences between databases.

Summary and Conclusions

The bibliographic record in its machine-readable format is very different from the traditional, manual record. The electronic environment has provided catalogue records with many opportunities and potentialities to carry out more functions in a variety of operations in bibliographic work. With the advent of online catalogues, the identification of data elements for inclusion in bibliographic records, which have gradually developed alongside the technology of catalogue construction, has reached a new era. To carry out different functions more effectively in the online environment, bibliographic records should be created with regard to a number of factors:

With ever-increasing developments in information technology and telecommunications and, consequently, ever-increasing availability of bibliographic files online or on-disk, an increased potential exists for bibliographic records to be created and used cooperatively in a variety of environments. This would result in more standardisation as well as economy in record creation.

In response to the various needs of different users, the bibliographic record will require a minimum set of data elements included for carrying out different functions such as the finding function, the identifying function, the relating function, the organising function and the choosing function. The increase in the number and type of data elements that make up electronic records illustrates the variety of their uses in the online environment. It can be concluded that inclusion or exclusion of data elements depends directly on the functions of the record and that reducing the level of description may lead to a great loss of functionality of the bibliographic record. The more functionality we expect from the bibliographic record, the more data elements would be needed for inclusion.

The way in which cataloguing data are indexed and tagged in automated systems influences the functionality of bibliographic records. In library cataloguing and for optimal functionality of bibliographic records, the indexing of fields and subfields should follow a uniform approach. This would maintain effectiveness in searching, retrieval and display of bibliographic information both within systems and between systems. In this context and in terms of the identification and handling of data elements, cataloguing standards (codes, MARC formats and the Z39.50 standard) should be brought closer, in that they should provide guidelines for the designation of data elements for machine-readable records. If the rationale of cataloguing principles is to bring uniformity in bibliographic description and effectiveness in access, they should also address the question of uniform approaches to the indexing of cataloguing data.

In summary, developments in the electronic handling and in the exchange of bibliographic data have had, and will continue to have, significant effects on the bibliographic record. A major impact of such developments on catalogues is that the bibliographic record in its machine-readable format can enhance data functionality beyond that found in manual records. Various functions of the bibliographic record in the online environment are carried out through data elements whose choice and content are determined by cataloguing principles and rules, an issue which constitutes the content.

Cataloguing Principles in an Online Environment

It is often claimed that current cataloguing codes are based on concepts and principles from the pre-machine period and that they do not serve us well in giving guidance in the construction of electronic catalogues. Thus, in organising bibliographic information for an electronic environment, it is essential to examine the validity and adequacy of the principles on which current cataloguing codes are based. By assessing the extent to which cataloguing principles accord with the capabilities of the online environment, this chapter will answer some of the questions that have been highlighted in the literature of the last two decades on the relevance of current cataloguing principles (mainly the Paris Principles) to the online environment. To many writers, for example, Martin (1996b: 157) the online catalogue has meant a re-examination of the principles and practice of cataloguing. Carpenter and Svenonius (1985: 177) raise the issue that:

> *At the time the Paris Principles were composed, there was some awareness that computers might change cataloging; the direction of this change could not then be imagined. It remains to be seen whether this change will require the composition of a new set of principles, this time without ambiguity or compromise.*

Another aim of this chapter is to establish whether cataloguing principles for the online environment should encompass a broader range of information sources, *i.e.*, different bibliographic databases such as library catalogues, databases constructed by publishers, booksellers, library suppliers and A&I services. Boll (1990: 10) asks: whether there is now a need to include rules for A&I services, which constitute a major component of the online environment.

In general, the aim is to investigate whether the conceptual foundations developed over the last two centuries for the creation of bibliographic records and the construction of catalogues are still valid in the new environment. A similar question is posed by

Svenonius (1989: 99) who questions whether changes in technology call for changes in the conceptual foundations of cataloguing.

This chapter is in two parts. In Part one some of the basic cataloguing principles, which have been highlighted in the literature as those most likely to be influenced by the new technology, will be re-examined in the light of both the present and the potential characteristics and capabilities of the online environment. Part two will deal with a comparison of A&I conventions with library cataloguing principles and identify in what areas the same principles can be applied by both communities.

What are 'Cataloguing Principles'?

In terms of descriptive cataloguing, as defined briefly at the beginning, 'principles' are regarded as underlying concepts for the design and development of cataloguing rules and the construction of library catalogues. Principles can also be seen as general rules setting the pattern for more specific rules. Cataloguing principles do not necessarily mean that we must have a single standard for descriptive cataloguing, or that all cataloguing codes must be the same. Cataloguing principles mean that we can have different, but compatible standards within the same framework (Hagler, 1989: 199). The Paris Conference, was an international attempt to make national codes compatible.

The Paris Principles, which are the basis for discussion in this chapter, are, in fact, an expansion of a few basic concepts developed over the last two centuries. These concepts, which are repeated in various sections of the Statement of Principles (ICCP, 1963) are: 1) the functions of the catalogue, 2) the concept of multiple entries, 3) the concept of uniformity in the choice and form of headings and entry words, 4) the concept of functionality of entries and catalogues, and 5) the concept of authorship, personal and corporate. However, this chapter deals only with some of the principles that might be influenced by the new environment and that have been the subject of arguments among cataloguers for a long time, namely:

- The objectives and functions of the catalogue which influence all other principles,
- The structure of the catalogue and the kinds of entries and indexes, *i.e.*, main entries, added entries and references,
- Uniform headings for works (*i.e.*, uniform titles) and uniform headings for authors, and
- The form of personal headings and corporate headings.

The concept of main entry will be dealt with in detail, because it has been considered important in the literature on the impact of computerised catalogues on cataloguing principles.

There are other pre-existing principles, unstated or overlooked, in the Paris Principles, such as the general assumption that catalogued items are almost always stand-alone publications rather than 'dependent works'. This issue, and other related questions, such as the 'basic unit of description' and the 'edition' issue, in relation to their treatment in the online environment, particularly in shared cataloguing systems.

In the extrapolation of cataloguing principles, it is necessary to be aware of the context within which they were originally meant to operate. The Paris Principles have been indirectly influenced by both the characteristics and the limitations of the manual catalogue. They were principles for a catalogue which had limited capabilities in providing access to bibliographic information. Those who contributed to the formulation and compilation of earlier cataloguing principles implicitly assumed that the physical form of the catalogue would be the card or printed book catalogue, either as individual catalogues or national bibliographies. On the whole, the Paris Principles were formulated at a time when there was little perception of approaches other than the traditional ones of author, title and subject.

Major Developments and Changes in Descriptive Cataloguing Since the Paris Conference

Nearly thirty five years have passed since the Paris Conference and cataloguers have witnessed profound changes in many aspects of bibliographic control in general, and in descriptive cataloguing in particular, during this period of time. There has also been a considerable increase in unconventional forms of publications as well as various types of information sources and a considerable growth in different presentations of documents which demand increasing detail to retain precision in identification. Martin (1996b) reviews some of the major issues which influence bibliographic control and access in the new environment.

The cataloguing world has also faced major challenges such as the increasing costs of cataloguing and the need for simplified cataloguing or minimal level cataloguing (MLC), the question of duplicate records in cooperative cataloguing systems and the potential danger that cataloguing principles and concepts might be de-emphasised by those coming from the new technology environment.

The cataloguing community is now working in an environment totally different from that of the early 1960s. Given the influence of all these changes and developments in the world of cataloguing, a fundamental re-examination of cataloguing principles seems very necessary.

A Re-examination of Cataloguing

While current cataloguing principles deal with basic questions concerning the organisation of author/title catalogues, online catalogues have revolutionised access to bibliographic information beyond that approach. An important change in relation to providing access to bibliographic information in the online environment is that access is no longer controlled by cataloguing principles and rules to the same extent as previously but, to some extent, is now governed by various search/retrieval capabilities that were not available in the manual catalogue. For example, access through keyword searching, truncation, Boolean searching, hypertext searching and, most importantly, access to the full text of items, lie outside of cataloguing rules. This is one of the most fundamental differences between an online system and a manual system that should be taken into consideration when re-examining cataloguing principles. Furthermore, while the boundary between description and access has faded in the online environment, cataloguing principles have traditionally placed little emphasis on description.

In the following sections some of the principles mentioned in section 0.2 will be analysed with regard to the present and potential influences which the various capabilities of the new technologies might have upon them.

Objectives and Functions of the Catalogue in an Online Environment: In our re-examination of cataloguing principles, major consideration should be given to the objectives and functions of the catalogue. Most cataloguing principles, such as the basis for description, the structure of the catalogue and the choice and form of access points are, to a great extent, influenced by the objectives and functions of the catalogue.

The present cataloguing objectives, which were proposed by Lubetzky to the Paris Conference, have their origin in the work of Panizzi and Cutter dating from the nineteenth century. The traditional approach in the Paris Principles toward the functions of the catalogue has not been able to solve the controversies between the 'finding function' and the 'collocating function' of the catalogue. It is often stated that the first and second objectives are inherently in conflict, and to consider one as primary means to sacrifice the other. While the first function (*i.e.*, Statement 2.1) puts emphasis on the finding of specific items within a library collection, the second function (*i.e.*, Statement 2.2) focuses on collocation of the works of a particular author and the editions and manifestations of a particular work.

These two different approaches influence the choice and form of main and added entries, references and the linking devices to connect related entities. For example, in the finding function approach the focus of description and the basis for cataloguing data is the physical item in hand. Thus the main entry and added entries are provided according to the information on the title page because it is more familiar to readers. In this context, the relationship of the item to other works and its place in the bibliographic hierarchy is not identified and recorded. Wilson (1989) presents a well account of the conflict between the two objectives and their implications for the functions of the catalogue.

It is further stated that these objectives are not fully achieved in the manual environment because of its limitations in finding the actual location of items and the huge cost of making analytics and assembling all the works of a given author, *i.e.*, the collocating function (Wilson, 1983, 1989).

A general question raised in the literature is whether the objectives and functions of the catalogue as set forth in the Paris Principles are still valid in the online environment. Another question which has to be addressed in this regard is: whether the catalogue in the online network environment should still maintain the same functions formulated for a pre-machine environment or should widen its scope to include new functions? While it is claimed by some writers that the current objectives and functions of the catalogue continue to be valid in the new environment and even that the new technology may help fulfil them more comprehensively and accurately (Kilgour, 1979: 39; Malinconico, 1980: 26; Schmierer, 1989: 111; Brunt, 1992: 23), others have challenged the validity and adequacy of the traditional objectives of the catalogue in the new environment.

Ayres (1990: 246) states that the scope of the objectives must be expanded to include the impact that online catalogues have on the content of the catalogue. Buckland (1994: p. A) discusses the need to change our basic assumptions about the catalogue's purpose in order to design the catalogue of the future. He claims that we should pay more attention to bibliographic access and selection and should design the catalogue as a selecting aid. Heaney (1995: 135) notes that library catalogues function not solely as descriptive lists of books but as elements of library management systems and as sophisticated information tools.

In addition to the finding and collocating functions, which are valid in any environment, the online catalogue helps to better identify and characterise entities in terms of their nature, scope and orientation through different data fields such as intellectual level, document type, genre, language code, geographic area code and additional notes. Similarly, a fuller description of the item helps the online catalogue to be used as a means for different users to choose one item over similar items. The locating of items is another function of the catalogue and, in this respect, online catalogues are far more capable of showing the location and status of the item(s) being sought.

In the following section, the functions of the catalogue will be analysed with regard to the impact of some of the major characteristics of the online environment. These are: 1) the integration of library operations, 2) developments in networking and in global access to catalogues, 3) access to other types of bibliographic databases, and 4) online search/retrieval/display capabilities.

Integration of Different Library Operations: The integrated online library system has made it possible for different library modules to use the same bibliographic records within the same database management system. Acquisitions librarians, cataloguers, circulation librarians, serial librarians and reference librarians all have access to the same database and use it for different purposes. In an integrated system, the end user may have access to parts of acquisition status, circulations and holdings information. It is therefore necessary for the online catalogue to fulfil the various bibliographic needs of different operations, from housekeeping functions to reference services. In this context, not only should the catalogue function as a finding tool as well as a collocating tool but it should also help in the choice between one work and others.

The combination of approaches to an integrated catalogue not only makes it necessary to expand the current objectives but also to put more emphasis on principles for the choice and form of access points as well as for description, *i.e.*, data elements beyond author/title information. For example, a reference librarian may need to find a specific item and at the same time identify different editions and manifestations related to that item to provide more help to the user.

Networking and Global Access to Catalogues: The fact that the resources and bibliographic information of hundreds of libraries participating in national and international networks are now accessible to any remote user calls for a reconsideration of the functions and objectives of the catalogue. The concept of 'catalogues on demand' extends the functions of the catalogue beyond providing access to a library's own collections. With international access to individual catalogues, the question arises as to whether a catalogue should serve in the first place its local users, that is, to identify the holdings of a particular library, or to enable any user to access the collections of other libraries available through the network. Buckland (1994: p. B) asks: "What difference does it make that the catalogue now is concerned with the collectivity of collections rather than the local holdings of the individual library?" While catalogues should serve their local patrons well, they should also be useful to remote users. In such an environment, consideration should always be given to the fact that the item in hand for cataloguing may be a manifestation of another work known under a different title being held in another collection.

With respect to the network environment, there is some support for the precedence of the collocating function of the catalogue over its finding function. In a conceptual approach to a catalogue's functions as presented by Lubetzky to the Paris Principles, Wilson (1989) proposes that, with regard to the availability of different catalogues in an online network and with respect to the significance of 'work' over 'publication', priority should be given to the collocating objective. He proposes a redefinition of 'work' to be taken as the basic unit of cataloguing. Dempsey (1990: 64) points out that a lack of sufficient attention to the collocating objective of the catalogue has resulted in two problems in large shared databases: difficulty in authority control and an increase in duplicate records. Ayres (1990) supports a similar concept. In general, in a network, online environment and with regard to the needs of different users, we cannot give precedence to any function. Rather, all functions of the catalogue should equally be taken into consideration.

On the other hand, while in a large shared database the potential number of editions and manifestations of a work increases, it is more likely that access to a very specific bibliographic manifestation of a work, for example, a particular version, would be a common need for some users. The result of a study of MELVYL at the University of California using transaction logs of remote users showed that known item searches constituted 40% of searches (Milsap and Ferl, 1993: 335). It is evident that in a shared system or network of catalogues there will be a good chance for the user to select those that suit his/her needs best among different representations of a work. Copy cataloguing through bibliographic utilities, which is usually a known-item search, is another example of such a user approach.

With the availability of catalogues to different remote users, it is hard to give absolute priority to either of the two traditional functions of the catalogue. A catalogue accessible to all types of users through a network will be expected to satisfy, as far as possible, different needs.

Availability of Different Types of Bibliographic Database: With respect to the accessibility of different types of online and/or on-disk bibliographic databases (*e.g.*, library catalogues, book trade bibliographic databases, national bibliographies and A&I databases) to various users, a combination of approaches in terms of the functions of the catalogue should be considered.

With access to book trade databases, the catalogue goes beyond providing holdings information and becomes a gateway to explore what is newly published, what is to be published and what is in print. In such an environment, emphasis is also put on other functions such as the crucial choice of one item over another. From a different point of view, the functions of the bibliographic database in the library world and book trade world are similar in many respects, such as the finding function (principles 2.1 (a), (b) and (c) in the Paris Principles), the selecting function and housekeeping function. Even the bringing together of works by a particular author (Principle 2.2 (a)) and also collocation of series, are functions wanted by the two communities. A major difference is in the collocation of different editions and manifestations of a work, which libraries appear to consider important enough to control by rules of entry.

Online Search/retrieval/display and Functions of the Catalogue: All a catalogue's functions can be achieved more comprehensively through the search/retrieval/display capabilities of the online catalogue. An interesting aspect of the online catalogue which is duplicated from A&I services is the ability of the searcher to choose and/or combine a number of different searching options. For example, keyword searching on place of publication, name of the publisher, date of publication, series information and ISBN or ISSN not only facilitates the finding function but it can also help in the choice of one item over another. Boolean searching can facilitate both the finding function (*e.g.*, ANDing the author's name with date of publication) and the collocating function (*e.g.*, ANDing the author heading with the uniform title to assemble different editions of a work). Hypertext searching on any term or a combination of terms can extend a known-item search to other items which may be unknown to the searcher but may have some kind of relationship with the item first found.

There is an important difference between the manual environment and the online environment in terms of search/retrieval/display capabilities of the catalogue and their influence on the two objectives. Whilst collocation in the manual catalogue is achieved through the physical pre-arrangement of records of related editions and manifestations of a work, in the online environment it can be achieved through the pre-coding and display of search results.

With many more data elements in MARC records, additional indexes and extensive search and retrieval capabilities, the online catalogue can be used as a selecting aid to choose specific items. This function, *i.e.*, the choosing function, which is of interest to different users such as acquisitions and reference librarians as well as the book trade, can be carried out more effectively. For example, combining key data elements, such as author or title with date of publication, country of publication, name of publisher and language of the item is a useful way to choose appropriate items.

Conclusion

The catalogue in the global online environment is supposed to satisfy all possible approaches. From the preceding paragraphs, it can be concluded that the functions of the online catalogue go beyond those laid down in the Paris Principles. The online catalogue with its extensive capabilities can widen the scope and content of the functions and fulfil new functions. It is therefore necessary that cataloguing principles for the online environment should cover all these different functions equally and should also take into consideration the influence of each function on other principles.

Structure of the Catalogue and the Concept of Multiple Entries: The structure of the catalogue has an important role in the fulfilment of its functions. Sections 3

(Structure of the Catalogue), 4 (Kinds of Entry), 5 (Use of Multiple Entries), 6 (Function of Different Kinds of Entry) and subsections 8.1, 9.1, 9.2, 9.5, 9.6 and also sections 10 and 11 of the Statement of Principles relate to the structure of the catalogue. The principles underlying the structure of the catalogue and choice of entries in the Paris Principles include statements concerning the determination and construction of necessary entries for a linear, alphabetical catalogue. Such a linear catalogue consists of main entries, added entries and references.

Online catalogues, on the other hand, go far beyond the linear author/title catalogue; they permit dynamic linking, merging and rearrangement of files. The structure of an online catalogue usually consists of bibliographic, authority and holdings records linked to one another, each of which is arranged in a given order. Multiple access points and related index files in an online system are not limited to traditional author/title headings. Since it is possible to specify more data elements in a record as access points, the structure of online catalogues may include other index files such as keywords, author/any keyword from title, standard numbers, language of the item, country of publication, date of publication, type of material, genre and readership level.

Cataloguing principles should take into consideration the complex structure of the online catalogue and provide principles for the construction of different files (*e.g.*, bibliographic, authority and holdings) and also for the indexing of different fields and sub-fields concerning access to required elements in the record. They should also suit the structure of the catalogue including different indexes for searching and browsing. A possible approach would be to provide principles for the construction of browsable indexes which can help the searcher to get a clear idea of what sort of indexes are available for searching and retrieval. It is also useful to provide name authority files for browsing, like those offered by SIRSI and PALS systems and a uniform-title authority file for making the catalogue more effective in its collocating function. A possible development in the structure of the catalogue is through the concept of 'super records'.

The Concept of Main Entry: As a typical example of the impact of the online environment on cataloguing principles, it has been claimed that the concept of main entry has lost its value. It was indicated that with the advent of computerised catalogues the value of the main entry concept, which developed in the context of book and card catalogues, has been questioned, but no satisfactory and practical solution has emerged as to how its functions can be otherwise fulfilled. Svenonius (1989: 61) asks:

> *If the main entry were to be abandoned, what would replace its role in the construction of uniform headings? what would take its place in the structuring*

displays in online catalogs? how would abandoning the main entry affect single-entry and minimal-level catalogs?

A review of the related literature of the last two decades shows a developing discussion in favour of abandoning the main entry concept in the online environment. Although before the advent of automated catalogues there were some proposals for the no-main-entry concept such as 'Description Independent System (DIS)' (Mori, 1955, cited in Takawashi, 1989: 66; Mori, 1965), 'alternative entry' (Jeffreys, 1967), and 'title main entry' (Hicks and Tillin, 1970; Hamdy, 1973), developments in online catalogues of access to bibliographic information have given the issue a new dimension and the number of those who advocate the abandonment of the main entry concept has increased. To many writers (for example, Gorman, 1975, 1979, 1980a, 1980b, 1992; Kilgour, 1979; Ayres, 1978, 1981, 1990; Shoham and Lazinger, 1991; Jeffreys, 1993; Winke, 1993), the concept arose out of pre-machine systems and is said to be irrelevant in a developed online catalogue where the technology permits many more access points of equal value in the retrieving of bibliographic information. It is often also claimed that the process of determining main entries is one of the most complex, costly and time consuming processes in descriptive cataloguing (Mori, 1965; Hamdy, 1973; Gorman, 1989; Takawashi, 1989; Jeffreys, 1993; Winke, 1993).

In contrast to those supporting the simple abandonment of the main entry principle, others argue for its continued use in computerised catalogues (Scott, 1976; Malinconico, 1977, 1980; Aroksaar, 1986; Carpenter, 1989, 1992b; Brooks and Bierbaum, 1987; Bierbaum, 1994; Martin, 1996a; Heaney, 1995). In a survey of the attitudes of cataloguers and cataloguing educators, Musavi (1986: 143) found that more than half of the respondents disagreed with the abandonment of the main entry concept even in the online catalogue. The majority of respondents believed that online catalogues will not devalue the concept of main entry. Baughman and Svenonius (1984) assessed the implication of the possible abandonment of main entry in AACR2 and found that a number of problematic rules would result. Exploring the definitions and functions of main entry, Carpenter (1989, 1992b) stated that some of the functions of main entry, particularly its collocating function, are still valid in the online environment.

The following section is an analysis of the main entry concept in terms of its functions in an online environment. The focus of this section is only on main entries for personal names.

Functions of Main Entry: Discussions of the main entry concept have been mostly concerned with the objectives and functions of the catalogue rather than merely its definitions.' According to Verona (1963: 146) any consideration about the functions of the main entry has to be based on an evaluation of the general objectives and functions of the alphabetical catalogue. A similar idea comes from Carpenter

(1989: 84) who points out that: "If main entry is to have any function, it must be in the context of fulfilling an objective of a catalogue."

A major justification for the concept often lies in its collocating function, in bringing together both different editions of a work and the works of an author. Carpenter (1989: 84-85) states that other functions, *i.e.*, 1) naming a work, 2) providing credit to the principal author, 3) providing the only full entry, and 4) being the entry to which all others refer, are of historical interest. Looking from a database perspective, Brooks and Bierbaum (1987: 338) consider the uniform main entry as an essential device to link all the occurrences of a bibliographic mutation. Tillett (1995) emphasises the role of main entry in specifying the nature of the relationship between a work and the person associated with it. Heaney (1995: 137) notes that the issue of the main entry is more complicated than its being only considered as a primary heading; it involves not the idea of "main" entry but also the adequate identification, within the record, of related works.

As a collocating device, the concept of main entry has been retained not only in multiple-entry card catalogues but also with the same justification in automated catalogues. In terms of collocation, main entry has two specific functions: 1) Assembling and displaying works by an author, and 2) Assembling and displaying different editions of a work.

Assembling and Displaying Works by an Author

Assembling of the works of an author, which is presented as objective 2.2(a) in the Paris Principles, can be achieved through a uniform heading for the author, whether recorded as the main entry heading or as an added entry. This function is thus not exclusively achieved by the main entry heading. Furthermore, the main entry heading alone cannot assemble all the works by an author. In many cases where an author is a joint author, editor, compiler or author of one part, his/her name may be presented as an added entry heading.

Assembling and Displaying Different Editions of a Work

While the most important justification for the main entry is in its role of assembling and displaying, in a meaningful and logical order, the various editions of a work, it has been a complex and debatable concept in the history of descriptive cataloguing. Although this function is attributed to main entry, it cannot be fully achieved through the main entry heading alone. In assembling the different editions of a work, the main entry heading is dependent upon a second collocating device: the uniform title. Without the inclusion of a uniform title following the main entry heading in the record, the assembling function of the main entry is only partially achieved: it would be limited only to those works whose editions and manifestations have identical titles proper.

Thus, neither of the two functions perceived for main entry in the Paris Principles can be fully achieved through the main entry heading alone. As will be discussed further in this section, a combination of the author's uniform heading and the uniform title that is considered as a 'unifying mode of identifying' different editions of a work (Martin, 1996b) will fulfil the collocating function in a more comprehensive way.

Online Search/retrieval/display and the Concept of Main Entry

Keyword Searching: In an online database with keyword access, it is possible to retrieve a record through keywords, whether in main entries, added entries or any other significant word indexed from the text of the record. A major characteristic of keywords is that they are not controlled by cataloguing rules and they are not subject to authority control. Therefore, keyword searching on names will retrieve only those records that match the term(s) keyed in by the searcher. Keyword searching capability cannot replace the main entry in terms of its collocating function. It can, however, facilitate the collocating function: once access to one or more specific items has been provided through keywords, the searcher can extend the search by keying the exact form of the author heading or the uniform title found on the retrieved record(s) to search for related editions with the same terms only.

Boolean Searching: Boolean search is another capability for bringing together different editions of a work. This can be done by keying in two or more data elements such as the author heading and the title proper or the uniform title, by using the 'AND' operator. Since the title proper of different editions of a work may vary, titles proper in conjunction with author heading cannot be a useful element for the collocating function. The 'author/title' search key, which many systems provide, is an implicit Boolean search which has the same limitation. Instead, a Boolean search on the author uniform heading and the uniform title, including relevant qualifiers, can achieve the collocating function more effectively. This approach is another justification for the main entry concept.

Index Browsing: The browsing capability removes the burden of entering the exact search terms and enables the searcher to gain an overview of an index containing an alphabetical list of all headings. Browsing, for example, the author index will display together all the works by an author irrespective of his/her type of contribution (*e.g.*, primary author, joint author, editor, compiler). Nevertheless, for the uniform citation and display of entries in the browsable author index we need to identify the primary author. To link works, however, the primary author's name should be in a uniform heading. This is again another justification for the concept of main entry in an online environment. It can be seen that, even with browsing capability, a useful collocation of different editions of a work is not possible with the present structure of entries. Browsable indexes could help solve the collocation problem if the author and the title indexes are pre-coordinated for meaningful arrangement and display of related entities.

Online Display and the Concept of Main Entry: Since the display format in online catalogues is independent of the storage format, when a number of records are displayed (particularly in brief displays) in response to a query, the retrieved titles need to be displayed in conjunction with a second primary identifier such as the author heading. Otherwise, not only is the identification of the retrieved items not complete, but different works by an author are also not distinguished and assembled. This primary element is necessary in online displays of related works. Carpenter (1989: 81) states that the primary key provides a unique identification of the record. He also points out that: "Discussions about main entry have changed focus from records to useful displays" (Ibid: 90). Online displays, for instance, default listings in brief displays, require that, in addition to titles proper, another principal element must be displayed. The following example may help to make this idea clearer:

As the convention now exists in many OPACs, when there is an editor or a compiler for a work and the work goes under title main entry or a corporate heading and the editor or the compiler is given an added entry as opposed to main entry, his/her/its name would still need to be displayed in conjunction with the title proper in the brief display to uniquely identify the work and to differentiate between works with identical titles. From another perspective, that of the catalogue user who does not understand what main entry is, an editor or a compiler may seem to be the primary identifier or access point which should be displayed in conjunction with the title in brief displays and in single entry listings.

Conclusion

As a concept, the main entry relates rather to the nature of relationships between entities (authors to their works or works to their editions) than to the physical medium through which those entities are to be described. Many works, particularly in the fields of literature, law and music, require such a uniform construct for identification and collocation. Even if technology provides catalogues with sophisticated devices to link two or more related entities to one another, it would not help the user if catalogues do not show him/her the nature of these relationships. Without such a concept the catalogue, whether manual or computerised, would lose its integrity and usefulness.

From the preceding discussions concerning the possible influence of different online search/retrieval/display capabilities, it can be concluded that online catalogues still need a construct to carry out some specific functions which cannot be fulfilled thoroughly through other devices. Of great concern is the fact that the main entry concept is not meant to be a single function element but rather a concept that is essential to fulfil some basic functions. Thus it is in need of a re-definition that will focus on its multiple functions:

Main entry is a uniform construct for the naming and identifying of works and also for the useful collocation and arrangement/display of the different editions and manifestations of a work. In addition to the identification of the primary author, the concept of uniform citation, as defined above, is dependent on two key identifying elements: uniform titles for works and uniform headings for authors.

Uniform Headings for Titles

A work can potentially be produced in different editions, different versions, in various languages and/or in a variety of physical formats. This concept is intrinsic to the bibliographic universe and its control is an essential principle for catalogues. In this context, the name of the work, *i.e.*, the 'uniform title', has been devised in descriptive cataloguing to control the conditions of a work. For this reason, the use of uniform titles has greatly increased and their application has gone beyond anonymous classics, sacred Scriptures and works of music. However, the Paris Principles are less concerned with the concept of uniform titles: principles 7.1, 11.3 and 11.4 only deal vaguely with the choice and form of uniform titles. In the following sections, the rationale and the functions of uniform titles will be examined in the context of the online environment.

Functions of the Uniform Title: The functions of uniform titles are: 1) to standardise the original title of a work, 2) to standardise the form of the main entry heading for anonymous works, 3) to group together all editions and manifestations of a work under one particular title, and 4) to identify the relationships between an edition and a work. The rationale for the principle of uniform titles, however, rests mainly with two functions: 1) the uniform identification of a work and 2) the assembling of entities derived from or related to the same work. As indicated, uniform titles support at least four types of bibliographic relationship: equivalence, derivative, whole-part, and sequential relationships.

Online Search/retrieval/display and the Concept of Uniform Titles: No research has yet attempted to study the influence of different search/retrieval/display capabilities of online catalogues on the principle of uniform title. Tillett (1992a: 111) states that some Western cataloguing practices that arise from the physical limitations of manual catalogues do not make sense in the online environment and should be rethought. Of such practices, the uniform title is one of the most important. Tillett (Ibid) states that we should simplify the entire issue of uniform titles to make it relevant to the online catalogue in a network environment. Vellucci (1990: 59) emphasises the need to explore more fully the potential of uniform titles as linking devices and as foundation points for online catalogues. She states: As we move into the online environment, the uniform title will continue to evolve. The terminology might change again, and new functions might be identified. But the important role of the uniform title in identifying works and serving as a linking device for bibliographic relationships will no doubt be a primary focus for uniform titles of the future (Ibid, 56).

Boll (1990: 15) points out that, in an online catalogue, both the primary heading and the uniform title "are needed to recall, as a group, manifestations of the same work that have different titles proper". As in the case of the main entry concept, the examination of individual search/retrieval/display capabilities in online catalogues reveals that not only do those capabilities not diminish the need for the concept of uniform titles but they also emphasise their role in the effective collocation and display of related works and items.

Without the uniform title associated with the main entry heading, one can see that different editions of the same work are scattered among the retrieved records for other works by the same author. For example, translations or selections of a work, while being scattered among different works by the same author, are treated as if they are new works by the same author. This problem is highlighted in online catalogues: they may need a number of screens to list all retrieved items and the searcher may have to spend considerable time to find his/her needed item.

With regard to the catalogue's collocating function, uniform titles will play a more important role in the online catalogue. In an online environment, the linking of different editions and manifestations of a work is essential for increasing recall in response to user queries and could be a critical part of the file structure for new system designs (Vellucci, 1990: 45). While uniform titles alone increase the search results (*i.e.*, recall), the addition of other data elements, such as version, language, date and part of the work, to the uniform title will narrow down the search results and will increase precision. In their present state, formal or conventional titles, such as "Laws, etc." and "works", may not be useful in online retrieval unless in conjunction with, for example, a name or date. The search expression "Laws, etc. AND New South Wales" is useful in an online catalogue. In such systems some of the qualifiers can be specified by Boolean means or can be simplified into natural language terms, as in the concept of super records.

While the occurrence of editions of the same work with different titles and different works with similar titles increases in large catalogues and union databases, the concept of uniform titles can help control this problem. In the context of searching a large bibliographic database, there should be a means for the user to realise that what has been retrieved in response to his/her query may be different editions of the same work.

Conclusion

For the same reasons that a concept equivalent to the main entry will be needed in an online catalogue, the concept of uniform titles will remain a valid principle in the new environment. Even with the different search/retrieval/display capabilities of the online catalogue, there is still a need for a standardised form of the title of a work serving to identify and collocate different editions and manifestations of a work. These capabilities can also help to simplify and make the application of the concept in online catalogues more understandable.

Uniform Headings for Persons

As indicated in earlier sections, another principle that is essential to the fulfilment of the main entry's functions is a uniform heading for persons. A rigid ideal in modern cataloguing codes and one of the first principles in the Anglo-American cataloguing tradition has been to list all works by or about a given person under a uniform heading. In this context, uniform headings have been regarded as a necessary device for the integrity of the catalogue (Chan, 1983: 20).

While the need for uniformity of headings in an online environment and for links among variant forms of a name has been reaffirmed by a number of writers (for example, Taylor, 1984: 15 and 1989: 33; Takawashi, 1989: 69; Shoham and Lazinger, 1991: 62; Brooks and Bierbaum, 1987: 338; Bierbaum, 1994: 84), the necessity to enter an author's works under one uniform heading and the provision of references for other forms of a name for the same author has come into question in online catalogues. In terms of the implication of adhering to the principle of uniform headings in an online environment Chan (1983: 29) asks:

> *...does the principle of uniform heading have the same meaning or import in the automated catalogue as in the card catalogue?... What are the implications of the principle of uniform heading in the maintenance of the name authority file? To what extent does the designation of a focal point* (i.e., *the uniform heading) facilitate and economize such operations?*

However, as discussed in relation to the collocating function of the catalogue, the bringing together and display of an author's works require that all records be presented under a uniform heading for the author. Divergence in the form of headings is not consistent with the requirements of the online environment. Normalisation of names is a principle which is also essential to database management systems.

However, a major problem in the online environment is that there are different bibliographic databases and a wide variety of users. A difficulty in searching different databases is that, while there is a uniform approach in library cataloguing in relation to uniform headings, other communities such as the book trade and A&I services are less concerned with this principle. In many bibliographic databases it is often the case that the same person has been entered under a variety of unlinked names leading to irretrievability of all the works by a particular author.

Online Search/retrieval/display and the Principle of Uniform Headings

Keyword searching: Keyword searching facilitates the finding function of the catalogue through the form of an author's name that appears on the title page or in information sources, *i.e.*, the form which is usually familiar to both the book world and the searcher. However, with keyword searching it is possible only to search names under the form in which they have been recorded in the bibliographic record. Keywords are not subject to authority control and therefore cannot always collocate all the works by or about an author in a catalogue, especially if the form of name differs. However, keyword searching facilitates the collocation of an author's works: once access is made to a record through any form of the name, it is possible to assemble works by or about a particular author through a further search on the uniform author heading.

Truncation. With right-hand truncation, the online catalogue is able to retrieve those names which begin with the characters defined by the searcher. In other words, names must be uniform, at least for the few beginning characters, to retrieve all the works by a given author. For example, truncation on a surname will retrieve works by those authors whose forenames or initials may differ from one another. Truncation, particularly automatic right-hand truncation, influences uniform headings in two ways: 1) it retrieves all the works by an author when only the surname is known to the searcher, 2) it increases the number of retrieved records, some of which may not be relevant to the needs of the searcher. In effect, not only does truncation not devalue the principle of uniform headings, but it also emphasises it, in that the more complete the uniform heading is, the more chance there will be for retrieval precision.

Index Browsing. In systems allowing the browsing of name indexes, it is necessary, in general, that works by an author be assembled under a single form of name. The browsing capability thus reinforces the need for the principle of uniform headings. The value of uniform headings can also be seen in single-entry printouts and lists both in library cataloguing and in publishers' activities. The 'author index' volume in the *Books In Print* is a good example of a name browsable index.

Authority Control Systems. In an online catalogue utilising name authority files, access to the works of a given author by any variant forms of the name would be as effective as access by the uniform heading. The distinction between the established form of a name and any cross reference to it is invisible to the user. It has been said that in future catalogues a complete listing of an author's works under any form of the author's name is quite feasible (Carpenter, 1992a: 95).

Even in authority control systems there is still a need to establish one form of a person's name as the uniform heading and others as references. In fact, uniform headings are still considered to be an important principle in authority work (Taylor, 1984: 15). While name authority systems make it possible to achieve the finding function in a one-step search for any work by a given author, adherence to the principle of uniform heading is a means to maintain the one-to-many relationship (*i.e.*, one name to many works) in bibliographic databases and, thus, to achieve the collocation of all works available by a given author in the catalogue.

Online Displays and the Principle of Uniform Headings. With regard to differences in the physical forms of the manual catalogue and the online catalogue, the very rigid ideal in the card catalogue of assembling *in one place* all the works a library has by a given author has shifted, in the online catalogue, to the ideal of the system's ability to retrieve all the works of an author through any searched form of his/her name and to display them together under one uniform heading for the author. Under whatever form of name the works by a given author have been searched, the default listing of those works requires that the name of the author needs to be displayed in a uniform manner.

Networks and the Concept of Uniform Headings

Uniform headings are an essential principle in bibliographic control, especially in shared cataloguing environments and union catalogues, facilitating bibliographic cooperation between libraries (LeBlanc, 1993: 425). The communication of bibliographic records for cataloguing purposes, reference services and inter-library loan depends to a large extent on the uniformity of headings. In searching the different catalogues accessible in a network, the patron, the technical services librarian and the reference librarian usually look for the works of a given author under the same heading.

The ability to look for particular bibliographic information in different catalogues irrespective of their size, type and location requires an ever-increasing need for standard bibliographic records. Except for differences in user interfaces, a first requirement is to conform to the concept of uniform headings at the national level.

National name authority files would be the most desirable answer to complications in the forms of authors' names and can provide consistent access to catalogues and other bibliographic lists. It is then possible to share bibliographic and authority records on the international level. Criticising the way that cataloguers prepare headings as if they are cataloguing for a single library, Wajenberg (1992: 106) states that:

The cataloging code for the third millennium should rise above the parochial emphasis on the local catalogue. It should provide instructions for preparing headings for a national online authority file, and eventually for an international equivalent.

Conclusion

It can be said that although the very rigid ideal of uniform headings has undergone gradual modification, the principle is still valid and its maintenance can secure the integrity of catalogues particularly in shared cataloguing systems, union databases and network environments at the national level. Although name authority systems have made it possible to retrieve all the works of a given author through a one-step search in the catalogue, the necessity for collocation and particularly for display of an author's works together requires that one form of name be chosen as the established uniform heading.

In summary, while it seems that there may be no solution to the problem of the present conflict between different communities and within each community (due to important reasons to maintain differences across cultures), a possible solution is for all creators of bibliographic records to conform to national name authority files as a source of standardised name headings. This would bring more uniformity in the different environments and would make searching and retrieval of works by a given author easier in various files in the online environment.

Form of Headings in an Online Environment

In addition to the principle of uniform headings, which is essential to the integrity and the collocating function of the catalogue, the form of names in headings, as emphasised by IFLA/Unesco in 1961, should be agreed upon both nationally and internationally. This principle needs to be examined with respect to searchers' expectations and also to the searching/retrieval/display capabilities of the online catalogue. In the following sections, the form of personal and corporate names will be discussed with respect to the possible influence of the online environment.

Form of Personal Name Headings: The form of a name is an important factor in searching and retrieval, particularly in online systems in which the searcher has to key in the name as the search string. In online catalogues with many search/ retrieval capabilities it is important to see whether this principle needs a rather different approach. In a manual environment, a problem with the form of heading is that searches for works of authors must be in the exact form and order of their name headings. This requirement is no longer totally necessary since cross references in authority records and keyword searching allow for the searching of names in different ways. If the searcher is not sure as to which part of the name forms the surname for efficient searching, for example, Jean De La Fountaine, Walter De La Mare, Dante Alighieri, cross references or keyword access offers the possibility to search names in any order. Keyword searching capability also reduces the need for complete "surname+initials+(full forenames)+dates" headings as in AACR2R.

Truncation of headings, especially automatic right-hand truncation, can help retrieve works by authors whose complete heading (*i.e.*, surname, forename or initials) is not known to the searcher. Variations in the fullness of forenames seem unimportant in systems with a truncation capability. Using 'Price, H H' and 'Grossman, Allen R.' as examples, Arlene Taylor (1984: 11, 13) proposes that an online catalogue with keyword searching of headings and automatic right-hand truncation needs rather different rules for the formulation of headings and references.

Wajenberg (1992: 105) claims that, with keyword searching, the inversion of surnames and rules for the choice of entry-element in compound surnames and names with prefixes become unnecessary. Using the heading 'Mozart, Wolfgang Amadeus' as an example, he points out that the most useful form of name is the fullest form. Kilgour (1995b), on the other hand, proposes that for a single-screen miniature catalogue author entries can be reduced to surnames alone. His survey of two online catalogues in the North Carolina State University, containing approximately 3.4 million entries, showed that surname searches produced mini catalogues of one screen 12.6% of the time, two screens 22.5%, and three screens 30.1%. He claims that his finding, that nearly two-fifths of the cataloguing of books in a large university library produces entries that will be displayed in mini catalogues of one screen, demands revision and simplification of cataloguing practices in large research libraries (Kilgour, 1995b: 705) For example, he proposes that with keyword search function no added author fields will be necessary for multiple surnames (Ibid: 706).

As will be noted later in this section, there are other factors, such as the need for default listings of the works of an author and the needs of the book world, citation traditions and international exchange of bibliographic data, which require the standard order of 'surname, forename' in full form for personal headings. There is at present no consensus on the form of headings among the different creators of bibliographic records. There are, however, to some extent similarities between library cataloguing and the book world: both tend to use the best known form of name with library cataloguing more inclined to use the complete form.

Form of Corporate Headings: The issue of corporate headings was one of the problems on which there was no international consensus at the Paris Conference. Even today different national codes have different approaches toward the form of headings.

Searching, retrieval and display of corporate names in online systems are often frustrating to the user. Many of the problems concerning the searching of corporate bodies' publications relate to the form of headings for these bodies. Little has been written on the form of corporate headings in an online environment. Some of the implications of searching corporate names in online systems have been briefly addressed by Arlene Taylor (1984), Brunt (1992) and more fully by Greig (1995). The result of a study by Henty (1986), concerning unsuccessful keyword searching, indicates that the reasons for the users' search failures are, to some extent, due to the implications of variant forms of corporate names. Some of the problems concerning the searching, retrieval and display of corporate headings in online systems are:

1) It is particularly difficult to search under the exact form of corporate headings in online catalogues because the user has to key in the search string. How much of the heading should be keyed in by the searcher to initiate the search, since corporate names are usually long, often similar to one another and appear in different forms such as acronyms, initials and subordinations (*e.g.*, World Health Organization, WHO or W.H.O.)?
2) In some cases, headings for subordinate bodies associated with the same parent body do not follow a uniform approach. While the 'World Health Organization' appears as the heading for this body, a number of subordinate bodies incorporating the acronym 'WHO' are treated as headings in the catalogue; for example, 'WHO Collaborating Centre on Environmental Pollution Control', 'WHO Commission on Health and Environment', 'WHO Expert Group on Pesticide Residues'. The same problem exists with the 'Food and Agriculture Organization of United Nations' and some of its subordinate bodies beginning with 'FAO'.
3) Entering corporate bodies under the name of the higher body would often cause inconvenience for the searcher, especially in large catalogues and shared systems. The use of indirect corporate headings is not innate and could appear meaningless to catalogue users. They "can be considerably distorted because of re-arrangement of the elements of the name and, in many codes, by translating the name of the jurisdiction" (Greig, 1995: 387).
4) The addition of a geographic name to the heading for corporate bodies often does not make sense in the online environment. Exact searching and truncation on headings beginning with the name of the jurisdiction (geographic name) often result in too many hits. Headings like 'Australia. Australian Parliamentary Observer Group', 'Canada. Canadian High Commission' and 'Canada. Canadian Armed Forces' which are problematic for searching could be more straightforward if 'Australia' and 'Canada', were omitted from the heading.
5) Truncation on the name of the parent body will usually retrieve too many records that are not easy to distinguish from one another, especially in brief displays where, because of screen limitation, the name of the parent body alone may fill the allotted space.

6) Clustering of all the publications of different departments and divisions of a corporate body is not usually sought by searchers. Also, it does not make sense in brief displays where, because of screen limitation, only the first few elements of the heading are displayed thus obscuring the name of the actual issuing body. Consider, for example, how frustrating the retrieval of publications of different subordinates bodies of the United Nations would be in an online catalogue).

Conclusion

It can be concluded that direct headings, *i.e.*, subordinate bodies under their own heading, would eliminate these problems provided that the heading for the subordinate body is self-sufficient. There are a number of factors that also justify this:

— direct headings form a shorter string and are more suitable for online displays, especially for brief displays,

— most searchers are usually looking for the publications of a given subordinate body and are not interested in the parent body,

— automatic right-hand truncation on subordinate bodies is more relevant to direct headings than it is to indirect headings and would narrow the scope of search to the publications of the subordinate body only. A search for publications by WHO commissions, expert committees and working groups can be done through the names of those bodies or through truncation of 'WHO'.

— alternative approaches could be provided by means of authority control. As with advanced name authority files linked to the bibliographic file it is possible to search names in different forms, considerations should also be given to any form which may be looked under by catalogue searchers.

In general, while a fuller form of personal names seems more useful in the online environment, corporate names need a simpler approach in that, for example, direct headings for subordinate bodies are more responsive to the search/retrieval/display capabilities of online catalogues. Nevertheless, the problems of corporate headings in online catalogues such as the form and structure (*e.g.*, official name versus name most frequently used; most frequently used versus conventional or modified name; language transliteration; punctuation and display problems) require further research.

Abstracting and Indexing Services

Online and/or on-disk A & I databases are now a major component of the online environment. As indicated earlier, in the introduction to this chapter, one of the aims of this research is to acknowledge the impact of the merging, integrating and accessibility of different types of bibliographic files, particularly library catalogues and A&

databases, on cataloguing principles and to see in what areas and how far similar principles might be applicable to the practices of the two communities.

Library cataloguing has over a century's history of establishing standards for the exchange of information whereas, due to the production of abstracts and indexes by publishers rather than by libraries, there is less standardisation within A&I services. Many indexing rules in the first half of the twentieth century were practically identical with those used in the preparation of library catalogues such as Cutter's *Rules for a Dictionary catalogue* and the *ALA Cataloging rules for Author and Title Entries* (Wheeler, 1957: 8, 50).

Because of the introduction of new technologies, library cataloguing and indexing services now have more impact on one another than before largely due to three major factors:

1) The extensive and powerful searching and retrieval capabilities that computer technology has introduced to library catalogues, such as keyword searching, truncation, Boolean searching and hypertext searching, were first introduced in A&I services. Consequently, the indexing of more data fields, which requires the addition of more data elements such as language, type of material and readership level, is another indication of the impact of A&I services on cataloguing practices.
2) The accessibility of different online library catalogues and A&I databases through a single terminal and the increasing ability of the searcher to go from one bibliographic database/file to another and to navigate the whole bibliographic apparatus.
3) The evolution of CD-ROM versions of many A&I databases which are now available to end users.

These factors have now become a cause for concern over the possible use of the same or compatible standards for the creation of bibliographic records. Because of technological advances in providing integrated access to different bibliographic files and databases, it is time to think as to whether bibliographical control of these different practices should be done based on a single standard. A first step in a study of the possible use of a single standard in both communities is to acknowledge the similarities and differences between library cataloguing and A&I practices. Library cataloguing has come to a set of principles which are internationally agreed upon and has provided bibliographic standards for description of and access to bibliographic items and for the communication of bibliographic data, whereas A&I services have not. There are differences within A&I services about their approaches to description and there are different standards. Some of the major areas of differences/similarities between the two communities that have to be considered are: 1) objectives and functions of the catalogue/database, 2) structure of the catalogue/database and of the bibliographic record, and 3) choice and form of access points. These are being discussed more fully in the following sections.

Objectives and Functions of the Catalogue/database

Differences in the approaches of library cataloguing and A&I services towards creating bibliographic records are a result of different objectives which each of the two communities identifies for its bibliographic database. The major object of looking for an article's bibliographical citation in A&I databases is different from that of looking for bibliographic information in a library catalogue. While library cataloguing is traditionally concerned with the finding, identifying, collocating and organising of bibliographic entities, A&I services deal rather with the subject content of bibliographic entities and, to some extent only, the finding of works by a particular author.

In A&I databases, the assembling of all the works by a given author may be a common approach for some searchers, but there is usually no concept such as the assembling of all editions and manifestations of a work. Journal articles, patent documents, reports, dissertations and conference proceedings have fewer editions than books. Consequently, the concept of main entry, which is useful for bringing together different editions and manifestations of a work, has more justification in library catalogues than in A&I databases. A similar idea is present in the COSATI (the Committee on Scientific and Technical Information) standard with the policy of a main entry free environment: "The system works because only rarely are there technical reports that are about other technical reports and unrelated by contract number" (Carpenter, 1994: 110).

Structure of the Catalogue/database and of the Bibliographic Record

Because of the differences in their objectives and functions, library catalogues and A&I databases differ from one another in terms of the structure of the bibliographic record and the structure of the database. There is no concept such as multiple entries (main entries, added entries and references) in A&I databases. However, in terms of the structure of the record, there are similarities in some of the data fields which can potentially conform to the same standard: headings for persons and corporate bodies associated with an item, date of publication, title of analytic, title of monograph, title of collection or series, language of the item, ISBN/ISSN, conference identification information (name, location, date), abstract/summary, country of publication, target audience and subject headings. These data fields can be treated similarly by the two communities by using identical terms/phrases. The searcher can approach the catalogue or the database with the same search string.

Choice and form of Access Points

This is one of the most important areas of possible reconciliation between cataloguing principles and indexing conventions. Because CD-ROM versions of A&I databases are becoming increasingly available to end users and have larger cumulations of citations in them, there is more need to reconcile variant names. Since there is usually no retrospective editing of headings when a CD-ROM is produced, such discrepancies are simply left alone. Many A&I databases also include citations of monographs, such as conference proceedings, festschriften and books reviewed, that are duplicated in library catalogues. This also indicates the need for more consistency in name headings between library cataloguing and A&I practices.

In terms of the treatment of names for inclusion in the record for later retrieval, A&I conventions differ markedly both within themselves and from cataloguing conventions. In respect of the choice of names to be entered in the bibliographic record, A&I conventions usually provide author indexing in depth (Svenonius, 1989: 19). They do not conform to principles such as main entry and the 'rule of three'. The names of persons associated with an item are entered as they appear on the item in hand. For example, the UNISIST *Reference Manual* (hereafter referred to as RM) prescribes that the names of all individual authors associated with a given item are to be entered in the record, unless there is a clear indication on the original that the chief responsibility for authorship lies with choosing only one or less than all of the persons cited, in which case only those indicated as chief contributors are to be entered (Dierickx and Hopkinson, 1986: 2.A12.1). There are other similarities or differences:

- Since A&I databases are not searched through the exact titles of items, title is not as common an access point as in library catalogues. Instead, a title keyword index is provided for title as well as subject searching.
- As a first principle in the indexing of names, both communities invert names of persons to secure alphabetic arrangement by family names.
- A&I conventions regard the names of editors of collections as an essential element for the identification of monographs (RM: 2.A12.1) whereas cataloguing conventions put less emphasis on the role of such contributors, in that they no longer consider editors and compilers as main entries.
- In terms of the names of persons associated with a monograph, A&I conventions regard the form derived from the item as essential and other forms as optional (other forms may include the 'established form', *i.e.*, the form of name established by reference to an authority other than the item to which the bibliographic record refers, 'real name', 'pseudonym', 'former name', 'subsequent name', 'search name') (RM: 2.A12.3).

One reason why many A&I services do not conform to the principle of uniform heading may be that they are usually discipline-oriented and, therefore, the chance of similarity between the forms of names within a given discipline is not great. There are usually not many identical names with identical forenames or initials within a given A&I database; for example, there were only two authors with the surname 'Buckland' in the LISA database and three in ERIC but none with identical forename or initial.

— A&I conventions emphasise the addition to names of two other elements: 1) the 'role', *i.e.*, the type of intellectual responsibility, such as 'author', 'editor', 'compiler', 'translator', etc., and 2) the person's affiliation. Cataloguing rules, on the other hand, treat the role of persons in the statement of responsibility area and discard affiliations.

— With regard to corporate names, there are some similarities and differences between A&I conventions and cataloguing principles:

a) the full form of corporate names is entered by A&I services with the inclusion of an abbreviation or acronym of a corporate body as an optional element (RM: 2.A14.2). AACR2R (1988: rule 24.1A) prescribes a similar approach without the optional inclusion of an abbreviation or acronym.

b) if the official or formal name of an organisation is usually quoted in the form of an acronym (*e.g.*, IBM, ASLIB), this may be entered as the full form (RM: 2.A18.2). AACR2R (1988: rule 24.1A) has the same approach.

c) the name of a corporate body should be entered in the language of the document, unless the name shown on the document is itself a translation, and the name in its original language is known, in which case the latter form should be entered if better known (RM: 2.A18.2). AACR2R (1988: rule 24.3A) prescribes that the official language of the body should be used.

d) where several levels of an organisation are cited, they should be given in descending order of scale from the larger unit to the smaller. In terms of entering at the intermediate levels, if their inclusion does not add significant information to the entry, they may be omitted provided always that the most specific unit is cited and that the entry provides an unambiguous identification of the organisation (RM: 2.A18.2). Similarly, AACR2R (1988: rules 24.13A and 24.14A) prescribes that a subordinate or related body should usually be entered as a subheading of the main body.

Conclusion: Although the application of a single standard to all kinds of bibliographic databases is neither applicable nor desirable, divergence in standards has significant implications for a common approach to bibliographic control in the online environment. If the different standards can be based on compatible principles for the creation, exchange and searching, retrieval and display of bibliographic records, user convenience should then be taken into account.

Therefore, a major issue for the profession will be the creation of compatible principles for bibliographical control in a global online environment. In this context, consistency between index entries and catalogue entries is an important issue as many indexing rules used headings identical to headings in library catalogues a few decades ago. In general, since the names of persons and corporate bodies are a common element for searching in different types of bibliographic files, library cataloguing and indexing services could now conform to the principle of uniform headings and use similar forms of names. They could use similar rules concerning, for example, pseudonyms, changed names, compound names, names with preposition and geographic names. It would be good if all communities involved in the creation and use of bibliographic records could at least benefit from uniform author headings through national name authorities.

Similarly, library cataloguing could learn from some of the A&I principles such as additional author access points, *i.e.*, discarding the Paris Principles 10.21 and 11.12, *i.e.*, the 'three names limitations'. The two communities could further designate the roles and responsibility functions of persons associated with the item, *i.e.*, the relator concept, *e.g.*, editor, compiler, illustrator, annotator, commentator, reviewer and translator. This would help different users to better understand the relationship between names cited and the item and would thus lead to better identification and retrieval of items.

Summary and Conclusions

The following conclusions are derived from the examination of a number of cataloguing principles carried out in this chapter, in the light of the various capabilities of the online environment.

Functions of the Catalogue

- Conceptually, the objectives and functions of the catalogue are independent of its physical form and arrangement. Technology can, however, influence the way in which these functions are carried out: the more developments there are in the technology of catalogue construction and in the online environment, the more possibilities there are to achieve those objectives and functions.
- Due to the potential use of bibliographic records by a variety of users, the scope of catalogue functions should be expanded to encompass additional functions. The two basic functions (*i.e.*, the finding function and the collocating function) remain valid in the online environment but the catalogue also can serve additional functions: to further identify entities, to choose one item over similar

items, to locate items and copies of items and to maintain databases in terms of record updating.

— While the finding function is a general approach in almost all bibliographic databases, the collocating function is more important to library catalogues and, to some extent, to publishers' databases than to other communities such as A & I services. However, in the online environment, with a variety of users, all the functions of the catalogue need to be considered important. It is therefore necessary to elaborate on this issue and arrive at an international agreement, since the delineation of the objectives and functions of the catalogue influences other cataloguing principles.

The Concept of Main Entry: Rather than being the locus of complete information for the bibliographic record or the primary access point, main entry is an important concept that maintains some basic functions of the catalogue, that of identifying and collocating, in a uniform way, different editions and manifestations of a work. In other words, if a major function of the catalogue is to identify and collocate works as well as their editions and manifestations, there is a need for a concept such as main entry. The lack of such a concept could result in failure to place a publication in the context of its bibliographic relationships. Unless we devise new mechanisms for the uniform identification and collocation of the different manifestations and editions of a work, it would be unwise to abandon the concept of main entry. Nevertheless, in order to delineate the concept more clearly and to avoid confusion as to its functions, main entry is in need of re-definition. The new functional definition should address the validity of the concept in terms of its various functions, irrespective of the catalogue's physical environment. Main entry is particularly needed in the online environment for the useful retrieval, display and arrangement of search results.

The Concept of Uniform Titles: Similarly to the concept of main entry, uniform titles are needed to perform some basic functions such as providing links between different editions and manifestations of a work and to distinguish among works with identical titles proper. Because of present problems in the online retrieval of the various editions and manifestations of works, a concept such as a standardised form of the title of a work can serve to identify and collocate them. However, uniform titles need to be simplified in order to avoid online retrieval problems.

The Principle of Uniform Headings: It is difficult to fulfil the collocating function of the catalogue/database without maintaining the principle of uniform headings. Uniformity of headings for authors and titles is especially important in network environments, where different catalogues and other bibliographic databases are accessible to the user through the same terminal. The principle is also of particular significance in shared cataloguing systems and union databases. Library cataloguing, book trade bibliographic databases and A&I services should at least be consistent or compatible in certain areas such as uniform headings. In effect, standardisation or compatibility in the form of headings is an essential requirement for universal bibliographical control (UBC), particularly in the global online environment.

Form of Name Headings: In terms of the form of personal and corporate name headings for effective searching, retrieval and display, online catalogues need a simpler approach. The form of headings needs to be reconsidered in terms of its suitability for different searching patterns (exact as well as keyword searching) and for display. For example, given adequate software, full forms of name should satisfy searchers seeking either that form, or only the surname plus initials. But searching under single letters, such as initials, is still a problem for many library systems. For subordinate corporate bodies direct headings are usually more responsive to online search/retrieval/displays.

Number of Contributors: As a consequence of the potential of the online system to incorporate more names as access points, the 'rule of three' is not sensible in the online environment. Removal of this outdated principle would add to the functionality of the catalogue, in that it would enhance access to and identification of works of all authors.

Wider Application of the Principles: Current cataloguing principles are not based on the overriding requirements of different users in a variety of environments. There are advantages if we can arrive at a body of principles which can serve to reconcile the bibliographical practices of publishers and booksellers with those of libraries, bibliographic utilities, national bibliographies and the archival community. It would also be advantageous if A&I services and library cataloguing practices could come closer in terms of providing consistent access to bibliographic information, particularly in terms of the form of name headings. Although the objectives and functions of book trade databases, A&I databases and library catalogues are different from one another, the entries created by each community need to be consistent or at least compatible for the purposes of record exchange and database searching. A possible solution is for each community to conform to national name authority files.

As indicated earlier in this chapter, in terms of some fundamental questions such as the 'basic unit of description', 'the edition issue' and the display of bibliographic data, current cataloguing principles are not adequately responsive to the requirements of the new online environment. In considering basic concepts for further investigation, attention should be paid to a possible resolution of such questions.

Representation of the DDC System in MARC 21 Formats

Background

The Dewey editorial team is converting from a proprietary representation of the DDC into one based on the MARC 21 formats for Classification and Authority data in conjunction with the development of a new editorial support system at OCLC. The new system needs to support new models of representation, efficient editorial operations, interaction with translations, seamless delivery of DDC data to demonstration and research projects, version control, and derivative products.

The record format used for entries in the schedules, tables, and Manual will be based on an enhanced version of the MARC 21 Format for Classification Data. The record format used for Relative Index (RI) heading records and records for mapped headings from other vocabularies will be based on an enhanced version of the MARC 21 Format for Authority Data.

We are making this conversion because we want the data in the new Dewey Editorial Support System (ESS) to be available in a format supported by an international standard, and one that supports flexible data representation. We also want the data to be more fully integrated with data in OCLC's WorldCat and in the related authority files, all of which use MARC 21. In addition, the system is being developed by people familiar with the MARC 21 Bibliographic and Authority Formats and using tools based on the MARC 21 formats.

The development team has identified several changes to the Classification and Authority Formats to improve the representation of DDC data. Some of these changes are being proposed below in section 2 of this discussion paper. Others are likely to be used primarily by DDC editors and translators, and thus will be local additions to the Classification and Authority Formats.

The German and Austrian communities are converting to MARC 21 from the MAB format and have proposed several changes to the MARC 21 Bibliographic Format related to the representation of DDC numbers. The Dewey editorial team and the team from Deutsche Nationalbibliothek (DNB) have agreed to work together on a proposal to address improvements to the representation of Dewey information across the MARC 21 formats. Changes are needed along a number of dimensions to address specificity and consistency in the representation of data.

MARC 21 and DDC

MARC 21 contains provisions for Dewey numbers in all the formats, with the Classification Format having the most detailed provision and the holdings format having the least. Outside of the Classification Format and field 083 in the Authority Format, the representation is limited to full classification numbers and call numbers. There is little or no support for representation of notation from the external Dewey tables, notation from internal tables or elements of synthesized numbers, and limited information about the type and source of the number. The Bibliographic and Community Information Formats represent Dewey numbers in the 082 field. The Authority Format represents Dewey numbers in field 082 which contains a Dewey call number for a series and field 083 which contains a Dewey classification number associated with the 1XX heading. The Holdings Format represents Dewey numbers in the $h subfield (Classification part) of field 852 field.

The Classification format contains far more details for the representation of Dewey numbers. In particular, it has conventions for the representation of notation in external tables and for ranges of Dewey numbers. Notation in internal tables is represented within the record for the number or span of numbers under which the table appears. Elements of synthesized numbers are documented within the record for the number. The format also provides detailed information about the type and source of numbers.

Discussion

This section includes issues that the Dewey team and DNB have found in the representation of DDC in the MARC 21 formats, and suggested changes to accommodate these needs.

Identification of External Table Numbers

The full edition of the DDC contains six auxiliary tables (Table 1-6), referred to in this document as "external tables." The notation from the six tables is applied across the DDC to represent forms, genres, geographic areas, languages, ethnic groups, etc. At present, only the Classification and Authority Formats allow for indicating the external table that has been used to construct a Dewey number. The Dewey editorial team recommends adding the Classification Format representation of external table notation to the Bibliographic Format to support the identification of and access to external table information, as will as the recording of component parts of numbers.

The Classification format uses subfield $z for the external table number. For example,

153 ## $z 2 $a 73 [Dewey notation 73 in Table 2]

153 ## $z 2 $a 74 $c 79 [Dewey notation 74-79 in Table 2]

Proposed Change:

- Add subfield $z - Table identification

  Bibliographic Format, field 082 - Dewey Decimal Classification Number (R)

Identification of Internal Add Table Numbers

The DDC also includes tables of notation within schedule and table records. These are referred to in this document as "internal add tables." In the current Dewey editorial support system and MARC Classification Format, internal add tables are represented using a single record for the internal add table. In the new ESS, the Dewey editorial team plans to use separate records for each entry in internal add tables. In addition to making it easier to support references to and from notation within add tables, the provision of separate records will support external identification of and access to the notation in internal add tables.

The Dewey editorial team recommends an extension to the Classification format to provide a separate MARC record for each entry of an internal add table in a 153 field. The Dewey editorial team proposes representing the internal add table notation within the 153 field using the existing subfields ($a and $c) both for the number or span at which the internal add table is located and for the table notation itself.

The Dewey editorial team recommends using a new subfield $y with the internal add table number immediately before the add table notation. Subfield $y will have the value 1 for the first internal add table at that location and values 2, 3, etc. for additional internal add tables at the same location.

153 ## $a 290 $y 1 $a 071 [Dewey notation 071 in the internal add table located at 290]

153 ## $a 362 $c 363 $y 1 $a 01 [Dewey notation 01 in the internal add table located under 362-363]

There can also be a span of notation within an internal add table in addition to a span for the table designation.

153 ## $a 333.7 $c 333.9 $y 1 $a 01 $c 09 [Dewey notation 01-09 in the internal add table located under 333.7-333.9]

Internal add tables are also located under Dewey notation in external Tables.

153 ## $z 1 $a 08 $y 1 $a 01 [Dewey notation 01 in the internal add table located under Dewey notation 08 in Table 1]

Number spans can be found as notation within internal add tables, and at the location of internal add tables.

153 ## $z 3B $a 1 $c 8 $y 1 $a 901 $c 907 [Dewey notation 901-907 in the internal add table 1 under Dewey notation 1-8 in Table 3B]

If there were multiple internal add tables at the same location, the value of subfield $y changes:

153 ## $a 810.1 $c818 $y 2 $a 3 [Dewey notation 3 in the second internal add table under 810.1-818]

Proposed change:

- Add subfield $y - Internal add table identification (R)

  Classification Format:

  153 - Classification Number

  253 - Complex See Reference (R)

  353 - Complex See Also Reference (R)

  453 - Invalid Number Tracing (R)

  553 - Valid Number Tracing (R)

  680 - Scope Note (R)

  683 - Application Instruction Note (R)

  684 - Auxiliary Instruction Note (R)

  685 - History Note (R)

  761 - Add Or Divide Like Instructions (R)

  765 - Synthesized Number Components (R)

  Bibliographic Format :

  082 - Dewey Decimal Classification Number (R)

  Authority Format

  083 - Dewey Decimal Classification Number (R)

Inclusion of Component Parts of Numbers in Bibliographic Records

In the MARC Classification Format, the component parts of numbers are represented in field 765 (Synthesized Number Components). The information in the 765 field is useful to show how a number is built, to show the meaning of the component parts of a built number, and to enable searching of particular component parts in classification number records. For example:

153 ## $a 346.0469516 $h Social sciences $h Law $k Branches of law; laws, regulations, cases; law of specific jurisdictions, areas, socioeconomic regions $k Branches of law $h Private law $h Property $h Government control and regulation of specific kinds of land and natural resources $h Other natural resources $h Biological resources $h General topics $k Management and control $j Conservation and protection

765 0# $b 346.046 $a 346.046 $r 333 $s 95

765 0# $b 346.04695 $a 333.7 $c 333.9 $w 333.7 $c 333.9 $t 16

The first 765 field indicates that Dewey notation 95 comes from 333.95 Biological resources. The second 765 field indicates that Dewey notation 16 comes from notation 16 Conservation and protection in the internal add table at 333.7-333.9.

Dewey numbers are usually associated with bibliographic records in a precoordinated form, but the components parts of those precoordinated numbers contain a rich array of information. For retrieval, DNB wishes to provide easy access to the component parts of Dewey numbers in bibliographic records, in association with the 082 fields containing Dewey numbers. There would be two ways of providing this:

- Specify component parts in the Classification Format and then create links between that data and its representation in the bibliographic file.
- Provide such information directly in the bibliographic record, especially when the bibliographic file is not linked to the classification file.

We do not see this as a choice between one method and another-if we adopt a consistent representation of classification number components, then data can be easily exported or imported between bibliographic files and classification files. We recommend continuing to represent the component parts of Dewey numbers using the 765 field in the MARC Classification Format, and propose using the structure of field 765 as the basis for a new field in the Bibliographic Format that can be used when importing or exporting data in a bibliographic record. The Bibliographic Format field would be specified as follows:

The Dewey editorial team suggests:

- Defining a new 085 field in the Bibliographic Format containing the same subfields as the 765 field in the Classification Format.
- Using subfield $8 to link the 082 field with the appropriate 085 field(s) and to provide information on the sequence of the steps.

For example, for the number illustrated above, there could be the following 082 and 085 fields:

082 0# $8 1 $a 346.0469516 $2 22

085 ## $8 1.1 $b 346.046 $a 346.046 $r 333 $s 95

085 ## $8 1.2 $b 346.04695 $a 333.7 $c 333.9 $w 333.7 $c 333.9 $t 16

A more complex example would be the following successive 082 fields with LC-assigned numbers from the full and abridged editions, respectively, together with a DNB assigned number.

If 085 fields were added for the two built numbers, the record would contain the following:

082 01 $8 1 $a 346.0469516 $2 22

085 ## $8 1.1 $b 346.046 $a 346.046 $r 333 $s 95

085 ## $8 1.2 $b 346.04695 $a 333.7 $c 333.9 $w 333.7 $c 333.9 $t 16

082 11 $a 346.04 $ 2 14

082 04 $8 2 $a 346.0469514 $2 22/ger $5 DE-101b

085 ## $8 2.1 $b 346.046 $a 346.046 $r 333 $s 95

085 ## $8 2.2 $b 346.04695 $a 333.7 $c 333.9 $w 333.7 $c 333.9 $t 14

Proposed change:

- Add new field 085 for number-building to the Bibliographic Format

  085 - Synthesized DDC Number Components (R)

  Indicators - Both indicators undefined, contain blanks

  Subfield Codes

  $a - Number where instructions are found—single number or beginning number of span (R)

  $b - Base number (R)

  $c - Number where instructions are found—ending number of span (R)

  $f - Facet designator (R)

  $r - Root number (R)

  $s - Digits added from classification number in schedule or external table (R)

  $t - Digits added from internal subarrangement or add table (R)

  $u - Number being analyzed (R)

  $v - Number in internal subarrangement or add table where instructions are found (R)

$w - Table identification—internal subarrangement or add table (R)

$y - Internal add table identification (R)

$z - Table identification (R)

$6 - Linkage (NR)

$8 - Field link and sequence number (R)

Classification Number Edition and Source Information in the Bibliographic Format

Currently, in field 082 in the Bibliographic Format, the edition number is carried in subfield $2. For the expansion of Dewey, the edition information needs to be expanded to include language of edition. In addition, the DNB wishes to document the agency assigning the number in the same field as the number itself. The second indicator already reports LC/non-LC as the assigning agency. In the case where the assigning agency is another agency, the subfield $5 (Institution to which field applies) is proposed, as in field 083 (Dewey Decimal Classification Number) in the Authority Format.

For edition information, The Dewey editorial team proposes to develop and maintain a registry of edition identifiers in which each edition would have a standard representation in subfield $2:

Examples:

$2 22 [latest version of DDC 22 file (currently available in WebDewey)]

$2 22/ger [latest version of German DDC 22 file (currently available in Melvil)]

The assigning agency information in the new $5 subfield would be coded:

082 04 $a 004 $2 22/ger $5 DE-101b

Proposed change:

- Add subfield $5 - Assigning agency of a Dewey number subfield
  Bibliographic Format, field 082 - Dewey Decimal Classification Number
  Classification Format, field 084 - Classification Scheme and Edition

Designations for Optional Numbers in the Bibliographic Format

The Dewey editorial team would like to investigate a provision for the designation of optional numbers in the Bibliographic, Authority, and Community Information formats. Many optional numbers are already coded in existing bibliographic records as if they were standard Dewey numbers. One example is optional numbers in 340 Law, which used to be assigned by the Library of Congress:

082 00 $a 345.730772 $a 347.305772 $2 20

In the example above, 345.730772 is the standard Dewey number for sentencing in US criminal law, and 347.305772 is an optional number. Another example is optional numbers for Australian literature and Canadian literature in records coming from the National Library of Australia and from Library and Archives Canada:

082 04 $a A823.30108 $2 21

082 04 $a C811.008005 $2 21

In the two examples above, an optional letter denoting the literature ("A" for Australian English literature and "C" for Canadian-American literature in English, respectively) has been inserted before the literature number. The rest of the Canadian number is a standard Dewey number, but the Australian number has been extended by notation from an optional period table. Optional numbers may be represented by a MARC Classification Format record where they are encoded with value b (Optional) in 008/09 (Standard or optional designation).

There are many optional numbers in bibliographic records in WorldCat, but no special designation exists to label the optional numbers as such. The Dewey editorial team considered coding optional numbers in a separate subfield in the Bibliographic Format, but rejected this approach because of the large number of optional numbers already coded in subfield $a in legacy data. In section 2.6 discusses approaches to addressing "type of number" issues.

Multiple Numbers in the Bibliographic Format

The MARC 21 Bibliographic Format already supports the addition of multiple Dewey numbers to bibliographic records. Field 082 is repeatable, and subfield $a within field 082 is also repeatable. The current convention is to use a single 082 field for numbers assigned from the same DDC edition cited in subfield $2. For example, a number assigned from DDC 22 is put in a different 082 field from a number assigned from Abridged Edition 14:

082 01 $a 346.0469516 $2 22

082 11 $a 346.04 $2 14

LC also routinely adds optional Dewey "numbers" (*e.g.*, notation "B" for biographical works) in addition to the standard Dewey number in successive $a subfields in the same 082 field:

082 10 $a 780.92 $a B $2 22

And until recently, the Library of Congress had routinely added a number for a series as a whole to records for specific works in a series; these two numbers were distinguished by the addition of an "s" after the series number:

082 10 $a 081 s $a 327.7 $2 21

In addition the DNB is also interested in adding table notation in a separate subfield where further addition to the full DDC number is not permitted by the rules; German virtual libraries are interested in assigning partial numbers instead of undertaking the process of number building; and there is general interest in providing multiple numbers for works with aspects in more than one Dewey category.

The Dewey editorial team welcomes these additional access points. At the same time, in order to support interoperability and choice of shelf location for physical items, it remains desirable to be able to identify the single DDC number that would be assigned following the instructions in the edition cited in subfield $2. The Dewey editorial team recommends the following actions:

- Cease use of repeated $a subfields in the same 082 field in the Bibliographic Format to represent multiple Dewey numbers in favour of successive 082 fields for each number.
- Introduce coding to represent numbers provided for access, including external and internal table numbers
- Introduce coding to distinguish between the primary number and additional numbers provided for access, and between standard and optional numbers.

Use of 082

The Dewey editorial team proposes the addition of subfields $m and $o in the 082 field in the Bibliographic Format that can be used to indicate the nature of the number in subfield $a in relation to the edition cited in subfield $2. They would be specified as follows:

$m Standard or optional designation

a - standard

b - optional

$o Primary or access designation

a - primary

b - access

Subfields $m and $o are not required, and the default is for them to be absent.

In the following example, the first 082 is the "primary" number; the second is optional; and the third and fourth represent the German virtual library approach of just entering the elements in successive 082 fields without building the number. Without the proposed coding, one cannot distinguish primary numbers from access numbers (except in the case of the third number, with its $z), and one cannot distinguish standard numbers from optional numbers.

245 00 $a Criminal sentencing / $c edited by Robert Emmet Long.

082 00 $a 345.730772 $m a $o a $2 20

082 00 $a 347.305772 $m b $o a $2 20

082 04 $z 2 $a73 $m a $o b $2 20

082 04 $a 345.0772 $m a $o b $2 20

Proposed change:

- Define subfields $m and $o as described above
  Bibliographic Format, field 082 - Dewey Decimal Classification Number

Use of 085 for Direct Assignment of Component Parts of Numbers : Another option for this information would be to use new field 085 (Number components) to represent the direct assignment of component parts of numbers (external table numbers, internal table notation, partial notation derived from Dewey numbers) in addition to its proposed use for the explanation of component parts of numbers found in the 082 field. The reason would be to limit the use of the 082 field to the representation of full Dewey numbers to avoid making this widely used field confusing and complicated.

The absence of $8 subfields linking field 085 to a specific 082 field could be interpreted as a sign that field 085 is being used for direct assignment of component parts of numbers rather than to explain how a number in field 082 was built. If used to represent the direct assignment of component parts of numbers, the 085 field would also need to include aspects of 082 information not previously specified for the 085 field—first and second indicators for edition and assigning agency, respectively; subfield $2 for edition; subfield $5 for assigning agency; subfield $m for standard or optional designation (subfield $o is not needed, since it would be by nature "access only"). While this approach removes some complexity from the 082 field, it does so at the expense of adding complexity to the 085 field.

Proposed Change: If the 085 field is used both for direct assignment of component parts of numbers as described in section 2.6.2 above and for number building information, the indicators will need to be defined as in field 082 and additional subfields ($m, $2, and $5) will be needed.

Segmentation Information in the Classification Format

The current ESS encodes segmentation information, and this is shared with users of DDC in WebDewey. Currently the segmentation mark indicates the end of the number used in the abridged edition. (Formerly a second segmentation mark could be used to indicate the start of standard subdivision (Table 1) notation.) Segmentation marks are used in the 082 fields in bibliographic records created by the Library of Congress.

In the ESS, seg and set fields are used for segmentation information. The seg field is used for records for a single Dewey number or number span to show where the segmentation mark appears. The set field is used for Dewey number records that contain number-building instructions to give segmentation information that cannot be expressed using a single number or number span. New fields 653 and 654 in the Classification Format are proposed for segmentation information, to encode seg and set fields, respectively.

Examples from the old ESS of seg and set fields are:

In the record for 025.431:

seg: 025.4/31 [025.4 is the abridged edition number][old ESS]

653 ## $a 025.4/31

In the record for 636.9:

set : Segment as shown in 599.2-599.8, *e.g.*, 636.9205, 636.92/9, 636.935/6

[There is an add instruction at 636.9 to add notation from 599.2-599.8][old ESS]

654 ## $i Segment as shown in$a599.2$c 599.8$i, *e.g.*,$a 636.9205 $i,$a 636.92/9$i,$a 636.935/6 [MARC proposal]

Proposed Change:

- Add new fields 653 and 654 to the Classification Format

  653 - Segmented Classification Number (NR)

  Indicators — Both indicators undefined, contain blanks

  Subfield Codes

  $a - Classification number—single number or beginning number of span (NR)

  $c - Classification number—ending number of span (NR)

  $y - Internal add table identification (R)

  $z - Table identification (NR)

  654 - Segmentation Instruction (R)

  Indicators — Both indicators undefined, contain blanks

  Subfield Codes

  $a - Classification number—single number or beginning number of span (R)

  $c - Classification number—ending number of span (R)

  $i - Explanatory text (R)

  $y - Internal add table identification (R)

  $z - Table identification (R)

Encoding Topic Information in some Classification Format Fields

The Dewey editorial team wishes to use subfield $t for topics named in examples in the 680, 683, and 761 fields. The $t subfield is already used for this purpose in fields 453, 553, and 768, *e.g.*:

768 0# $i Unless other instructions are given, class a subject with aspects in two or more subdivisions of $a 641.563 $i in the number coming first, *e.g.*, $t low-carbohydrate, low-calorie cooking for persons with diabetes $e 641.56314 $i (not $n 641.5635 $i or $n 641.5638)

Subfield $t is needed to distinguish topical information from "canned text" (canned text being text that remains the same for particular kinds of fields, regardless of topic), and to enable automated identification of the meaning of DDC numbers given in examples. Examples of the proposed use of the $t subfield are:

680 1# $i An area is classed in its present number even if it had a different affiliation at the time under consideration, *e.g.*, $t Arizona under Mexican sovereignty $z 2 $a 791 $i (not $z 2 $a 72)

683 0# $i In building numbers, do not add by use of 0 or 1 (alone or in combination) more than twice, *e.g.*, $t history of rock protest songs $a 782.421661592 $i (not $a 782.42166159209)

761 #0 $i Add to base number $b 025.29 $i notation $z 2 $d 1 $c 9 $i from Table 2, *e.g.*, $t acquisition of materials from Latin America $e 025.298

Proposed Change:

- Add subfield $t - Topic information

  Classification Format:

  680 - Scope Note (R)

  683 - Application Instruction Note (R)

  761 - Add Or Divide Like Instructions (R)

Number Hierarchy

Currently in field 153 of the Classification format only the upward caption hierarchy is given, in subfields $h and $k. The Classification numbers associated with those captions are not given. For example:

153 ## $a 616.8001 $c 616.8009 $h Technology $h Medicine and health $h Diseases $k Specific diseases $k Diseases of specific systems and organs $h Diseases of nervous system and mental disorders $j Standard subdivisions

DNB recommends using a new subfield $e (Classification number hierarchy — single number or beginning of a span) in field 153 to link to the next number or number span upwards in the Classification number hierarchy. This will provide the link to the appropriate headings and the appropriate notes with hierarchical force. It will also indirectly provide for links to the downward hierarchy.

Examples:

$a 616.8001 $c 616.8009 $e 616.8

$a 616.8 $e 616.1 $c 616.8

$a 616.1 $c 616.8 $e 616.1 $c 616.9

$a 616.1 $c 616.9 $e 616

$a 616 $e 610

$a 610 $e 600

Proposed Change:

- Add subfield $e - Classification number hierarchy—single number or beginning number of span

  Classification Format, field 153 - Classification Number

Summary of Changes to Bibliographic 082

The following changes would be needed for field 082 - Dewey Decimal Classification Number

New subfield codes:

$c - Classification number—ending number of span (R)

$m - Standard or optional designation (NR)

$o - Primary or access designation (NR)

$y - Internal add table identification (R)

$z - Table identification (R)

$5 - Institution to which field applies (R)

On the Classification of Books and Text Files, Particularly Fiction

Purpose

This essay is about how publishers, bookstores and libraries go about classifying books, how bulletin-board services (BBS's) classify textfiles, how readers with more than a few books classify their collections, and what merits there are in their respective systems.

It also considers whether bookstores, librarians, and BBS sysops can learn anything from one another in the way they sort books and text files.

Some Personal Experiences

A couple of years ago I decided to spend some of my spare time sorting, arranging, and cataloguing all the books our family owns. I began with my own books, which I had been sorting by different arrangements since I was eight or nine years old. At different times, I had my books arranged by publisher, by author, by title, by genre or type, and not sorted at all. At last I settled upon sorting all the fiction strictly by author, not separating science fiction from miscellaneous fiction, and putting my nonfiction together in shelf categories based roughly on the Dewey Decimal system. Eventually I got the idea of arranging all our family's books by subject and author in just this way, and cataloguing them all by title, author, and subject in a database file. I received some encouragement, though no help (not that I asked for any) from my parents and brother. I traversed the house, toting large stacks of books to the computer to be catalogued, and then putting them back where I found them.

When I had seen what all sorts of books we had in the house, I began devising a system to arrange them all rationally. At that time, there was some fiction in every room of the house, and the nonfiction was similarly scattered. So I started by taking all the fiction from all over the house (except for each of our personal favourites, which stayed in the bedrooms), sorting it by author, and putting it all on just two bookcases. The nonfiction I sorted out, roughly, into the Dewey Decimal categories; the more books we had in a given area, the deeper I went in sorting them. I had science and mathematics in my room; economics, politics, language, literature, biography, health, all in their own places in the computer room; devotional and theological books and bibles (other than our personal bibles) all together in the living room, and so on. When I had been at this for several days, my mother inquired how things were going with it, and I showed her how I had arranged things.

She expressed pleasure, but had a few nits to pick: to wit, several books with beautiful bindings (the Gustave Dore edition of Dante's Divine Comedy and the New York Times Book of Money among others) had been placed with other books of the same sort (epic poems and economics respectively) instead of in prominent view of guests in the living room; and a number of tattered old paperbacks, which happened to be of a theological or devotional persuasion, *were* in prominent view of guests in the living room. This situation had to be remedied. I argued as much as I could without dishonoring my parents, and perhaps more; but to no avail.

On another occasion my brother Brian hired me to sort out his books, and told me how he would like them sorted. He wanted most of the fiction sorted by the author's name, but with a couple of exceptions: books of cartoons and comics (Peanuts, Archie, etc.) were to be separate, as were decision novels (Time Machine, Choose Your Own

Adventure, Grailquest, etc.). I sorted them thus and they have been shelved that way most of the time since.

During my first visit to a friend's apartment, I looked over his shelves of books and inquired by what method he had sorted them. He asked if I could figure it out by inspecting the shelves for myself; so I went to the job. Parts of it were easy to see. Books by G.K. Chesterton on all subjects were shelved together, and books by C.S. Lewis were all together on another shelf. Below this were two or three shelves of miscellaneous Christian books, followed by a shelf of different Bible translations. On another bookcase there were books on economics and political science; below this were non-Christian philosophers. There was a shelf of science fiction and non-fiction about science fiction, which did not seem to be sorted by author. Then there was a shelf of books of all sorts — philosophy, government, fiction, theology, devotion, and several other matters. In another room was another shelf of miscellaneous books, most but not all fiction.

I spoke to him again and asked if my observations were correct, and asked particularly about the two shelves which seemed to be a hodgepodge of unrelated books. He affirmed most of my observations, adding that he sorted the Christian books into theology and devotion; with the devotional books shelved more handy to his reading chair, as he had been neglecting them of late. As for the two hodgepodge shelves, he said that the one was all books which he had bought recently and hadn't read yet; the other was old and rare books.

Fiction

.Fiction and Literature

.Forms and Genres

.Marketing Categories

.Bookstores' and libraries' shelving convenience policies

.Should science fiction and fantasy be shelved separately?

.Myths and legends

."Classics and Literature"

.Series by more than one author

.Anthologies of several authors

.Sorting by genre: difficulties

.Ways libraries sort fiction

.Should essays, letters and diaries be placed with fiction?

.Problems about sorting by nationality of author

.Literary criticism

One of the main shelving classifications used by libraries is "Literature." It is supposed to include books of essays (but not if the essays are all on the same subject), letters and diaries, poetry, satire, drama, novels, short stories, and jokes.

I have tried to figure out what essays have in common with fiction, what letters and diaries have in common with fiction, and why nonfiction written in verse should be placed with fiction written in verse. My brother suggested it might be that essays are subjective, so they should go with fiction. But all books are subjective to some degree. Man can't write something completely objective no matter how hard he tries. I have seen some relatively objective essays placed with Literature while some very subjective essays, which were all on the same subject, were shelved with that subject. Perhaps the generalities would be a better place for miscellaneous essays, rather than "Literature."

Diaries and letters are more like autobiography than fiction. So whether they should be placed with fiction depends on how the library shelves biography. See the section on Biography under Nonfiction, below.

It seems that fiction (*i.e.*, narrative) poems should probably go near prose fiction. Whether nonfiction poems (lyric poetry) should be placed near prose fiction is less clear. Maybe we can consider them as essays written in verse? If so, perhaps they should be placed next to the miscellaneous essays in the generalities. Or, perhaps, within the "Literature" shelves we could have separate shelvings for nonfiction poems and narrative poems.

It will first be good to note two ways of separating fiction: by forms, and by genres.

Forms are such as Joke, Parable, Poetry (Epic, Lyric, Comic), Novel, Short story, Drama (Plays, whether for stage, radio, or television), and Satire. Other forms include Decision novels, Role-playing game scenarios, Computer adventure games, and Hypernovels. These latter forms have been invented but lately and have not yet been recognised in classification systems by libraries. However, many bookstores recognise them as distinct forms and shelve them separately.

Genres, on the other hand, include Historical (Gothic, Western), Mystery, Science Fiction, Fantasy, and Horror. Genres are similar to Marketing Categories, which are used by publishers and bookstores. However, sorting by genre means placing books of a similar nature together, while sorting by Marketing Category means placing books likely to be bought by the same readers together. For example, when sorting by Marketing Category one would place non-fiction about science fiction together with science fiction, and some non-fiction by authors known for their science fiction would be placed with science fiction, such as Robert Heinlein's book about his travels around the world, Tramp Royale.

Some Marketing Categories used by publishers and bookstores include Horror, Gothic, Western, Science Fiction and Fantasy, Romance, War, Mystery, and Historical. Children's Fiction is usually shelved separately; but it is not as often subdivided by genre as grown-up books are. Rather, it is subdivided by age group or reading level. Young-Adult fiction for young teenagers and older children is often shelved separately as well. Remarkable things I see here are that Horror, which deals as often as not with the supernatural, is not always classed with other fantasy; and Westerns and Gothics are numerous enough to often be in a separate shelf from other Historical Novels.

Both bookstores and libraries usually shelve new books in a special place, often up front in a prominent spot, until they are displaced by still newer books. Bookstores often place books which are on sale in a prominent spot, unsorted by category. It may be said that new books and reduced-price books are considered separate marketing categories in their own right.

To conserve shelf and floor space, bookstores usually place hardbacks and trade paperbacks of a particular genre on a top shelf above standard-sized paperbacks of the same subject or genre. Both retail and used book stores do this. Libraries, on the other hand, usually have shelves tall enough for all but the very tallest books, and if a book is too tall even for this shelf it may be shelved lying on its back to avoid placing it in an oversized books section. However, some libraries have oversized book sections and indicate in a book's card catalogue entry that it is shelved in the oversized book section.

The question has been raised whether science fiction and fantasy should be shelved separately from one another, rather than together as they are in most bookstores and many libraries. The usual objection, which seems to me very strong, is that many books treat traditional fantasy plot elements scientifically, many more books treat traditional science fiction plot elements unscientifically, and many more deliberately mix science fiction and fantasy plot elements, sometimes using the concept of alternate worlds which is common to both fantasy and science fiction; and all these trends tend to make it difficult for readers (much less bookstore managers and librarians, who have not time to read every book through) to say whether some books are fantasy, or science fiction. In addition, many readers enjoy both science fiction and fantasy. However, with this reason we are treating "science fiction and fantasy" as a marketing category rather than one or two genres.

Books of myths and legends also pose a sort of problem. These fall into at least two main categories: those treating them as ancient religions, and those treating them as collections of stories. Books of the latter sort should, it seems to me, be placed with fantasy and science fiction, or with children's fiction, and not with books on religion (as libraries do) or "Classics and Literature" (as most bookstores do). Of course, there is a fair amount of overlap between the two categories, and perhaps all books on mythology should be shelved together, since it is sometimes difficult to tell which class a book falls into without reading the whole thing, which librarians and bookstore managers scarcely have time for.

One category used by bookstores is "Classics and Literature". It commonly includes most of the oldest fiction, most of the poetry, recent fiction praised by literary critics, and sometimes old books on history, philosophy and miscellaneous subjects. A more appropriate unifying title might be "Books Likely to be Assigned for School Reading," though that might be a bit unwieldy. Perhaps old books which are not fiction should not be placed here.

Publishers have an advantage in that they can place an entry for a book under several headings in the catalogue when there is some uncertainty about which category it fits best in. Libraries have a similar advantage with their card catalogue, in which a book has at least three entries (for author, title, and subject) and sometimes more (if by multiple authors or on multiple subjects).

A characteristic difference of libraries and bookstores may be seen in the way they shelve series of books by more than one author. Star Trek, Doctor Who, and Dragonlance novels; Oz, The Three Investigators, and Horatio Hornblower; all were or are written by several authors. Most bookstores place all the books in these series together, sometimes according to the author who began the series, sometimes according to the series title. Libraries, on the other hand, treat these books as works of the author who wrote each particular book, and not (as bookstores may be said to do) as collaborations with the authors of other books in the series, particularly with the author who began the series. In this way Star Trek novels are shelved in two dozen different places, Oz in two places, the Three Investigators in three or four, and so on. In addition, the fact that few libraries have subject information on fiction means that one cannot search in the card catalogue for "Star Trek" and find all the authors whose Star Trek novels are in this library: one must browse carefully through all the shelves of science fiction, or, worse still, all the shelves of fiction.

Some of the reasons for this are plain. Bookstores depend more immediately and directly on their customers' satisfaction, and shelve the books where their readers expect to find them. Libraries, on the other hand, as many are operated by the government, are only indirectly affected by their customers' wants, and many may not have given this problem the thought it deserves; also, many of the series I have mentioned are considered "vulgar" or "popular" fiction, and are seen as less a reason for the library's existence than the "serious" fiction and the non-fiction.

In all the libraries I have observed personally, fiction books are arranged by author without any exception being made for series which are written by more than one author. However, I have heard that some libraries do make an exception for them.

Whether libraries should try to imitate bookstores more in this matter is open to some question. It may be argued that it is too difficult and time-consuming difficult to keep track of all the series written by more than one author, and to decide whether to shelve each one according to the series' creator's name or according to the series title. I may modestly comment that the bookstore managers, whose livelihood is at stake, don't think it is too much trouble.

With some (Oz and the Three Investigators) I would favour using the series's creator's name (L. Frank Baum and Robert Arthur respectively), but with those such as Star Trek (Gene Roddenberry, who created the series, only wrote one of the novels) I am not sure that this is the best course. Some bookstores shelve Star Trek by its series title among the authors in the science fiction section. Others place Star Trek at the end of the science fiction section. These observations apply also to Doctor Who, Dragonlance, and some other series.

How should anthologies of fiction by several authors be shelved? Most libraries and bookstores shelve them with the fiction, by the editor's name. Libraries place some anthologies in the 800's and some in the popular fiction. A few place all such anthologies at the head of the fiction, and sort them there by title or by the editor's name. It seems that this last method is perhaps best. Perhaps it might be better to subdivide them according to their themes, whether general (Best Short Stories of the Year), more specific (Best Science Fiction of the Year), or more specific still (12 Classic Time-Travel Stories); but to do this consistently and systematically would require an extensive analysis of the actual and possible themes, perhaps as extensive as the analyses of all knowledge found in the Library of Congress and Dewey Decimal Systems.

If we decide that all multi-author anthologies are to be placed together, then we still have to decide how they are to be sorted within this grouping — whether by the editor's name, or by the title. Sorting by the title has this merit: that it places all anthologies in a single series together, even if the different anthologies in the series have been edited by different people. For example, the Nebula Awards anthologies have been edited by several different authors, but when multi-author anthologies are sorted by title all the Nebula Awards stories are placed together.

There is also some merit in placing an entry in the card catalogue for every author represented in the anthology, as well as for the editor. (I hear some librarians shudder as they think of "100 Short Short Science Fiction Stories".) However, there would need to be a way to show that the anthology is shelved with anthologies under the title or editor's name, whichever the library uses, and not with the author's fiction.

Bookstores (and the publishers, and most readers) place J.R.R. Tolkien's The Lord of the Rings, David Eddings's Belgariad, and Stephen Lawhead's Pendragon Cycle with fantasy. However, many libraries place them with the general fiction. Dover Books places G.K. Chesterton's The Club of Queer Trades and The Man Who Was Thursday with other mysteries in their mail-order catalogue; however, some libraries place them with general fiction. There is also some confusion about such novels as A Connecticut Yankee in King Arthur's Court by Mark Twain, Time and Again by Jack Finney, and Lest Darkness Fall by L. Sprague de Camp. They are time travel stories, but also historical novels; should they be shelved with science fiction or with historical novels or general fiction? Hal Clement's Needle and Larry Niven's The Long Arm of Gil Hamilton are usually shelved with science fiction but there is some reason to shelve them with mysteries. Disagreements and confusions such as these are the main reason in favour of placing all fiction together, and not separating science fiction and fantasy, mystery, and so on from the general fiction.

Next we shall consider the several systems libraries use to sort fiction. The Library of Congress and Dewey Decimal systems each have two provisions, one for "serious fiction" and one for "popular fiction." The Library of Congress system sorts first by the nationality or language of the author, then by the author's last name. Books of all forms (poetry, novels, etc.) by a single author are shelved together, sorted by title. For popular fiction, the Library of Congress system sorts first into authors who began writing before 1950, and authors who began writing after that date. Within each group it sorts by author's name and then by title. The Dewey Decimal system sorts first by the nationality or language of the author, then into several forms: poetry, drama, novels and stories, humour and satire, letters, diaries, and essays. Within each form classification, it sorts books by the author's name.

Both the Dewey Decimal and Library of Congress systems place essays, diaries, and collections of letters together with the different kinds of fiction, which seems a bit odd. Essays are nonfiction, and letters and diaries are much more like autobiography than they are like fiction. It seems more logical that books of essays on several subjects should go with the "generalities" or miscellanies, and letters and diaries should go with biography and autobiography.

It seems that sorting by form is much easier than sorting by genre, considering the disagreements and confusions above noted. However, which meets readers' needs better is less clear. There is something to be said for having, say, science fiction poetry placed with science fiction short stories.

Sorting fiction by language is a fairly straightforward matter, and it is a minor question whether to place translations with the language of the original or the language into which translated. (Most libraries place translations with the language of the original.) Sorting by nationality is somewhat more difficult. J.R.R. Tolkien lived in England most of his life but was born in South Africa. Isaac Asimov lived in America most of his life but was born in Russia. W.H. Auden was born in England and began writing there; he moved to America and continued writing until he died. Rudyard Kipling was born in India, lived in England awhile, lived in India again and began writing there, lived in England again, then in America, then in England again, and lived in South Africa for awhile too, besides extensive travels in other places, writing all the way.

Besides, sorting fiction by the nationality of the author does not seem to me so useful to the reader as dividing genres from the general fiction, despite the problems of when to distinguish mystery or science fiction from general fiction and when to leave it there. Isaac Asimov (an American Jew) has more in common with Arthur C. Clarke (an Englishman living in Sri Lanka) than he has with, say, Chaim Potok (another American Jew); at least their fiction has more in common.

Considering these difficulties regarding sorting by nationality, and the previously mentioned difficulties in sorting by genre, it is no wonder that many libraries think it is best to put all fiction together. (The Stockbridge library has recently decided to place all fiction together, where formerly it was divided by genre.)

Where should nonfiction about fiction (also known as literary criticism) be placed? In its own place beside the fiction but not mixed in with it, or mixed in with it? And, if mixed in with it, how should they be sorted together?

The Library of Congress system places specific literary criticism (books about a particular author's books) immediately after the author's books. For instance, first come all G.K. Chesterton's fiction and essays, then all nonfiction books about Chesterton's books. The Dewey Decimal system has a less fortunate way of shelving literary criticism. As books are shelved within each classification number (such as 823 for English novels and stories), they are sorted by the author's name. Thus, a book by Lin Carter about J.R.R. Tolkien's stories would not be shelved with Tolkien's books, but with Carter's other books about English novels and stories.

Bookstores sometimes use a similar system to the Library of Congress method. For example, nonfiction books about Star Trek are usually shelved with the Star Trek novels.

Nonfiction

.Computer programmeming, telecommunications, computer applications

.Essays, Letters, Diaries

.Biography and Autobiography

In the Dewey Decimal system the 000's are "Generalities;" books about broad subjects like the nature of knowledge, books about many different subjects (such as encyclopaedias), and books of library science. As cybernetics is considered to be a branch of the study of knowledge, and is shelved with the "Generalities," *computer programmeming* has been considered a branch of cybernetics, and shelved with the generalities. (001.64) This is not right. Computer programmeming is an applied science, a useful art. It should go with the 600's, which includes agriculture, mechanics, and manufacturing. With it should go, perhaps, books on telecommunications and on various computer operating systems and application software. This should be taken into account in the next edition of the Dewey Decimal system. The Library of Congress systems puts computer programmeming in QA, near mathematics. I don't know where the Library of Congress system puts all books on application software; some of it (desktop publishing) goes in Z, library science.

Both the Dewey Decimal and Library of Congress systems place essays, letters, and diaries with fiction and poetry. My brothers, these things ought not to be so. Are essays fiction? Are letters and diaries? Is a man ever more honest and truthful than when he writes in his diary which he hopes will never be published until he is too dead to be embarrassed by it? But libraries place diaries with fiction. How about if we start placing them (and letters as well) with autobiography? And as for books of essays, which often treat of many different subjects, and in an informal way, even so they are not fiction. Perhaps they should be placed with generalities such as books of trivia and encyclopaedic works, instead.

Bookstores sometimes place books of essays with "classics and literature," and sometimes in a place of their own.

Biography and autobiography are usually treated similarly, whether by bookstores or by libraries. From here on I shall call them both "biography."

If all biographies are placed together (and they are not always), they are usually sorted by the name of the subject. Some bookstores do this.

The Dewey Decimal system advises placing biography with the subject or discipline the person is associated with. Some libraries using the Library of Congress system do the same thing. In the Library of Congress system biographies of fiction authors are placed with fiction written by the author.

Should biographies be divided according the kinds of men they are about, scientists, preachers, politicians, writers, etc.? Probably not, since so many men are difficult to pigeonhole like that. Is Albert Schweitzer a missionary or a philosopher? Is Benjamin Franklin a scientist, an entrepreneur, a humourist, or a statesman? Yet the Dewey Decimal system asks librarians to pigeonhole men every time they shelve a new biography. Shelving all biography together, sorted by the subject's name, is more sensible and less presumptuous.

Classification of Text Files

.How BBS's do it now

.How general-purpose BBS's ought to do it

.How text-file BBS's ought to do it

.Hypertext books and hypertext software

.Text files in bookstores and libraries

How should bulletin-board services (BBS's) classify and sort the text files which they offer for download by their users?

Many BBS's have a single directory for text files, and sometimes one more for text files relating to the BBS's focus: for example, general text files and role-playing game text files. Some have no text file directory at all, which is a major oversight.

Probably the exact method of classification should depend on the number of text files a BBS offers. If more than about 5 or 10 text files fall into a single classification category, a new file directory should be added for them; assuming that the BBS software allows enough file directories to do this.

I would recommend that general-purpose BBS's use at least three directories for text files: one for computer-related nonfiction, one for other nonfiction, and one for fiction and humour. If a BBS has a particular focus or specialty, of course one or more directories should be added for text files relating to the focus. And if the sysop of a BBS wishes to specialise in textfiles and hypertext, he would do well to have many directories containing different nonfiction subjects and fiction genres. Probably he will want to go deeper in classifying computer-related nonfiction than general bookstores or most libraries do. For example, he may wish to have several sets of directories with technical text files about different operating systems. In general, the problems of a BBS sysop who wishes to specialise in text files (may his tribe increase!) are very like those of a bookstore manager or librarian, with a few added difficulties: as, how to sort by author, when the BBS software is designed to sort by filename or by upload date. Perhaps he can encourage uploaders to include the name of the file's author in the description, so that other users can do a text search for the author's name and find the file.

Hypertext books should probably be placed in the same directories as text files. Hypertext reader software should perhaps go in the same directory with text file utilities, or perhaps (if there are many of them) in a separate directory for hypertext software. Of course, each file requiring a particular hypertext reader should say so in its file description. Since hypertext books are limited to a single operating system, and potential readers who use a different operating system or a different kind of computer than the author cannot read such hypertext books, probably sysops should encourage uploaders to upload books in plain text as well as in hypertext format, out of consideration for users of other operating systems.

Bookstores and libraries should take advantage of the large amounts of reading matter available as textfiles on BBS's and online services, and take an active role in making some of these textfiles available for printout to their customers and patrons. Or they may want to make many text files available on a hard disk and allow their customers to come in with blank disks and copy off text files to take home.

Libraries' Removal from Reality

A curious thing about libraries in our society today is that nearly all of them, whether they are run by governments, non-profit organisations, or even businesses, are not directly accountable to their readers. Government-run libraries can listen to patrons' suggestions if they like, but they are under little incentive to do so, since the tax money will continue coming in regardless of how well they serve their patrons. Non-profit organisations are accountable to those who donate to them, who may not be the same persons as those who patronise their libraries.

And most libraries run by businesses are part of private schools and colleges, and, thus, select books with a view to their customers' educations. Their customers have paid for education, not for reading pleasure, and the librarians use the expert judgement they have been paid for to decide which books are most useful to their customers' education.

It doesn't seem that this is a necessary property of organisations lending rather than selling books. Consider the numerous videotape stores which both rent and sell all sorts of videotapes. It is possible for a store to both rent and sell books, though whether it would be profitable in the presence of so many government-subsidised libraries is unknown and probably varies from one area to another.

Whether such library stores would find it most expedient to sell an annual membership which allows customers to check out so many books for so many weeks, or charge a separate rental fee for every book checked out, or some combination of the two, can only be found out by experiment. Also, they may wish to allow customers to pay all or part of the membership or rental fees by trading in used books. They may wish to offer additional incentives, such as: older books may be checked out longer (perhaps four weeks rather than the traditional two); five or six years' membership fees up front will buy a lifetime subscription; library members may buy books in the store at a discount; and so on.

Another possibility is that of privatising the public libraries: that is, selling this branch of the state or county government to one or more private persons or companies, who will then run the libraries as they see fit. These private persons and companies will have to serve their customers well, or they will lose money. Under this system, those paying for the library's services are the same people who benefit from the services. Such is not the case in most counties of America today. The taxpayers of the county (mostly the land-owners, and to a lesser degree the people who spend money in retail stores in the county) pay for the library; but the bookworms of the county are the main ones who benefit from its services.

Sampling Method Used

Libraries which I have observed mainly: Dekalb, Henry, and Clayton counties; Clayton State College and Emory University; Fernbank Elementary and Stockbridge Jr. High School.

Bookstores which I have observed mainly: The Book End, B. Dalton, Zondervan's, Waldenbooks, Cole's, Oxford and Oxford Too, the Book Nook, Wall's Paperback Exchange (special thanks to Ganelle Wall), Kendall's Books, Read Once, Fischer's, and the Moth's Wing.

BBS's whose text file directories I have observed: Disktop Publishing Association, Faster-than-Light, Pallas Athena, Poorly Sick World (special thanks to Jeffrey Scott).

When I use the words "all," "most," "some," "a few," and so forth with respect to libraries and bookstores, I speak with regard to several years of wandering and browsing in the libraries and bookstores above mentioned, and often thinking of their systems and comparing them. In a few places I have been able to supplement this experience with information from people in other areas of the country about their hometown's library.

The "Amherst Method" : The Origins of the DDC Scheme

In 1996 OCLC published the twenty-first edition of the 120-year-old Dewey Decimal Classification. By that time over 200,000 libraries in 135 countries were using the classification to organize their collections. In the United States alone, it was being used by 95 percent of public and school libraries, 25 percent of special libraries, and 25 percent of aca- demic libraries (mostly at small colleges). From the slim forty-four-page book Melvil Dewey initially published in 1876, the scheme grew to over four thousand pages in its twenty-first edition. It is probably fair to say that at some time in their lives, a substantial majority of Americans living in the twentieth century have used the system. Few would argue the scheme has not been influential, yet our knowledge of its origins remains unsettled.

A debate surrounding the origins of the Decimal Classification has been going on for generations; reasons for a lack of consensus are not hard to find. Dewey himself established some parameters by dropping inconsistent hints during his lifetime and scattering inconclusive bits of information throughout his publications. In a 1920 Library Journal article entitled "Decimal Classification Beginnings," both student and assistant librarian at Amherst College and deeply involved in conceptualizing the best classification system for any library. "After months of study," he wrote, he was listening to a Sunday sermon, and while I look stedfastly at [the pulpit] without hearing a word, my mind absorbd in the vital problem, the solution flasht over me so that I jumpt in my seat and came very near shouting "Eureka!"

It was to get absolute simplicity by using the simplest known symbols, the arabic numerals as decimals, with ordinary significance of nought, to number a classification of all human knowledge in print; this supplemented by the next simplest known symbols, a, b, c, indexing all heds of the tables, so that it would be easier to use a classification with 1000 heds so keyd than to use the ordinary 30 or 40 heds which one had to study carefully before using. Because the quote is so colourful-especially in the simplified form of spelling Dewey used variously throughout his life-scores of cataloguing teachers assigned thousands of library school students to read the article over subsequent decades.

Despite its wide circulation, however, the article fails to clarify the classification's origins. Dewey did acknowledge a debt to Sir Francis Bacon (who nearly three centuries earlier had hypothesized that all knowledge derived from memory, reason, and imagination, and that these three invariably produced works of history, philosophy, and belles lettres), but he failed to locate his scheme in the continuum of library classification history and thus generally ignored the contributions and influences of his predecessors.

Ever since, library historians have been trying to clarify and contex- tualize the classification's origins. In the last half-century they have seized upon one or more of the informational tidbits Dewey left behind, assigned each a relative value, and drawn upon these values to create their unique interpretations of the scheme's beginnings. On one thing they all agree, however. All believe Dewey did not create a decimal classification out of whole cloth, and for the past half-century the historiography addressing its origins has tried to identify debts Dewey owed predecessors and contemporaries in classification history that he at one time or another acknowledged, overlooked, forgot, allegedly even deliberately ignored.

The debate was initiated in 1945 by Kurt F. Leidecker. In the course of researching a biography of William Torrey Harris in the early 1940s, Leidecker discovered what he believed was a debt Dewey owed his protagonist. As a superintendent of the St. Louis Public Schools from 1868 to 1880, Harris was also responsible for the St. Louis Public School Library. There he crafted a classification scheme from Bacon's original structure by inverting and slightly expanding it. He summarized his scheme in an 1870 Journal of Speculative Philosophy article that, Leidecker notes, Dewey read in spring of 1873, while contemplating a new system for Amherst. To prove it, Leidecker quotes a 9 May 1873 letter Dewey wrote to Harris, in which he inquired about Harris's system. Concerning Dewey's debt to Harris, Leidecker is diplomatic, perhaps even reluctant to besmirch the reputation of librarianship's most famous pioneer. "Complete originality was never claimed by Dewey in the establishment of his library classification system," he writes, but Leidecker's irritation with Dewey for only "somewhat ambiguously" acknowledging his debt to Harris is quite evident.

The next contributor to the debate was Eugene E. Graziano, who had read Leidecker's biography of Harris. Because Dewey had adapted so heavily from Harris, and because Harris had studied the philosophy of G. W. F. Hegel, Graziano concluded that Hegel's philosophy, whether Dewey knew it or not, constituted the philosophical foundation on which the Decimal Classification ultimately was based. In a master's thesis done at the University of Oklahoma and in an article he published subsequently in Libri in the 1950s,

Graziano demonstrates convincingly how Harris's classes were influenced by his exposure to and belief in Hegel's philosophy. Like Leidecker, however, Graziano seems reluctant to challenge Dewey's status as professional icon. He is gracious toward Dewey's relative lack of attribution to Harris's contribution to the classification, but amused at Dewey's apparent ignorance of its own underlying philosophical base.

John Maass, however, is neither gracious toward Dewey nor awed by his historic stature. While doing research on the United States's Centennial Exhibition of 1876 in Philadelphia (at which, Maass correctly notes, the American Library Association was founded and the newly published Decimal Classification much discussed), Maass studied William Phipps Blake, a geologist and mining engineer whom the Centennial Commission had engaged in 1872 to organize its exhibition. On 25 May 1872, Maass notes, Blake submitted a scheme to the commission that organized the exhibition into ten "departments," each of which was subdivided into ten "groups," each of which was further divided into ten "classes." Maass notes that Blake's classification was published as a leaflet in February 1873 and likely was sent to Amherst. He also notes that a forty-two-page pamphlet elaborating the scheme was "mailed to professional men throughout the U.S." a month later. Based on this evidence, Maass argues that "Dewey copied that decimal notation from Blake. .. and cunningly covered his tracks." Although Maass cannot cite evidence directly linking Dewey to Blake or his publications, he nonetheless concludes, "It is certain beyond a shadow of a doubt that Melvil Dewey studied this pamphlet by Blake (dated February 27th, 1873) and derived from it the draft of his Decimal Classification (dated May 8th, 1873)."

The most recent and most thoroughly researched entry into the historiographical debate surrounding the origins of the scheme is John Comaromi's book, The Eighteen Editions of the Dewey Decimal Classification (1976), which many scholars regard as the most definitive work so far on the subject. In his first chapter Comaromi evaluates arguments made by Leidecker, Graziano, and Maass, but for additional clues he also analyzes the preface to Dewey's first edition of the DDC, the ideas of other classification experts like Leo LaMontagne, W. C. Berwick Sayers, and Henry Evelyn Bliss, and various classification systems already in use at the time Dewey crafted the decimal scheme-especially a system devised by Jacob Schwartz at the New York Mercantile Library that Leidecker, Graziano, and Maass had not discussed. In addition, Comaromi studied some primary source material in the files of Forest Press (twentieth-century publishers of new editions of the DDC) in Albany and New York, and in those boxes and files in the Dewey Papers at Columbia University that an archivist had labelled

"Decimal Classification." Regarding the latter, Comaromi indicates, "Information pertaining to the early years [of the DDC]. .. is scanty."

Comaromi judges the evidence Maass presents for his thesis "inconclusive," but finds Leidecker and Graziano's arguments highly plausible. He acknowledges Dewey probably drew on strong points from the classification schemes of Harris and Schwartz, the former because he used Arabic numerals for classes (and within classes arranged materials alphabetically by author surname), the latter because he used Arabic numerals for first and all subsequent divisions beyond the major classes to which he assigned numbers. Comaromi also acknowledges that Hegel's philosophy constituted the theoretical basis for Harris's system, and because Harris's system was "the most fruitful source of Dewey's conception," he concludes, Hegel "provided the philosophical underpinnings" of Dewey's system.

But Comaromi introduces two new elements absent from previous discussions. First, he notes that in the preface to the DDC's first edition Dewey acknowledges an unspecified debt to Natale Battezzati, author of Nuovo Sistema di Catalogo Bibliografico Generale, published in Milan in 1871. Comaromi argues, however, that Dewey here refers to Battezzati's recommendation for an early cataloguing-in-publication system for all books, and not to the notion of assigning Arabic numerals in decimals to classify books. Second, Comaromi guesses that "members of the Amherst faculty and experts elsewhere probably provided the substance and order of most of the divisions and sections."

Curiously, however, he does not elaborate, nor does he pursue the possibility in further research. Although Comaromi's work constitutes the most complete analysis of the origins of the Dewey Decimal Classification, it still falls short of definitive for two reasons: (1) failure to widen the scope of his research to include the socio-institutional context in which Dewey developed his scheme; and (2) failure to analyze all relevant primary source materials-in this case bits of evidence scattered throughout more than one hundred boxes of Dewey Papers Comaromi did not peruse. The following is an attempt to contribute further to the historiography on the origins of the scheme-on the one hand by grounding an account of Dewey's thinking as he crafted the Decimal Classification on an analysis of a larger body of primary sources, on the other by expanding and deepening our understanding of the contextual forces influencing his decisions on the classification's structure.

In order to reduce the debt he was accumulating at Amherst, in the fall term of his junior year Dewey agreed to keep account books for the college library. For Dewey the opportunity opened up a whole new world. By this time he had already decided to dedicate his life to educational reforms but had not yet identified which reforms nor located the institutional arena in which he would effect them. After joining the library's staff, however, he quickly recognized what he thought was the library's potential for educating the masses. He immediately volunteered to expand his responsibilities, and then tackled them all with the intensity of a crusader.

First he read systematically the limited amount of literature on libraries available to him, keeping notes on most of his reading and rereading much of it twice. For example, in January 1873 he read Charles C. Jewett's "A Plan for Stereotyping Titles."

Dewey liked Jewett's recommendation for building a common catalogue. "This would secure accuracy & uniformity.. ., save expense after the first few libraries were catalogued," and because some central institution could print from its plates "a full & perfectly accurate catalogue of all books in the libraries of America. .. a Universal Catalogue would be feasible."

In February he visited Boston to study the Boston Public Library, the Boston Athenaeum, and the Harvard College Library. In his diary Dewey recorded that Athenaeum Director Charles Ammi Cutter was at the time "in the throes of catalogue printing." Dewey peppered him with questions, especially concerning classification. "He puts the books on the horse under 'horse' & not under 'zoology.'" Dewey believed most people with only rudimentary reading skills would think the same way.

When Dewey returned to Amherst, he reviewed the library's operation and arrangement more carefully. He also continued to pore over library literature. On 22 February he read William T. Harris's 1870 Journal of Speculative Philosophy article on "Book Classification." After carefully considering Harris's discovery that books arranged alphabetically under each subject forced a relative rather than fixed location, Dewey noted, "of this I am inclined to be a friend."

Then, on 7 March, he read a pamphlet he had "blundered on" in the collection entitled A Decimal System for the Arrangement and Administration of Libraries. It had been privately printed in 1856 and donated to the library by its author, Nathaniel Shurtleff, a Boston Public Library employee. "Of course [I] took it home. My heart is open to anything that's either decimal or about libraries."

Dewey admitted liking Shurtleff's concept of marrying a decimal system to library administration and arrangement, but criticized its details because he thought the author laid "altogether too much stress" on the decimal system at the expense of efficiency and saving time. A second reading on 29 April did not change his mind. He thought some of the ideas "out of date," and noted that at the Boston Public Library "where it originated," the library had quickly "abandoned the unfeasible part of the plans." He later wrote, "My idea is a brief Index for finding a known work & a full scientific for classed catalogue showing the resources in any given subject & having a full alphabetical index with numerical reference to the scheme & catalogue."

Further reading led to further refinement of a developing idea. He disliked the New York State Library's system of organizing its collections-"They arrange the books alphabetically paying no attention to subjects"-but liked the practice of recording the library's holdings on cards (one card per title) that Jacob Schwartz used at the New York Mercantile Library. On 20 February he also wrote Schwartz that he was "favourably impressed" with the classification scheme Schwartz had created for the Mercantile. Five days later Schwartz thanked him for the compliment and encouraged Dewey to adopt his classification scheme for Amherst.

Cutter, Harris, Shurtleff, Jewett, and Schwartz-all had developed firm ideas about classification schemes or cataloguing practices which Dewey thought showed strengths and weaknesses, and in the spring the schemes and practices used by all were swimming around his head as he contemplated the most useful methods of bibliographic organization suitable not only for Amherst but also for all libraries. Such was the context in which he "came very near shouting 'Eureka!'" during that Sunday sermon and concluded to "use decimals to number a classification of all human knowledge in print." His approach was characteristic of much previous personal behaviour and most subsequent professional behaviour. Adopt from existing practice only those features that promised to make a new system easy to use, and centralize that system to avoid duplication of effort. At this point the scheme as he conceived it joined strong points from Cutter, Harris, Shurtleff, and Schwartz. Dewey's contribution to classification was in joining and adjusting them, not in creating anything new. He quickly outlined the first draft of his decimal scheme and submitted it to the Amherst College Library Committee on 8 May 1873.

Conceptually, it was constructed on the premise that all knowledge could be divided into nine main classes (he had originally proposed ten, but abandoned that because use of ten added another digit to one of the numbers and reduced the scheme's simplicity). Each of the main classes could be subdivided into nine more subclasses by adding a decimal to separate the subclass from the main class signifier. Further divisions of subclasses could be added by assigning a second digit to be placed after the first subclass signifier. "Thus the subclasses may be increased in any part of the library without limit; each additional decimal place increasing the minuteness of classification tenfold." Within each of these classes, Dewey then proposed a subarrangement alphabetically by author under that class, but if this included more than one book by that author, books would "stand in the same order on the shelves as the titles of the same in the catalogue." Thus, the call number for any item in the scheme as Dewey originally conceived it would consist of a single-digit class number to the left of a decimal point, followed by one or more digits to the right of the decimal point, under which cataloguers would add author surnames. "Readers will call for books thus located by their 'class number' (instead of 'shelf')," he explained, "and author's name as printed in the catalogue (instead of 'number on shelf.')" Books of a general character on more than one topic-like a dictionary of science-would receive no subclassification but would sit on the shelf with only the main class number. The committee agreed in principle with Dewey's proposal and encouraged him to pursue it for Amherst's collections.

Although Dewey had settled on a basic outline for his scheme, he still sought outside advice, especially for identification of appropriate classes. Harris responded four days later. "Perhaps the main advantages of my scheme are my plan of numbering such classes and the ease with which one masters the details after getting a glimpse of the general plan," he told Dewey. "It gives in the classified index a view of all the literature on a given subject & in the alphabetical index all the advantages of ordinary catalogues."

Harris had built his scheme on two sources: (1) ideas of Sir Francis Bacon, who had argued that the three faculties of the human mind-memory, imagination, and reason-produced three categories of learning-history, poetry, and philosophy-each of which could be further subdivided; and (2) the ideas of G. F. W. Hegel, who inverted Bacon's order to give a more prominent role to philosophy, and from which the rest of the structure follows. From philosophy (the science containing all sciences), Harris saw a natural structure of knowledge progressing to theology (the science of the absolute), government, philology, nature (including mathematics, physics, chemistry, and the natural sciences), the useful and the fine arts, and finally, geography, biography, and history.

That Dewey largely tapped Harris's structure as the broad blueprint for his own decimal scheme (in order-philosophy, theology, sociology, philology, natural science, useful arts, fine arts, literature, and history) is hardly debatable, but in defining and identifying a hierarchy of divisions and sections he created beyond that structure Dewey looked elsewhere for guidance. His own priorities were dictated by a commitment to simplicity. "My ideal," he recorded in his reading notebook on 19 June 1873, "is a brief index for finding a known work & a full scientifically classed catalogue, showing the resources on any given subject & having a full alphabetical index with numerical references to the scheme & catalogue." In April 1874 he noted in his diary: "Conciseness in statement as much as possible consistent with clearness will be the first thing. Careful arranging in the right order for easy understanding & reference, & most important of all their substance." "Here the most rigid economy must rule; our free libraries will all need to exercise their straight economy & any system that does not allow such saving must be defeated for users."

Dewey clearly demanded first and foremost that his decimal scheme be simple and concise; beyond that, however, he looked mostly to the Amherst College community for guidance in identifying and arranging divisions and sections under the broad Bacon-Hegel structure of knowledge that Harris used and he himself found acceptable. Guidance-both direct and indirect-came from two sources: (1) the Amherst College tradition into which Dewey had assimilated and the curriculum through which he passed between 1870 and 1874; and (2) the Amherst faculty (especially Julius H. Seelye and John W. Burgess) and the texts they assigned in their courses. And because Amherst hired him as Associate Librarian after he graduated in June 1874, Dewey had ample opportunity to exploit both while he worked on the Decimal Classification.

First, the Amherst College tradition and curriculum. In 1875 Amherst College was a small, comfortable, almost family-like school nestled in the scenic Connecticut Valley. Founded in 1821, it was strongly tied to orthodox Christianity, and much more interested in discipline than research and intellectual inquiry. One of the jobs of any nineteenth-century institution of higher education was to build character, and at Amherst-like most other New England colleges-the building blocks used to construct character came from a combination of Protestant orthodoxy and Western culture and classics. The curriculum was designed to communicate universal truths already known and unquestioned, not to expose students to contemporary political issues or even to sample contemporary literature. It influenced students toward a particular world view, inculcated a definition of the role of education, and identified the rules to which and the authorities to whom they should look in later life for guidance in making sense of their world. The curriculum also reinforced the concept of "mind as vessel"; education was a process by which the student would passively "fill" the "vessel" with the best that a patriarchal White Western (and, of course, Christian) civilization had to offer.

That Dewey agreed wholeheartedly with the concept is obvious from his subsequent activities; it formed the foundation for all his educational reform schemes. More important for understanding the origins of the Dewey Decimal Classification, however, the Amherst tradition did nothing to contradict the hierarchy Harris defined for his classification. Because the world as viewed through the eyes of an 1874 Amherst graduate fairly well matched the world as viewed by William Torrey Harris in 1870, Dewey had no philosophical or ideological reservations about its suitability for his scheme. He probably regarded it as "common knowledge" or even "natural," and so he simply appropriated it. For Dewey the simplicity and efficiency offered by superimposing the decimal system on any suitable general plan was paramount. Harris's divisions provided what he considered sound educational rationale for a structure of knowledge he would cement into the Decimal Classification. Its moral centre was located in "Anglo-Saxonism," a doctrine that defined "objectivity" and touted the unique virtues, mission, and destiny of the Anglo-Saxon "race."

Student coursework at Amherst was typical for a classical curriculum. Freshmen took Latin and Greek prose composition, geometry, algebra, and trigonometry, and read Cicero, Homer, Livy, and Horace. Sopho-mores continued reading the Latin and Greek classics, began learning French and German, and took some chemistry. Juniors expanded coverage of Greek and Latin classics, and supplemented these with courses in philosophy, botany, chemistry, and astronomy. Seniors were introduced to psychology, geology, biblical history, logic, constitutional law, political science, and history. Amherst offered few electives, and all of those came in the junior or senior year. Like the rest of his classmates, Dewey looked upon the world reflected in this curriculum as objective and absolute. He was there to fill his mind with the best that Western civilization had to offer, not to question basic values. And like the Amherst tradition, the Amherst curriculum did little to challenge Harris's structure of knowledge. Between the tradition and the curriculum, Dewey found little to disturb the hierarchy of Harris's arrangement. Both were elements of a cultural milieu that reflected priorities already inherent in the system.

Amherst faculty who taught the curriculum were a dedicated, albeit conservative and traditional lot. Most were Amherst alumni. Among them Edward Hitchcock taught physical education and hygiene, Elijah Harris' chemistry, Edward P. Crowell, Latin, William S. Tyler and Richard H. Mather, classics, Julius H. Seelye, philosophy, and beginning in 1873 John W. Burgess, history and political science. Most faculty relied upon recitation as a standard method of pedagogy, most honoured the tradition of pointing to a moral as each day's assignment was recited, and most thought the truth of life had already been discovered and was located in the Bible. The strength of their convictions was evident everywhere at Amherst and reinforced the doctrine of Anglo-Saxonism Dewey found so natural.

Hitchcock exemplified the Amherst tradition and curriculum. He had graduated from Amherst in 1849, went on to receive an M.D. from Harvard, then returned to Amherst in 1861 to carve out a reputation as the "father of college physical education in America." In and out of class, Hitchcock emphasized that in order to live an efficient, well-balanced life, one had to give proper attention to the body. Underlying this conviction was his belief in the Pauline dictum that the body was temple to the soul. He constantly stressed the importance of exercise, especially to his students who were required to gather in the gym four mornings a week for calisthenics. Hitchcock's ideas about exercise probably had a major influence on the way Dewey treated hygiene and physical education in his classification scheme, including the location of Medicine (610) under Useful Arts (600), and especially the placement of Hygiene (613) and Public Health (614) after Anatomy (611) and Physiology (612) but before Materia

Medica and Therapeutics (615) and Pathology, Theory and Practice (616). "There is no logical reason" for this order, Comaromi notes, "unless we assume that a normal state of health and how to maintain it should logically precede a pathological or unhealthy state." Without knowing it, Comaromi echoed the message Hitchcock hammered into his students in his classes.

Second, Amherst college texts and faculty. Most of Dewey's professors required their students to use textbooks that outlined a structure of knowledge in particular subject areas. Walker Professor of Mathematics and Philosophy Ebenezer Snell, for example, required a natural philosophy text he had recently revised that was originally written by Denison Olmsted.

In his Introduction to Natural Philosophy Olmsted divides coverage of the subject into nine parts, each of which he subdivides into chapters. In order, the nine parts include mechanics, hydrostatics, pneumatics, sound, magnetism, frictional (or statical) electricity, dynamical electricity, heat, and light. Dewey took the course-and read the textbook-in his junior year. When he identified subdivisions for Physics (530) two years later (Snell himself says in his preface to the 1871 edition of the textbook that the book's subject was really about "physics"), Dewey included Mechanics (531), Hydrostatics (532), Pneumatics (533), Acoustics (534), Optics (535), Heat (536), Electricity (537), Magnetism (538), and Molecular Physics (539). Thus, the only changes Dewey made from the textbook he used for Snell's class were to move the science of light (optics) to follow the science of sound (acoustics-Olmsted had in fact listed these two in that order in his introduction), to add "molecular physics" as a catchall category, and to marry frictional and dynamical electricity into one category titled "electricity" that preceded rather than followed magnetism.

Dewey was more heavily influenced by Julius H. Seelye and John W. Burgess, in part because their pedagogy contrasted sharply with that of their colleagues. Seelye was regarded by most students as Amherst's most stimulating teacher. He had graduated from Amherst in 1849 and for the next three years studied at Auburn Theological Seminary under the tutelage of his uncle, Laurens P. Hickok. After a brief stay at the German University of Halle, in 1858 Seelye returned to Amherst, where as professor of philosophy he began dispensing a steady diet of Hickokian thought to his students that one historian characterizes as "a potpourri of Kantian psychology, Puritan ethics, evangelical religion, Calvinist theology, and Hegelian idealism."

It was Hickok who turned Seelye into a Hegelian. All his life Seelye worshipped the concept of the state and encouraged a patriotic nationalism. For his Psychology, Moral Philosophy, and History of Philosophy courses-all of which Dewey took as a senior-Seelye routinely assigned readings from Hickok's Empirical Psychology and Moral Science (both of which he was editing into new editions for Ginn & Heath).

He then engaged his students in discussions of their readings "to develop the power of their thinking." A former student recalled that Seelye "was eclectic, individualistic, but with a decided bent toward Hegelianism." It is likely that the Hegelianism to which Dewey was exposed in Seelye's classes made Harris's structure of knowledge, heavily influenced as it already was by Harris's Hegelianism, seem "natural" to Dewey. At this time in his life, it will be remembered, Dewey was still "filling his mind" as an undergraduate in what he perceived to be an absolutist world. That he probably saw a clear connection between Seelye's and Harris's ways of looking at the world may have made Harris's general plan the most suitable one available in 1874 upon which to superimpose his decimal scheme. At the very least Seelye would have had little reason to object to the broad outlines Harris wove into his classification. Both were Hegelians, and when Dewey called on Seelye for advice, the latter probably felt comfortable with Harris's broad scheme and paid most attention to filling out the divisions and sections.

On 5 February 1875, for example, Dewey noted in his diary that Seelye "came into the library and helpt me classify books for an hour or more and did a good job for which I was very grateful." On 2 and 7 June Dewey wrote that Seelye had spent part of each day in the library "working on his heads" (*i.e.*, classification subject headings). That Seelye exercised influence over Dewey is obvious from the order in which he ultimately listed and named divisions for Mental Faculties (150) in his decimal scheme-Intellect (151), Sense (152), Understanding (153), Memory (154), Reason (155), Imagination (156), Susceptibility (157), Instincts (158), and Will (159). It is hardly a coincidence that this order bears a striking similarity to the way Hickok arranges his discussion of these subjects in Empirical Psychology. Under a "First Division" Hickok titled "Intellect," for example, he discusses "Sense" in the first chapter, "Understanding" in the second (where "Imagination" receives four pages of attention), "Reason" in the third. His "Second Division" is titled "Susceptibility" (in which he discusses "Instincts"), and his "Third Division" covers "Will."

An even more striking connection between text/faculty and the structure of the DDC's first edition can be found in the way Dewey treated Temperaments (137), which Comaromi notes was based on an already outdated theory that differences among body fluids produced particular human temperaments. In a section entitled "Differences of Temperament" within a larger chapter on "Anthropology," Hickok identifies four basic temperaments-"sanguine," "melancholic," "choleric," and "phlegmatic." Hickok believed the sanguine temperament was most influenced by the nervous system, the choleric temperament by the muscular system, and the melancholic and phlegmatic by the digestive system. Like Seelye, John W. Burgess worked actively with Dewey on listing and naming the Decimal Classification's divisions and sections. Burgess introduced Dewey to academic research and the seminar method of instruction. Known to his students as "Weltgeist," Burgess taught mostly seniors his first year. He had graduated from Amherst in 1867, then studied history and political science in Germany. Burgess, like Seelye, was convinced by Hegel that private property was the logical conclusion of human development, and that the law proceeded from it. Like Seelye he believed with Hegel that history represented an unfolding story of the development of the state that was authored by God and which, in its most absolute form, had been developed by Teutonic peoples. When Burgess brought this German training back to a college steeped in religious orthodoxy, only his ability to lace a strong sense of patriotism through a belief in Calvinism, capitalism, and the American form of democracy made his ideas palatable to his colleagues. America, Burgess believed, was the most perfect realization of humankind's quest for liberty, in large part because a direct correlation existed between Protestant successes and the advance of democracy.

While Dewey was identifying and refining divisions and sections in Sociology (300) and History (900) between 1873 and 1875, Burgess had assumed responsibility for teaching the Amherst College freshmen Greek and Roman history. Unlike his predecessors who taught it "as contributory to the linguistic discipline," however, Burgess looked at Greek and Roman history as a "record of political development." In 1874-5 Burgess was also running a bootleg seminar in modern European political history without compensation or institutional permission. Several members of Dewey's graduating class had purposely stayed at Amherst to take it, including John Bates Clark. Dewey also participated, but in a unique way. He made the literature of the subjects Burgess was teaching "accessible" to Burgess's students "by his new method of subject cataloguing." Burgess later recalled that Dewey "worked with me most successfully in that branch of my instruction during the years I taught at Amherst."

It is not unlikely that Dewey used Burgess's and his students' reactions to the headings of subclasses and subdivisions on which he was working to refine the 300 and 900 classes. It is also possible that his experiences with Burgess's seminar gave Dewey the idea to change "Government" in Harris's scheme to "Sociology" in his own. His decision to use "Sociology" as a major heading under which to list subclasses like Statistics, Political Science, Political Economy, and Law was unusual given the chronology of the discipline's development. Although few American colleges offered sociology courses and none supported sociology as a separate department in 1875, contemporary thinkers often used the terms "sociology" and "social sciences" synonymously. Considering what Dewey stuck in the 300s, it appears he agreed with them, and he probably got the idea from Burgess and/or his seminar students. On 1 and 8 June (one day before and one day after Seelye had been in the library to help him), Dewey noted in his diary that Burgess had just "finisht with work" Dewey had asked him to do on two classes within the decimal scheme.

Thus it was that the Amherst College tradition, curriculum, faculty, and assigned texts provided Dewey with much of the information he needed to structure a hierarchy, and name divisions and sections within the major classes he had appropriated from Harris's scheme. Dewey gives no indication in his diary that he ever questioned or disagreed with advice given him by Seelye, Burgess, or any other Amherst faculty member. He once even complimented Seelye for "giving me quite a lift." He seems to have accepted the world they presented to him as an absolute. Because, like most other students at classical colleges in 1875, he was still at a stage in his life where he was expected to "fill his mind" with the best his instructors had to offer, he regarded them as the experts on the structure of knowledge, and he had confidence that whatever they told him was the best advice he could get; his only response was to fit that advice into the decimal scheme in order to create the simplest, most efficient classification for all American libraries. As a result, the hierarchical arrangement of headings Dewey ultimately devised for the decimal scheme had the effect of framing and cementing a worldview and knowledge structure taught on the tiny Amherst College campus between 1870 and 1875 into what became the world's most widely used library classification.

In mid-1875 Dewey began sending drafts of the Decimal Classification to librarians like Jacob Schwartz; W. T. Harris; Walter Stanley Biscoe of the Taunton, Massachusetts Public Library; Frederic Beecher Perkins of the Boston Public Library; William Isaac Fletcher of the Watkinson Library in Hartford, Connecticut; John Fiske and Ezra Abbott of Harvard; Emeline Hutchins of the Sturgis, Massachusetts Public Library; and Annie Godfrey of the Wellesley College Library. He also sent proofs to Amherst faculty like Edward Hitchcock and Edward P. Crowell, and to graduate student John Bates Clark. By the end of November 1875, he had completed his scheme and was ready to have it printed.

In mid-March 1876 Dewey wrote the Register of Copyrights in Washington, D.C., asking permission to copyright "a little work just passing thru" the press entitled "A classification & subject index with direction for their use." He enclosed one dollar to cover the cost of copyright. By this time Dewey had seen initial page-proofs for the scheme and on 27 March wrote the "explanations for my classification and index" which ultimately went into the introduction.

By this time the scheme had also evolved to its more familiar ten classes with an ill-defined initial section (000) for bibliographies, periodicals, and encyclopedias that preceded Philosophy (100), Theology (200), Sociology (300), Philology (400), Natural Sciences (500), Useful Arts (600), Fine Arts (700), Literature (800), and History (900).

Each class accommodated divisions and sections, subsections and sub-subsections (some classifiers would argue ad infinitum) by utilizing both of the remaining digits, then expanding the capacity of the system even more by adding numbers after a decimal following the third digit. In 1876 it was hard for Dewey to believe library collections would ever outgrow the Decimal Classification's ability to organize them bibliographically.

So what were the origins of the Decimal Classification? Evidence presented in this essay suggests that on 7 March 1873 Melvil Dewey was introduced to the concept of a decimal classification when he read Nathaniel Shurtleff's 1856 pamphlet. Two months later he had decided to superimpose a system of decimals on a classification scheme William Torrey Harris had refined for the St. Louis Public School Library, that was based upon a structure of knowledge articulated by Sir Francis Bacon but inverted by German philosopher G. W. F. Hegel. That was about as much as Dewey appropriated from classification history. The rest he appropriated from Amherst and the Anglo-Saxon world in which it operated. Dewey chose decimals because he was convinced the metric system offered simplicity, efficiency, and an unlimited potential for expansion; he chose Harris's hierarchy because it fit the Anglo-Saxon world into which he was born, a world further refined by the Amherst tradition, curriculum, and faculty. Between May 1873 and November 1875 Dewey filled out the divisions and sections of Harris's hierarchy by appropriating from Amherst textbooks and faculty. The Hegelianism evident in Hickok's works and Seelye's and Burgess's teaching probably reinforced and expanded the Hegelianism already inherent in Harris's hierarchy, and all fit very neatly into the doctrine of Anglo-Saxonism then forming in late-nineteenth-century America.

For the most part, historians of library classification have looked for the origins of the Dewey Decimal Classification only in classification systems that preceded it. What they have not realized was that beyond Harris's basic structure, most of the scheme emerged from a worldview defined on the Amherst College campus between 1870 and 1875. And because Dewey regarded this as a "natural" world-an integral part of the discourse of his culture-he felt no more need to cite his sources than contemporary scholars feel the need to verify "general knowledge."

At the last session of the conference at which the American Library Association was organized in Philadelphia in October 1876, Lloyd P. Smith, librarian of the Library Company of Philadelphia, asked Dewey to elaborate on the system of cataloguing and classification he had recently "devised" at Amherst. Smith described it as "the most valuable idea" he would "carry away from this conference." Dewey acknowledged the compliment Smith paid to his "Amherst method," but referred conference attendees instead to his article in a just-published government report on public libraries in the

United States. By referring to the Decimal Classification as the "Amherst method," however, he characterized it more than he knew.

Melvil Dewey certainly did not invent his decimal scheme out of whole cloth, but he did craft its pattern by selecting the threads from which its essential fabric was woven. For the most part these threads came from two locations-the St. Louis Public School Library classification system and Amherst College. Dewey's genius was in weaving them into a simple system most libraries could easily adopt. His good fortune was that he presented it at the beginning of a public library movement in the United States that significantly benefited from a common classification scheme, and since in the twentieth century the American public library became a model other countries emulated, worldwide adoption of Dewey's scheme followed easily. His legacy, however, is mixed.

On the one hand the scheme has over the decades saved millions of dollars and countless hours of time. Because it has become so widely accepted throughout the world it has permitted one person to classify one title for the hundreds of thousands of libraries using the decimal system. In addition, the system itself has become familiar to millions of people who can feel relatively confident that their knowledge of the system used in one library will serve them well in another. On the other hand the doctrine of Anglo-Saxonism Dewey wove so tightly into his system has over the years resisted the introduction of new threads with more culturally pluralistic origins.

Because it is probably fair to say that at sometime in their lives a substantial majority of Americans living in the twentieth century have used the DDC, it is probably also fair to say that for the past century the scheme itself has quietly-almost invisibly-occupied an influential position as one of the forces sustaining the discursive formations of a Eurocentric patriarchy. The extent to which the DDC has as a result disadvantaged other discourses has yet to be analyzed. It is hoped that some scholar with a deep understanding of twentieth-century American intellectual, social, and cultural history will write this much-needed book sometime in the near future.

Comparison of Dewey and Library of Congress Subject Classification

This is a comparison chart showing how the Dewey Decimal system and the Library of Congress organize materials by subject for the purpose of assigning call numbers. These two systems account for over 95% of the call number classification in libraries in the United States, and are widely used in many other countries.

The chart includes all ninety-nine second level (two-digit) DDC classes (040 is not assigned), and should include all second level (two-digit) LCC classes. Where a class in one system maps to several classes in other system, it will be listed multiple times (*e.g.* DDC class 551).

Additional information on these classification plans are available at:

Dewey Decimal Classification —high level categories, with recursive links to lower level categories

Library of Congress Classification —high level categories

Chart

DDC	LCC	Description
000	A	Generalities
010	Z1001-8999	Bibliography
020	Z665-718.8	Library & information sciences
030	AE	General encyclopedic works
050	AI	General serials & their indexes
060	AM111-160	General organization & museology
070	AN	News media
070	PN4699-5650	Journalism
070	Z278-549	Publishing

080	AC	General collections
090	Z105-115.5	Manuscripts
090	Z1019-1033	Rare books
100	B	Psychology & Philosophy
111	BD300-450	Ontology
115	BD493-701	Time
120	BD143-237	Epistemology
120	BD?	causation
120	BD?	humankind
124	BD493-701	Teleology
130	BF1404-2055	Paranormal phenomena / Occult sciences
150	BF	Psychology
152	HM1041-1101	Perception
152	QH?	movement
152	BF511-593	Emotions
155	BF712-724	Developmental psychology
160	BC	Logic
170	BJ	Ethics (moral philosophy)
180	B108-708	Classic philosophy
181	B850-5739	Oriental philosophy
182	B108-708	Ancient philosophy
183	B108-708	Sophists & Socratic philosophies
185	B108-708	Aristotelian philosophy
186	B108-708	Skeptic & Neoplatonic philosophies
187	B108-708	Epicurean philosophy
188	B108-708	Stoic philosophy
189	B720-765	Medieval western philosophy
190	B790-5802	Modern western philosophy
200	BL	Religion
210	BL175-265	Natural theology
212	BL205-216	Nature of God
220	BS	Bible
221	BS701-1830	Old Testament
225	BS1901-2970	New Testament
226	BS2547-2970?	Gospels & Acts of the Apostles

227	BS2640-2765.6	Epistles
228	BS2547-2970?	Revelation
229	BS2547-2970?	Apocrypha
230	BR	Christian theology
232	BT198-590	Jesus & his family
236	BT819-891	Eschatology
250	BR?	Christian orders & local church
260	BR?	Christian social theology
270	BR140-1510	Christian church history
280	BR?	List of Christian denominations
282	BR?	Roman Catholic Church
283	BR?	Anglican churches (English and Protestant Episcopal)
284	BR?	Protestants of Continental origin
286	BR?	Baptist, Disciples of Christ, Adventist
287	BR?	Methodist & related churches
290	BL660-2680	Non-Christian religion
292	BL700-820	Greek mythology and Roman mythology
295	BL1500-1590	Zoroastrianism
296	BM	Judaism
297	BP	Islam, Bábísm, Bahá'í Faith
300	H	Social sciences
301	HM	Sociology
301	GN	Anthropology
310	HA154-473	General statistics (of parts of the world)
320	J	Political science
330	HB	Economics
331	HD4801-8943	Labour economics
332	HG	Financial economics
333	HD101-1399	Economics of land
333	HD9502	Economics of energy
336	HJ	Public finance
339	HB?	Macroeconomics
340	K	Law
341	KZ	International law
345	K5000-5582	Criminal law

346	KB479	Private law
347	K2201-2385	Civil procedure
347	K2100-2385	Courts
350	JF	Public administration
352	JS	City government
353	JK1-9593	U.S. federal government
353	JK2403-9593	U.S. state governments
355	U	Military Science
360	H	Social services; association
361	HN	General social problems & services
362	HN	Social welfare problems & services
363	HN	Other social problems & services
364	HV6001-7220	Criminology
365	HV8301-9920	Penal & related institutions
366	HS	Association
367	HS	General clubs
368	K1960-1973	(Social) Insurance
370	L	Education
371	LB3011-3095	School management
371	LC3950-4806.5	Special education
372	LB1501-1602	Elementary education
373	LB1603-1699	Secondary education
374	LC5201-6661	Adult education
376	LC1401-2572	Education of women
377	LC321-951	Schools & religion
378	LB2300-2430	Higher education
380	HF	Commerce, communications, transport
382	HF1	International commerce (Foreign trade)
383	HE6000-7500	Postal communications
384	HE	Communications
384	HE7601-8700.9	Telecommunication
385	HE1001-5600	Railways
386	HE380-560	Inland waterway
386	HE5751-5870	Ferry transportation
387	HE380-971	Water transportation

387	HE9761-9900	Air transportation
387	TL787-4050	Space transportation
388	HE	Transport
390	GT	Customs
390	BJ1801-2195	Etiquette
390	GR	Folklore
391	GT500-2370	Costume and Personal Appearance
392	GT2400-3390.5	Customs of life cycle & domestic life
393	GT2400-3390.5	Customs of Death
395	BJ1801-2195	Etiquette
398	GR	Folklore
400	P	Language
410	P101-410	Linguistics
411	P327-327.5	Writing systems
412	P321-324.5	Etymology
414	P?	Phonology phonetics
415	P201-299	Grammar
419	PM8001-8995	Sign language
420	PE	English language
430	PD	Germanic languages
440	PC2001-3761	French language
449	PC3201-3366	Provençal
449	PC3801-3976	Catalan
450	PC1001-1977	Italian language
459	PC601-872	Romanian language
459	C901-986	Rhaeto-Romanic language
460	PC4001-4977	Spanish language
469	PC5001-5498	Portuguese language
470	PA2001-2915	Latin language
480	PA201-899	Greek language
490	P501-769	Indo-European Languages
492	PJ991-995	Afro-Asiatic languages
494	PL1-481	Altaic languages
495	PL3521-4001	Sino-Tibetan languages
496	PL8000-8844	African languages

497	PM101-2711	North American languages (Native American languages)
498	PM3001-4566	Central American Languages (Native American languages)
498	PM5001-7356	South American Languages (Native American languages)
500	Q	Natural sciences & mathematics
510	QA	Mathematics
512	QA150-272	Algebra
513	QA101-145	Arithmetic
514	QA612-699	Topology
515	QA299-433	Analysis / Calculus
516	QA440-611	Geometry (excluding Topology)
519	QA273-299	Probability, Statistics, Numerical analysis
520	QB	Astronomy
521	QB349-421	Celestial mechanics
530	QC	Physics
531	QC120-168.85	Classical mechanics; Solid mechanics
532	QC120-168.85	Fluid mechanics; Liquid mechanics
533	QC120-168.85	Gas mechanics
534	QC221-246	Sound & related vibrations
535	QC350-467	Light & paraphotic phenomena
536	QC251-338.5	Heat
537	QC501-721	Electricity & electronics
538	QC750-766	Magnetism
539	QC770-798	Modern physics
540	QD	Chemistry & allied sciences
541	QD450-801	Physical & theoretical chemistry
542	QD1-65	Techniques, equipment, materials
543	QD71-142	Analytical chemistry
544	QD71-142	Qualitative analysis
545	QD71-142	Quantitative analysis
546	QD146-197	Inorganic chemistry
547	QD241-441	Organic chemistry
548	QD0001-0999	Crystallography
549	QE351-399.2	Mineralogy
550	QE	Earth sciences

551	QE	Geology
551	GB651-2998	Hydrology
551	QC851-999	Meteorology
552	QE420-499	Petrology
553	QE?	Economic geology
560	QE701-760	Paleontology
560	QE7601-899	Paleozoology
570	QH301-705.5	Life sciences -Biology
572	QD415-436	Biochemistry
572	GN	Anthropology
573	GN49-298	Physical anthropology
574	QH301-705.5	Biology
575	QH359-425	Evolution
575	QH426-470	Genetics
576	QH573-671	Microbiology
577	QH540-549.5	Ecology
578	QH201-278.5	Microscopy in biology
579	QH1-199.5	Collection and preservation
580	QK	Botanical sciences
581	QK	Botany
582	QK474.8-495	Spermatophyta (Seed-bearing plants)
585	K494-494.5	Gymnospermae (Pinophyta)
586	QK504-638	Cryptogamia (Seedless plants)
590	QL	Animals
591	QL1-355	Zoology
592	QL360-599.82	Invertebrates
593	QL360-599.82	Protozoa, Echinodermata, related phyla
594	QL360-599.82	Mollusca & Molluscoidea
595	QL360-599.82	Other invertebrates
596	QL605-739.8	Vertebrata (Craniata, Vertebrates)
597	QL614-639.8	Fishes
597	QL640-669.3	Reptiles and amphibians
598	QL671-699	Aves (Birds)
599	QL700-739.8	Mammalia (Mammals)
600	T	Technology (Applied sciences)

607	T61-173	Education
607	T175-178	research
608	T201-342	Invention & patents
608	Q	Invention & patents
610	R	Medicine
611	QM	Human anatomy
611	QH573-671	Cytology
611	QM550-577.8	Histology
612	QP	Human physiology
615	RM	Pharmacology & Therapeutics
617	RD	Surgery & Related Topics
618	RG	Gynecology
618	R	Other medical specialties
619	R735-854	Experimental medicine
620	TA	Engineering & allied operations
621	TJ	Mechanical engineering
621	QC	Applied physics
622	TN	Mining & related operations
623	UG1-620	Military engineering
623	VM	Nautical engineering
624	TA	Civil engineering
625	TF	Engineering of railways
625	TE	Engineering of highways
627	TC1-978	Hydraulic engineering
628	TD	Sanitary & engineering
628	TD159-168	Municipal engineering
629	T	Other branches of engineering
630	S	Agriculture
631	S1-972	Techniques, equipment, materials
632	SB599-990.5	Plant injuries, diseases, pests
633	SB317.5-319.864	Horticulture
634	SB354-402	Fruits
634	SD	Forestry
634	SB169-172.5	Orchards
636	SF	Animal husbandry

637	SF250.5-275	Processing dairy & related products
638	SF518-561	Insect culture
639	SK	Hunting, fishing,
639	S604.5-604.64	conservation
640	TX	Home economics
650	HD28-70	Management & auxiliary services
653	Z53-102	Shorthand
657	HF5601-5689	Accounting
658	HD28-70	General management
659	HF5801-6182	Advertising
660	TP155-156	Chemical engineering
670	HD9720-9975	Manufacturing
680	TT	Handicrafts
690	TH	Buildings
700	N	Arts
708	N400-3990	Museums
710	SB469-476	landscape art
720	NA	Architecture
730	NB	Plastic arts, Sculpture
736	NB0001-1952	Carving & carvings
738	NB0001-1952	Ceramic arts
739	NB0001-1952	Metalwork
740	NC	Drawing
740	NK	Decorative arts
746	NK8800-9505.5	Textile arts
748	NK5100-5440	Glass
749	NK2200-2750	Furniture & accessories
750	ND	Painting
760	NE	Graphic arts, Printmaking & prints
761	NE1330-1352	Relief processes (Block printing)
763	NE2250-2570	Lithography
764	NE2236-2240.6	Chromolithography & serigraphy
765	NE1400-1879	Metal engraving
767	NE1940-2232.5	Etching & drypoint
770	TR	Photography & photographs

780	M	Music
781	MT	General principles & musical forms
782	M1495-5000	Vocal music
783	M1528-1529.5	Music for solo voice
784	M1000-1075	Orchestras, ensembles
785	M1000-1075	Ensembles with one instrument per part
786	MT180-255	Keyboard instrument
787	MT259-338	strings
788	MT339-533	Wind
790	PN1560-1590	Performing arts
790	GV	Recreation
792	PN2000-3307	Theater and other stage presentations
793	GV1221-1469.63	Indoor games & amusements
795	GV1301-1311	Games of chance
796	GV557-1198.995	Sport
797	GV750-770.27	Air sports
797	GV770.3-840	Aquatic sports
799	SK	Fishing, Hunting, Shooting
800	P	Literature & rhetoric
810	PS	American literature
820	PR	English literature
830	PT1-4897	German literature
840	PQ0001-3999	French literature
850	PQ4001-5999	Italian literature
860	PQ6001-8929	Spanish literature
869	PQ9000-9999	Portuguese literature
870	PA6001-8595	Latin literature
880	PA3050-5660	Greek literature
890	PN	World literature
900	G	Geography
900	D	History
910	G	Geography
911	G141	Historical geography
912	GA	Graphic representations of earth
914	G1791-2196	Geography of Europe

915	G2200-2444	Geography of Asia
916	G2445-2739	Geography of Africa
917	G1105-1692	Geography of North America
918	G1700-1779	Geography of South America
919	G2740-2799	Geography of Oceana
920	CT	Biography
920	CS	Genealogy
920	CR4480-4485	Insignia
930	D51-90	History of ancient world
938	DE	History of the Greco-Roman World
938	DE	History of the Greco-Roman World
940	DAW1031-1051	History of Europe
942	DA	History of Britain
943	DD	History of Germany
944	DC	History of France
945	DG	History of Italy
946	DP	History of the Iberian Peninsula
947	DJK	History of Eastern Europe
947	DK	History of Russia, Soviot Union, and former Soviot republics.
948	DL	History of Northern Europe; Scandinavia
949.?	DAW	History of Central Europe
949.?	DB	History of Austria -Liechtenstein -Hungary Czechoslovakia
949.?	DF	History of Greece
949.?	DH	History of Low Countries -Benelux Countries
949.?	DJ	History of the Netherlands
949.?	DJK	History of Eastern Europe (General)
949.?	DQ	History of Switzerland
949.?	DR	History of the Balkan Peninsula
950	DS	General history of Asia and Far East
951	DS701-799.9	History of China
952	DS801-897	History of Japan
953	DS201-248	History of Arabian Peninsula (History of Saudi Arabia, etc.)

954	DS401-486.8	History of India
955	DS251-326	History of Iran (Persia)
960	DT	History of Africa
961	DT211-239	History of Libya
961	DT241-269	History of Tunisia
962	DT154.1-159.9	History of Sudan
962	DT43-154	History of Egypt
963	DT371-390	History of Ethiopia (Abyssinia)
963	DT391-398	History of Eritrea
965	DT271-299	History of Algeria
966	DT470-671	History of West Africa & offshore islands
967	DT?	History of Central Africa & offshore islands
968	DT1701-2405	History of South Africa
969	DS349.8-349.9	History of South Indian Ocean islands
970	F	History of North America
971	F1001-1145.2	History of Canada
972	F1421-1440	History of Central America
972	F1201-1392	History of Mexico
973	E	History of United States
980	F2201-3799	History of South America
981	F2501-2659	History of Brazil
982	F2801-3021	History of Argentina
983	F3051-3285	History of Chile
984	F3301-3359	History of Bolivia
985	F3401-3619	History of Peru
987	F2301-2349	History of Venezuela
988	F2351-2471	History of Guinea
990	DU	History of Oceania
993	DU400-430	History of New Zealand
994	DU80-398	History of Australia
995	DU490	History of Melanesia
955	DU739-747	History of New Guinea
803	AG	Dictionaries and other general reference works

069	AM	Museums. Collectors and collecting
	AP	Periodicals
	AS	Academies and learned societies
	AY	Yearbooks. Almanacs. Directories
	AZ	History of scholarship and learning. The humanities
	BD	Speculative philosophy
	BH	Aesthetics
	BL	Mythology
	BL	Rationalism
	BT	Doctrinal Theology
	BV	Practical Theology
	BX	Christian Denominations
	C	Auxiliary Sciences of History (General)
	CB	History of Civilization
	CC	Archaeology
	CD	Diplomatics. Archives. Seals
	CE	Technical Chronology. Calendar
	CJ	Numismatics
	CN	Inscriptions. Epigraphy
	CR	Heraldry
	DX	History of the Gypsies
	GB	Physical geography
	GC	Oceanography
	GE	Environmental Sciences
	GF	Human ecology. Anthropogeography
	HA	Social science statistics
	HC	Economic history and conditions
	HD	Industries. Land use. Labour
	HQ	The family. Marriage. Women
	HT	Communities. Classes. Races
	HV	Social pathology. Social and public welfare. Criminology
	HX	Socialism. Communism. Anarchism
	J	General legislative and executive papers
	JA	Political science (General)
	JC	Political theory

JJ	Political institutions and public administration (North America)
JK	Political institutions and public administration (United States)
JL	Political institutions and public administration (Canada, Latin America, etc.)
JN	Political institutions and public administration (Europe)
JQ	Political institutions and public administration (Asia, Africa, Australia, Pacific Area, etc.)
JV	Colonies and colonization. Emigration and immigration. International migration
JZ	International relations
KB	Religious law in general. Comparative religious law. Jurisprudence
KD	Law of the United Kingdom, Ireland, America. North America
KE	Law of Canada
KF	Law of United States
KG	Law of Latin America -Mexico and Central America -West Indies. Caribbean area
KH	Law of South America
KJ-KK	Law of Europe
KL-KW	Law of Asia and Eurasia, Africa, Pacific Area, and Antarctica
LA	History of education
LB	Theory and practice of education
LC	Special aspects of education
LD	Individual educational institutions -United States
LE	Individual educational institutions -America (except United States)
LF	Individual educational institutions -Europe
LG	Individual educational institutions -Asia, Africa, Indian Ocean islands, Australia, New Zealand, Pacific islands
LH	College and school magazines and papers
LJ	Student fraternities and societies, United States
LT	Textbooks

Library of Congress Classification (LCC)

The Library of Congress Classification (LCC) is a system of library classification developed by the Library of Congress. It is used by most research and academic libraries in the U.S. and several other countries -most public libraries and small academic libraries continue to use the Dewey Decimal Classification (DDC). It is not to be confused with the Library of Congress Subject Headings or Library of Congress Control Number.

The classification was originally developed by Herbert Putnam with the advice of Charles Ammi Cutter in 1897 before he assumed the librarianship of Congress. It was influenced by Cutter Expansive Classification, DDC, and was designed for the use by the Library of Congress. The new system replaced a fixed location system developed by Thomas Jefferson. By the time of Putnam's departure from his post in 1939 all the classes except K (Law) and parts of B (Philosophy and Religion) were well developed. It has been criticized as lacking a sound theoretical basis; many of the classification decisions were driven by the particular practical needs of that library, rather than considerations of epistemological elegance.

Although it divides subjects into broad categories, it is essentially enumerative in nature. It provides a guide to the books actually in the library, not a classification of the world.

The National Library of Medicine classification system (NLM) uses unused letters W and QS-QZ. Some libraries use NLM in conjunction with LCC, eschewing LCC's R (Medicine).

The System

Letter	Subject Area
A	General Works
B	Philosophy, Psychology, and Religion
C	Auxiliary Sciences of History
D	General and Old World History
E	History of America
F	History of the United States and British, Dutch, French, and Latin America
G	Geography, Anthropology, and Recreation
H	Social Sciences
J	Political Science
K	Law

L	Education
M	Music
N	Fine Arts
P	Language and Literature
Q	Science
R	Medicine
S	Agriculture
T	Technology
U	Military Science
V	Naval Science
Z	Bibliography, Library Science, and General Information Resources

Melvil Dewey and the Development of the Dewey Decimal System

Melvil Dewey, born in 1851 in upstate New York, was an interesting guy. He was named Melville Louis Kossuth Dewey after the Hungarian reformer Lajos Kossuth, a popular lecturer in exile after the failed revolutions of 1848. Uprisings occurred throughout Europe that year (including the famous one in France that was the subject of Victor Hugo's Les Miserables), aimed at overthrowing the monarchies. Americans were enamored of these revolutions, being "predisposed to judge hereditary rulers harshly," as library historian Matthew Battles puts it, so it was not surprising to find parents naming their children after revolutionary heroes.

From childhood, Dewey was fascinated with books. In 1868, when his school caught fire, he rescued as many books as he could from the school library; but inhaled a great deal of smoke in the process and consequently had a cough that lasted for months. Told by his doctor that he would be dead within a year or so, he tried to make the most of what he thought would be limited time, according to the recent and fascinating biography by Wayne Wiegand. Efficiency became his obsession. He urged simplified spelling, shorthand, the metric system, and similar reforms. He later dropped his foreign-inspired middle name and shortened his first name to Melvil to dispense with extraneous letters. (He considered simplifying his last name to Dui but gave up on that.)

At Amherst College Dewey worked his junior year (1872-73) in the Amherst College library, where he was frustrated by the disarray of the book collection. As noted in the Staff Report on public libraries, it was an era when libraries were spreading rapidly, and their collections of books were growing. There was no uniform or consistent system for organizing books, sometimes not even within a single library. Each library simply assigned a spot on a shelf for each book, and recorded in its catalogue where the book was.

Some libraries adopted the British Museum's method of numbering the shelves, in which a book would be filed on shelf 132A (or whatever). This "fixed location" approach was useful up to a point—if you were looking for a book, you could look up its shelf location in the catalogue. However, deciding what books went on which shelves was pretty arbitrary. In some libraries, shelves were arranged to "look nice" -books of the same size would be put on the shelf together, regardless of subject matter. Seriously.

One big problem with the "fixed location" approach was that it was difficult to integrate new acquisitions. Adding new books to a shelf meant other books would need to be rearranged, perhaps pushed off to different shelves, and that meant changing all the relevant catalogue records.

The New York State Library organized its books alphabetically by title, without regard for subject. Imagine the problem every time a book was acquired! Jacob Schwartz of the New York Mercantile Library got around that problem with a card system. Rather than cataloguing in a ledger, he assigned one card per title, with the shelf location in the upper left-hand corner. However, Dewey wrote that Schwartz thought location was "not essential to the system" and could be "omitted or used, at the discretion of the librarian."

Many librarians thought it would be useful to organize books by subject matter. The problem was, what does "subject matter" mean? Francis Bacon, in the 1600s, said there were three branches of knowledge: history (deriving from memory), poetry (from imagination), and philosophy (from reason.).. That formed the basic classification system of the few libraries that bothered with such things. The Vatican library, for example, used only two classifications: sacred and profane.

In 1873 Dewey discussed the matter with Charles A. Cutter, director of the Boston Athenaeum. Cutter had developed a classification scheme that Dewey liked; Dewey wrote in his diary that "book on the hourse [were put] under 'horse' & not under 'zoology.'" [All quotes from Dewey's diary are taken from Wiegand's biography, listed below under Resources.]

A few weeks later, Dewey "blundered on" a pamphlet printed in 1856 by Nathaniel Shurtleff that suggested a decimal arrangement for libraries. Dewey wrote, "My heart is open to anything that's either decimal or about libraries." But he disliked Shurtleff's approach, which he felt was inefficient.

Another influence was William F. Poole of the Cincinnati Library, who dared to suggest that fiction was important and needed to be arranged for use.

Dewey found all these systems had strengths and weaknesses. Many years later he wrote, "one Sunday during a long sermon ... while I lookt stedfastly at [the pulpit] without hearing a word, my mind absorbd in the vital problem, the solution flasht over me so that I jumpt in my seat and came very near shouting 'Eureka!'" (Note the simplified spelling.)

Dewey's innovation was to combine a numbering system (like at the British Museum) with classification by topic. However, the numbers didn't indicate a shelf but rather a field of knowledge. Battles says, "Thus he joined the analytical simplicity of decimal numbers to an intuitive scheme of knowledge, one that would fluidly accommodate all the books ever written, and all the books that could be written as well." Thus was born the Dewey Decimal Classification system.

Wiegland comments that Dewey's contribution to classification was joining together the strong points of systems developed by others, not creating anything new. So, to answer your question, Dewey's genius wasn't the creation of something new, but the consolidation of diverse ideas.

By the way, Dewey was interested not just in standardizing book classification, but everything else, down to the size and margins of the catalogue cards. He wrote about what we would now call economies of scale applied to "cataloguing, indexing, and the score of things which [can] be done once for all the libraries." The money saved by standardized administration could be used for more acquisitions.

The main innovation and advantage of DDC is that it's an indirect, rather than a direct, reference to a book's location. When you look up a book in the catalogue, you're not told which shelf to go to; instead you're told a location relative to other books, and you need some second reference (such as a chart of where numbers are stored, or numbers marked on the sides of shelves) to find the book itself. This separation avoids the problems of the "fixed location": if the library adds books, so that some books are shifted to different shelves, only the chart of location needs to be changed, not the whole card catalogue.

One of the beauties of Dewey's system is that it provides an easy way to introduce new subjects—there have been lots of new subjects since 1876!. The key was the use of decimals. Dewey began by establishing a broad division of knowledge into basic categories, to which numbers were then assigned—crudely put, these are the numbers to the left of the decimal point. That done, it was easy to add new subjects by dividing the original categories into progressively finer gradations—these are the numbers to the right of the decimal point. DDC is what today we'd call scalable—it has readily accommodated the explosion of knowledge since Dewey's day. By the way, it's not just the development of science but also globalization that has brought enormous additional information. And it was easy for both librarians and readers to learn how to use the system.

Dewey largely created library science and is rightly known as the "Father of Modern Librarianship." Without DDC, each library would have to create its own system at vast expense. Now it's a simple matter. That's the reason Dewey is so beloved by librarians.

We feel obliged to note that Dewey was no saint. He was racist, antisemitic, anti-black, anti-everything not white male Anglo-Saxon Christian. He died in 1931.

How Dewey Decimal Classification (DDC) Works

Dewey divided knowledge into nine classes plus one "Miscellaneous," each assigned a numerical range:

000 General Works (Miscellaneous)

100 Philosophy

200 Religion

300 Social Sciences

400 Languages

500 Pure Sciences

600 Technology (Practical Arts) including medicine, engineering, business accounting, agriculture, salesmanship, etc. 700 Fine Arts (including architecture, painting, photography, music, amusements, etc.)

800 Literature

900 History, Geography, Biography

Each item that comes under one of these disciplines is assigned a number in that range, called a class number. The logic is hierarchical: that is, within a main class, there are various subdivisions (called subclasses), and these are subdivided further, getting more specific. For example, within 700 (the arts) we have 790 ("Recreational and Performing Arts"), and within that is 795 for games of chance. After the three leading numbers, decimals can be used for as much further subdivision as needed, so 795.4 is card games, 795.41 is card games "based chiefly on skill," 795.415 is contract bridge, and 795.4152 is the bidding process (auction) in contract bridge.

A hallmark of DDC is the use of consistent subclassifications and mnemonics regardless of category. For example, 73 usually refers to the U.S., on both sides of the decimal point; thus, U.S. cooking is 631.5973 and U.S. history is 973. In contrast, LCC subclassifications have no consistency from one class to the next.

A derivative of the DDC is the Universal Decimal Classification (UDC), an international adaptation of the Dewey system used extensively in Europe. It's more detailed, but the principles are pretty much the same. There is an abridged version for small local libraries, and a more detailed/complex version if the library grows, or for larger libraries.

Library of Congress Classification (LCC)

You didn't ask, but the Straight Dope Science Advisory Board got into a discussion about DDC vs. Library of Congress Classification, so we might as well go whole hog. The Library of Congress was established in 1800 to provide members of Congress with information needed in making legislative decisions. By law, all books registered for copyright in the U.S. must submit a copy to the Library of Congress, which accordingly has become the de facto "national library" and the largest in the country.

The LC originally used a "fixed location" system started by Thomas Jefferson, with 44 subdivisions. However, at roughly the same time as the explosion in libraries (1890s) that led to the Dewey Decimal System, the Librarian of the Library of Congress and his Chief Cataloguer started a new classification system. Basic features were taken from Charles A. Cutter's "Expansive Classification"—you'll recall that Cutter influenced Dewey.

The Library of Congress Classification (LCC) system is based on 21 major classes (as compared to DDC's ten). Each class is arbitrarily assigned one of the letters A through Z, with five exceptions (I, O, W, X, and Y are assigned at second or third level subclasses). Within each major class, the subclasses were independently developed by specialists in each field, so the system was decentralized, with different topics having different arrangements of subclasses.

Beginning in 1902, with Class D, two-letter combinations were used for subclasses. The basics of the system were developed between 1899 and 1940. Here are the broad categories:

A = General Works

B = Philsophy and Religion

C = Auxiliary Sciences of History

D = Universal History

E and F = American History

G = Geography, Anthropology, Recreation

H = Social Science

I = Political Science

K = Law

L = Education

M = Music

N = Fine Arts

P = Language and Literature

Q = Science

R = Medicine

S = Agriculture

T = Technology

U = Military Science

V = Naval Science

Z = Bibliography, Library Science

The first subdivisions within a class are indicated by two-letter combinations—for example, under class G, we have GV for "Recreation and Leisure." Then, decimals are used to refine the discipline, so GV1199 -1570 is devoted to "Indoor Games and Amusements," within which the range GV1232 -1299 is set aside for card games. In that range, GV1282 is for Contract Bridge, and then GV1282.4 for bidding. LCC classifications and their descriptions fill 40 volumes with over 200,000 headings, so I'm not about to give much more detail here.

Is GV1282.4 easier than Dewey's 795.4152? Well, for the example of contract bridge, there's probably no particular advantage one way or t'other.

The organization of the LC was primarily focused on the needs of Congress, and secondarily towards other government departments, agencies, scholars, etc. So more space is allowed for history (classes C to L) than for science/technology (Q to V). More important, the focus on the needs of Congress means the LCC pays less attention to non-Western literature, and has no classifications for fiction or poetry.

A peculiarity of the LCC is that subdivisions are often by country, rather than by subject, especially in the social sciences. This makes sense in light of the library's role as a research tool for Congress. In contrast, under the Dewey Decimal System, the subject is usually subdivided fully by topic before geographical divisions are added.

LCC is more technically oriented than DDC. For example, photography is under TR (a subclass under technology) in the LCC, rather than in the fine arts as with DDC. Although library patrons probably don't notice, critics say the technical focus often makes LCC cataloguing difficult for non-experts in a field. For instance, LCC lists "amicide" for the category of "friendly fire casualties" and "dysmenorrhea" for "menstrual cramps." Battles says that the LC classifications often "strike a tone of bureaucratic high-handedness." The Library of Congress places much emphasis on cross-referencing. Battles comments that "those nesting, cross-referenced rubrics make up an epistemological labyrinth unto themselves." The classification system emphasizes professional knowledge.

After the main classification, there's a usually a Cutter Number (after a decimal point). These were based on a system developed by Charles Cutter in 1891. Cutter numbers are used primarily to maintain alphabetization as needed, based on personal or corporate names, geography, titles, etc. Cutter Numbers are a letter followed by numbers, ordered like decimals in order, so .M395, .M4, .M47, .M5, etc..

The LCC changes slowly compared to the DCC. And changes are required on almost a continous basis, from geopolitics (Czechoslovakia splits into the Czech Republic and Slovakia) to societal growth (the category "Negroes" is now "Afro-Americans" for U.S. blacks, and "blacks" for non-U.S. blacks.) The change of "Moving Pictures" to "Motion Pictures" didn't occur until 1989.

Comparison of DDC And LCC

The two systems were developed around the same time, give or take a decade or so. Both were based on the perception of knowledge and the relationships between academic disciplines extant from 1890 to 1910. Both are enumerative systems covering all topics, all disciplines, all fields of knowledge. Both are updated regularly. Both use a "controlled vocabulary," that is, a list of preferred terms for cataloguing.

Intner and Weihns say that both systems reflect the bias of a nineteenth-century U.S. outlook, then a "Western" outlook, and reflect a "white, male, Anglo-Saxon Christian view of the universe." These biases are more obvious in the LCC, and have been largely eliminated in the UDC variant of the DDC.

The differences are more striking.

Size: The LCC is significantly larger—that is, LCC has more broad classes (21 vs. 10), with more and narrower subcategories.

Specificity: The LCC has far more specific subclasses and categories that tend to be technical in nature. In any classification system, from libraries to file drawers, the question is: do you have a lot of files with less material in each one, or fewer files with more material in each one? LCC opts for the former approach; DDC for the latter. (Note that there is still order in the DDC within each file, of course.)

Structure: The DDC has overarching principles (for instance, decimal division) and mnemonic notations. For the LCC, each of the 21 classes was developed independently by experts in that field, and continues to be expanded and updated independently. There is no consistency in LCC between the classes.

Notation: The DDC uses only numbers; combined with some mnemonics, it's much easier for librarians, students, volunteers, and so on to remember. The LCC, in contrast, uses both letters and numbers, allowing more classes, more categories, more classifications.

Indexing: The DDC Relative Index can bring all topics together, under one grand umbrella, regardless of what class they're in. This is lacking in the LCC, because of the inconsistency between classes.

In sum, DDC uses fewer categories and sub-classifications and is consistent across disciplines, while LCC is more highly subdivided with no consistency between disciplines. It's understandable, therefore, that DDC has proven more useful to libraries catering to a wide range of needs such as public libraries and schools, while LCC is more widely used in libraries focused more on technical areas like colleges, universities, and government.

Communications and Classification in the Next Century

On October 26, 1998, IA McIlwaine, Professor of Library and Information Studies at the University of London spoke at OCLC about the problems that are arising with the rapidly expanding growth of international communication. Dr. McIlwaine believes that it is vital that those concerned with knowledge organization across the world—in many different spheres and for many different purposes—should have a better knowledge and understanding of what others have done. There is a rise of many different classification enterprises in a variety of contexts that are for ordering and retrieval of information different from that with which we have traditionally been concerned. We, as librarians, are not sufficiently aware of what is going on in other circles, and we do not make known what we do sufficiently vigorously for others to benefit from our efforts.

For Dr. McIlwaine, this issue became very apparent with the publication of the Checklist of North American Birds. In the introduction, the editorial committee states that since the previous edition, "there has been an increase in publications on the systemic status and taxonomic relationships of birds, which are used by a variety of professional biologists, including museum curators, journal editors, state, provincial and federal government wildlife managers and scientists, law enforcement personnel and ornithologists in general." She is surprised that there is no mention of librarians or those responsible for creating tools for information about birds. This shows that people are not sufficiently aware of our activities and that we are not aware of what is going on elsewhere in fields other than our own.

Dr. McIlwaine takes Francis Miksa's premise that in the future individuals will need to create their own method of applying the tools available for knowledge organization (as outlined in his recent book The DDC, the Universe of Knowledge and the Post Modern Library), and provides a brief comparison of the adaptability for this purpose of both the DDC and the UDC. An examination of the wider issues of both knowledge structures and terminology for the retrieval of information in the future follows.

What is the UDC?

The UDC (Universal Decimal Classification) was developed directly from the DDC, the Dewey Decimal Classification. Two Belgians, Paul Otlet and Henri LaFontaine, created the UDC in 1895. Their task was to create a bibliography of everything that had appeared in print. In Dr. McIlwaine's estimation, this task is as enormous, in the days of 3x5 cards, as making a catalogue of the entire content of the Internet seems today.

Otlet and LaFontaine made arrangements with Dewey that allowed them to develop Dewey's scheme into greater detail, to extend a number of synthetic devices, and to add additional auxiliary tables. The results from these changes are a UDC that is highly flexible and consequently nonstandard, a classification scheme capable of expressing certain pieces of information, especially in the sciences and technology. Using the scheme can lead to extremely complicated looking notations, but it has the ability to express concepts in considerable depth. Also, to use the classification correctly, the classifier has to have a good grasp of fundamental classificatory principles, because no citation order is laid down. Therefore, the individual institution must decide on its own rules and maintain its own authority file.

Examples of UDC Complex Notations

628:463:692.758 Farm location in nature reserves

341.64(44:450) Arbitration of disputes between France & Italy

663.4(493)(075)=112.5 Textbook on the brewing industry in Belgium written in Flemish

One of the principal differences between the UDC and its parent, Dewey, lies in its flexible nature and its lack of uniformity across libraries that use it. UDC is not used much in North America. It is used, however, in special libraries, in mathematics libraries, and in science and technology libraries in other English-speaking parts of the world. It is also used extensively in Eastern Europe, South America and Spain. The UDC was the basis of the French National Bibliography until the 1980s and is still used for the National Bibliography in French-speaking Africa. It is required in all science and technology libraries in Russia. It is interesting to note that the first and second editions were published in French, the third in German, the fourth in English, and the fifth in Russian.

Management of the UDC

The initial organization to take responsibility for the bibliographic listing and subsequent publication of the UDC was the Institut International de Bibliographies, frequently referred to as the Brussels Institute. The headquarters was moved from Brussels to The Hague in 1931, and the name of the organization became the Federation International de Documentation (FID) in 1937. The name changed again, in 1988, to International Federation for Information & Documentation (also abbreviated FID).

In the early 1990s, a consortium of publishers took over the governance of the UDC. The membership of the Consortium is made up of five publishers of the UDC, who publish the classification in the world languages together with the FID. The members of the Consortium at the present time are BSI, the British Standards Institution; AENOR (Associacion Espanola de Normalizacion y Certificacion), the Spanish Standards organization; CELES, the Belgian publisher; Bohn Stafleu van Loghum, the Dutch publishers; and INFOSRTA-NIPDOC (Information Science and Technology Association), Japan. Each publisher has the rights to publish the UDC in its own language. Licenses are granted to organizations that wish to publish a version of the classification in a language other than a "world" language. This is the preferred route for many publishers issuing editions in languages that are not widely spoken, such as Czech, Polish, or Estonian. There is now one standard version of the classification, known as the Master Reference File, and it consists of just over 61,000 entries. It is updated once a year as the result of revisions, corrections, and amendments published in the annual Extensions and Corrections to the UDC. This is the authoritative version of the scheme, and at present it is only available in English. A long-term objective is to create a database that is multilingual. The most likely language to be added next is German.

UDC vs. DDC

The UDC is flexible and therefore lacks uniformity across libraries that use it. It is not applied in a standard fashion and is therefore rarely available on pre-created records. Nor would pre-created records be useful, even if available, since the greatest strength of the UDC, its flexibility, is also its greatest weakness, its lack of conformity.

The UDC, even though it has greater freedom of interpretation, is uneven in its coverage of modern topics. It can, however, be easier to manipulate UDC to accommodate advances in knowledge, because there is greater scope for creating new synthesized numbers for concepts or simply to insert a new number as required without the need to reach general editorial agreement. Many concepts that look new are in reality a combination of existing ones and so can be immediately expressed, which is a final advantage of providing greater freedom and autonomy than the editorial process currently enjoys.

Future Development of UDC

The future lies not in keeping the UDC and the DDC as competing classification systems. Rather, we should be thinking about them in conjunction with one another when attempting to cater to the needs of the twenty-first century. The flexibility of the one could well be used to complement the stability of the other, by allowing the user to search on words that were translated into the notation of the appropriate classification. UDC could provide extended detail, if a concordance to the two classifications was produced. Dr. McIlwaine believes this would require UDC to abandon some of its more "laissez-faire" attitudes, but would not necessarily interfere with the autonomy of the individual user. A stable means of approaching information, one which permits the user to make the combinations that they wish, is the approach that is going to be needed in the future for virtual rather than actual libraries.

Some of the future developments that are being considered include the production of a concordance of the Area Tables of the two classifications. There are beginning discussions about mapping UDC numbers onto DDC numbers.

Information classification, however, is not limited to bibliographic classifications that are the basis of the UDC and the DDC. Dr. McIlwaine notes that there are a great many classifications in existence used for many purposes. It would be important if we, as librarians, took note of their existence when we are constructing retrieval tools. Many international, national, and local organizations are creating classifications for specific purposes. Some examples include the UNCSS (United Nations Common Coding System < http://www.ext.grida.no/undp/doc/ >) the International Classification of Diseases of the World Health Organization, the classification of occupations produced by the International Labour Office and the Merck index of drugs. She wonders how many library classifications take note of these schemes, much less actually incorporate them into their tables as a means of expansion?

Dr. McIlwaine asserts that if we are to make sense of the information that is available to us today and if we are to create adequate tools for the retrieval of that information, then we must make far greater efforts to coordinate what we are doing with the work of specialists. She believes that librarians must reach some common agreement on the ways that we handle both the systematic arrangements of concepts and the control of vocabulary used in academic discourse. We also need to realize that any solution will be a pragmatic one that will not be universally accepted as the only one, for no such thing exists. Rather, in the common interest of improving communication and easing universal access to information, we must be willing to accept certain standards and make certain compromises.

DDC for the Organisation of National Bibliographies

Introduction

National libraries and agencies responsible for ensuring bibliographic control and issuing national bibliographies have faced many new challenges in recent years. The growing demands for making national bibliographies accessible through the Internet and the need to extend bibliographic control to Internet and Web documents have been issues that many national agencies have had to deal with, at least since the end of the 20th Century. The shift to making national bibliographies available online or through the Internet was well documented in Unni Knutsen's 2001 survey. By 2003, 32 national bibliographic agencies were already making their bibliographic data available through the Web.

At the same time, the issue of extending bibliographic control to electronic document on the Web and in particular Internet sites has also forced national libraries and bibliographic agencies to consider changes in legal deposit regulations and undertake studies on how to bring electronic documents under bibliographic control. Michael Gorman had already put the issue of bibliographic control of electronic resources on national libraries' agendas at the 2001 IFLA Conference and Marcelle Beaudiquez had proposed some solutions for the selection and capture of Web sites for inclusion in national bibliographies.

While much attention has been given to these issues, some others raised in the International Conference on National Bibliographic Services (ICNBS) held in Copenhagen in November 1998 were also being tackled by national libraries. The organisation and efficient information retrieval of data in national bibliographies have been and should always be a constant concern. As more and more national bibliographies are issued in electronic formats, the issue of arranging the bibliography in a "user-friendly" way and ensuring an efficient subject access to records is needed more than ever. The long standing UNESCO and IFLA recommendation to arrange the bibliography according to an international classification scheme has been progressively accepted and implemented. It is in this context that three national libraries decided to work together to develop a common Dewey Decimal Classification (DDC) arrangement for the national bibliographies of Austria, Germany and Switzerland.

This presentation will deal with this project to use the DDC to improve access in German to the national bibliographies of Switzerland, Germany and Austria. The reasons that led to the revision of the existing arrangement and the difficulties in adopting a common approach will be explained. In particular, the presentation will describe the experience of the Swiss National Library in using the 100 divisions and the results obtained. The challenges of incorporating existing domains in the new DDC categories in the national bibliography of Die Deutsche Bibliothek will be explained in detail.

DDC at the Swiss National Library

In the 1990s, the Swiss National Library (Schweizerische Landesbibliothek) undertook a major reorganisation of its operations and structures in order to improve its delivery of goods and services. Part of these changes involved the improvement of bibliographic access to the collections. Many of the bibliographic practices of the library had not kept up with current international standards and thus needed to be reviewed. This evaluation led, for example, to the introduction of USMARC (now MARC21) in 1993 as the communication format for its library automation system, to the replacement of the indexing system based on the UDC by the Schlagwortnormdatei (SWD) and the Regeln für den Schlagwortkatalog (RSWK) in 1998 and more recently to the use of the Anglo-American Cataloguing Rules (AACR2) for descriptive cataloguing.

In 1998, a study was conducted to select a classification scheme that would be used to organise and arrange documents in new public access collections being developed at the Swiss National Library. The study also looked at how a new classification scheme could be used for the systematic organisation of the national bibliography, Das Schweizer Buch (SB), that was organized at that time according to 24 subject categories (Sachgruppen). Revision of the bibliography was planned in 2001 for the one hundredth anniversary of the bibliography and the goal was to select a scheme that would meet IFLA and UNESCO recommendations. The decision to adopt the DDC as the classification standard at the Swiss National Library was officially taken in September 1999. Work started in early 2000 to modify the overall redesign of the national bibliography in time for the 2001 edition. An analysis was conducted to evaluate the classification arrangement requirements of the bibliography. The bibliography is published twice a month in a printed version and lists about 25'000 titles per year. There are 25 issues annually, issue 16 contains records of music sheets and issue 25 provides a cumulative list of serial publications. The printed version of the bibliography is available by subscription and with this service clients can access an online pdf format of the bibliography. The Library is presently planning an improved online access to the bibliography.

Based on the annual output of the bibliography, it was decided that the Dewey's Second Summary (Hundred Divisions) would give an appropriate subject access to the records in the bibliography. Two modifications to the standard 100 classes were made; 914.94 (Swiss geography) and 949.4 (Swiss History). The decision to use the standard organization of the DDC was motivated by two factors; the national bibliography is a bibliographic tool used by librarians and booksellers and should thus promote the correct use of standards and secondly, the use of the DDC in the bibliography should reflect the application of the scheme used at the library for its open stacks collections where all of the classes are represented. The issue 16 that lists sheet music uses a more precise Dewey outline. It contains deeper hierarchical levels below the Third Summary in 782, 784-788 and these were developed on the basis of the literary warrant.

The 100 classes are displayed in 5 languages (German, French, Italian, Rhaeto-Romanic and English) in the bibliography. The French, Italian and English versions were taken from the respective DDC21 versions. The German version was prepared in collaboration with Die Deutsche Bibliothek and the Rhaeto-Romanic version was prepared by staff at the Swiss National Library. The outline is used according to a licence agreement between the Swiss National Library and OCLC-Forest Press.

The task of assigning class numbers to the documents listed in the bibliography was assigned to the descriptive cataloguers. In the process of cataloguing documents for the bibliography, it seemed more efficient that they continue assigning the appropriate class for each document as they had done for the previous arrangement. A training programmeme and support tools were developed and by November 2000, the cataloguing staff was ready to use the Dewey classes. The subject indexing staff worked closely with the cataloguers to guide and revise the work. Periodic quality checks were done and in general the quality level was quite high. On average, the percentage of documents classed wrongly (within a main class or outside a particular class) has ranged between 5 -7% in each of the quality controls. Instructions to cataloguers are updated regularly in order to maintain and improve the quality level.

In 2002 and 2003, an analysis of the distribution of documents within the Hundred Divisions was conducted. The goal was to find out how the classes were used and if more precise classes should be added. The survey indicated that four main classes accounted for almost 75% of documents listed (300, 600, 700 and 800). More precisely, documents classed in the following 10 classes accounted for about 47% of documents listed: 150 (2%), 330 (6%), 340 (6%), 360 (6%), 610 (8%), 620 (2.5%), 790 (3%), 830 (8%), 840 (3%), 910 (2%). The survey clearly showed that documents were not spread out evenly in all of the classes and that while some classes could be merged (100-140, 160-190), others could benefit of more specific numbers (*i.e.* 333, 791, 792, 795, 796). This distribution of documents across the DDC classes reflects the Swiss publishing output and the content of Swiss National Library collection. This information is being used to evaluate the DDB outline proposal for its bibliography.

DDC in the German National Bibliography

Die Deutsche Bibliothek (DDB) decided to use a new scheme based on DDC for the Deutsche Nationalbibliografie (DNB) beginning with the bibliographic year 2004. This scheme is nearly the same as the one used in Das Schweizer Buch with notable exceptions in the geography and history notations. In the German national bibliography (DNB), geography of Germany is classed under 914.3 and German history is under 943 while in the Österreichische Bibliografie, Austrian geography is under 914.36 and history of Austria under 943.6. The Österreichische Nationalbibliothek (Austrian National Library) decided to follow the decision of DDB in 2004 and change to DDC at the same time, together with the complete reorganisation of the Austrian National Bibliography (ÖB) which is only available in an electronic version since this year. Other more substantial discrepancies will be presented and commented in the following pages.

The German national bibliography (DNB) is available in printed form as well as in pdf and html versions. The main series DNB, Reihe A is a weekly list for all documents from the publishing houses and listed about 106'000 titles in 2004. Other smaller series consist of titles from institutions and companies and grey literature (series B, issued also weekly), of university publications (series H, issued monthly) and maps (series C, issued quarterly) and of two series for printed (series M) and recorded (series T) music, both issued monthly. Two main reasons were responsible for DDB's decision to turn to Dewey for the organisation of the national bibliography. The first and most important was an initiative of German academic and university libraries to translate DDC and integrate DDC services in German bibliographic and online activities based on a feasibility study on Dewey in German libraries published in 2000.

DDB took over the responsibility for initiating a DDC German Consortium, for the raising of funds for the translation and for the negotiations with OCLC and the

German publisher, the K.G. Saur GmbH. So it seemed natural that DDC should also be part of DDB's activities in the field of classification as soon as possible. And this of course led to the second reason for turning to Dewey in the national bibliography: since 1982 the three German-language countries had used two different systems for organising their national bibliographies and with the adoption of Dewey in Das Schweizer Buch (Swiss National Bibliography) all three were different. This situation was seen as a constraint for the exchange of data and for the use of the bibliographies. Growing international acceptance of Dewey for national bibliographic services and the varieties of DDC applications in national bibliographies convinced DDB that a change to Dewey would improve the national bibliographic services and facilitate cooperation with foreign national libraries.

The Swiss and Austrian scheme of 24 subject categories in the national bibliography had already been given up in the Federal Republic of Germany since 1982. The increase in book production in Germany and the development of new disciplines and users' and librarians' needs for precise access in the weekly lists made it necessary to establish a more specific arrangement of titles. A classification arrangement of 65 subject categories based roughly on the arrangement of disciplines in the Universal Decimal Classification, but without using UDC notations was established. The classification made it possible to separate the different language families such as English, German, the Romanic, Classical and Slavic languages, to give access to new subjects such as environmental sciences, social and economic history and a more detailed organisation of technology with the different branches of engineering sciences. Based on literary warrant and following academic libraries' wish to exclude less "serious" publications in the fields of esoteric, occultism and parapsychology as well as comics and cartoons, two new extra subject categories for esoteric subjects and for comics and cartoons were added in 1993.

DDB evaluated the possibility of using the DDC scheme used by the Swiss National Library for Das Schweizer Buch. The goal was to use it without giving up some of the advantages the 65 categories scheme developed between 1982 and 1993 had brought. In particular, that scheme gave fairly specific access to titles and was considered quite efficient for the selection process. In many categories, there was a good match between the second Summary of Dewey and the former subject categories (as in all fields of science) or even more specific, especially in fields where literary warrant was already high. In other cases, the subjects were split in different disciplines. The separation between language and literature in the language families (in UDC in one class) or the splitting of economics in the more general and academic class 330 and the more practical class 650 Management (mainly covering the so-called Betriebswirtschaft in German) caused some concerns in providing the same type of access for book selection. There were also cases where specificity could not be retained within the structure of the 100 divisions. The most difficult is the melting of all branches of engineering sciences into one general class 620 and even considering the use of more specific third Summary of Dewey would not have solved the problem. The discipline base arrangement does not correspond with modern disciplines, such as electrical engineering and electronics, mechanical engineering or environmental technology that had been separate subject categories in the DNB until 2004. Another serious loss to university and state libraries of Austria, Southern and Eastern Germany was the specific class for Slavic languages and literature that disappeared in the more general categories of 490 and 890.

Modifications of the Second Summary in the DNB

A questionnaire was sent out to the customers of the DNB in spring 2003 in order to inform them of the planned change to Dewey and ask if the disadvantages mentioned above were acceptable and which other wishes for special arrangements, not necessarily part of the Second Summary and the Swiss scheme, should be followed. Out of 450 customers nearly 200 answered, and one general vote was for exclusion of school textbooks and juvenile literature from the Dewey arrangement. The DDC practice of classing all kinds of educational material with the subject and fiction for children with the language-based literature seemed to be of little use for librarians and book trade. It appeared that these categories of documents are better accessed by verbal subject access where the type of document can be retrieved. Another proposal favoured by most respondents was the division between literary history and criticism on the one hand, and fiction on the other hand. In a rough arrangement of 100 subject categories, the precision Dewey offers in the 800 by using Tables 3A and 3B could not be duplicated. More importantly, in all of the subject categories for American, English and German literature, the secondary literature would be lost among masses of fiction titles, most of them of little or no interest for academic libraries and users of the bibliography. The introduction of a letter B (for Belletristik = fiction) makes it possible to separate between 830 (Literary history and criticism of German literature) and 830;B (German fiction) and the same for the other literatures within the main 800 class.

Another modification that was introduced in reaction to the respondents wishes and in respect to literary warrant was the adoption of a flexible application of the general scheme "Second Summary" where in cases it was either too general or too specific in scope. The case of the 790 already mentioned in connection with the Swiss National Bibliography is a good example. The main class 790 "Sports, games & entertainment" which includes topics like film, broadcasting, theatre, dance have considerable literary warrant and is important for academic and special libraries, for archives of broadcasting companies, film archives etc. Therefore DDB decided to use an organisation based on the 1000 Dewey sections and particular sections such as 791 (Film, broadcasting, public performances), 792 (Stage performances), but afterwards combine 793-795 in 793 (Games) and 796-799 in 796 (Sports). The number of publications in DNB, Series A for 2004 demonstrated the relevance of this arrangement: 507 titles in 791, 220 in 792, 230 in 793 and 1'153 in 796. Access in one class only would have meant considerable extra work for selectors looking for titles in one of these subject domains.

The organisation of divisions within particular classes was also problematic for a completely different reason than the one of specificity. There are cases when the Dewey Second Summary is too precise. This problem occurs for the records created by the New Release Service, a bibliographic service of the DNB connected with CIP. This service receives very sketchy information from publishers regarding the content of forthcoming books. As DDB does not usually receive either a table of contents or an abstract from publishers, it is often nearly impossible to decide in which of the Second Summary divisions the titles should be assigned. This occurs mostly in the areas of philosophy and religion where title information also tends to be unspecific, fanciful or just useless in determining the subject. After consulting the Dewey editor on these modifications, an arrangement was made which combines all philosophical classes from 100-120, the 140, and again 160-190 in one general class 100 (Philosophy in the First Summary) and thus avoids also the separation of this subject by two different others, class 130 (Parapsychology & occultism) and class 150 (Psychology). Religion proved to be a similar case because it is not easy to subdivide the 230-280 classes by knowing only the titles of publications; so a one general class for religion 200 (including 210) and the categories 220 (for the Bible), 230 (including all classes up to 280) for Christian religion and theology and 290 for the other religions make a useful subdivision for German librarians who anyhow find the Dewey arrangement in the 240, 250, 260 and 280 classes rather inappropriate for German theological traditions.

The Use of Dewey in the Music Series for Printed and Recorded Music in the DNB

The decision to use Dewey for the organisation of all the DNB bibliographic series meant that particular solutions had to be found for special types of documents. This is the case for two DNB bibliographic series; series M which lists printed music (Musikalien) and series T which lists recorded music (Tonträger). Both series had been organised by a special scheme different from the main one used in the other series.

The decision to apply Dewey to these two musical series meant that a more specific application should be developed in order to offer a meaningful access to titles for music librarians. It also became apparent that a straight application of Dewey hierarchies could not be easily adopted. After doing a comparison with the previous musical scheme it was determined that a Dewey application using between four and six digits seemed to be the most appropriate method of organising the bibliographic series. At the same time, the new scheme had to take in account the specificities of both series. The interest in printed music (Series M) is mainly determined by aspects of musical forms, voices, instruments and size of ensembles, and for recorded music (Series T) it is the musical styles and traditions, the ethnic or national origin and the need to organise the high number of items in popular music that seemed to be more important.

The schemes for both series were developed in close contact with OCLC. This proved necessary not only because of the Dewey editors' rich experience and knowledge in this field but also to give advice in the context of the OCLC licence restrictions. The licence usually does not allow showing headings and class numbers together on hierarchical levels below the Third Summary. In the end, the decision was made to use a scheme of 51 subject categories in series M, which contains deeper hierarchical levels for sections 782 (vocal music) and for sections 786-788 (various kind of instruments). Series T did not need separate notations below the level of four digit numbers for the instruments in 786-788 and only five classes were needed for the different kinds of vocal music. After long discussions with the classifiers in the Deutsche Musikarchiv (German musical archives, the music collection of DDB situated in Berlin) it was suggested that a more detailed organisation of class 781.64 (popular music) would be needed. But due to limited personnel resources and the fact that popular music CDs, records, cassettes and DVDs do not offer enough information concerning musical styles, 781.64 was not developed.

Problems with Dewey Principles and Dewey's View on Certain Subjects

The broad Dewey arrangement of the DNB based on the Second Summary introduced in 2004 was a first step in the introduction of the DDC. Acknowledging that such a broad classification would not satisfy users' bibliographic needs, the DDB is planning to introduce full Dewey notations for titles listed in the DNB in a two-stage process during two years, beginning with the bibliographic year 2006. During that year, the German print edition of DDC 22 will be published and an online service called Melvil will be available. That online service will consist of a classification tool, MelvilClass, a German version of WebDewey, and a retrieval tool MelvilSearch which will offer German language access to classified documents in German libraries by browsing in Dewey categories as well as by precise search with all German index entries of DDC 22.

Some of the problems described in the implementation of the Dewey arrangement of the DNB will be solved when Dewey numbers at full length can be used for retrieval purposes. In working with the full Dewey, the German classification experts found some limits in the development of Dewey in some disciplines. For instance, the fact that subjects can be distributed in different disciplines and does not allow for these titles to be listed in one discipline was a cause for concern. The evolution of disciplines such as archaeology or environmental studies since the end of the 19th century where new objects of research has changed the way the discipline should be organised and a broad classification would give insufficient access to documents in these disciplines.

In the field archaeology, archaeologists concentrated on classical archaeology for a long time, and the position of the discipline within the history of the ancient world in 930.1 seemed natural. However, many fields of research on different continents (such as Africa and Latin America) and in different ages (like medieval archaeology in Europe) have changed the focus of the discipline. These different fields of research are organised in many classes in Dewey. And even from the beginning many archaeological studies have been classified with the objects they described in classes like the 722 (Architecture from the earliest times to ca. 300) or the 733 for ancient sculptures. For German librarians expecting to find everything under archaeology, there is not one Dewey subject category for archaeology assembling all titles on that discipline. Retrieval methods will have to be developed in order to lead users to the titles in the different classes covering their field of interest such as the 722, the 733 or certain parts of pre-Columbian archaeology in 972.01 (Mexico) or 985.01 (Peru).

Environmental research can be split up in many disciplines. Dewey has classed most aspects which are not strictly scientific or technological in economics (DNB subject category 330) and social services and problems (DNB subject category 360). The former DNB scheme had a specific subject category Umweltschultz (environmental protection) that had additional entries in other disciplines such as life sciences, environmental engineering, political science etc. According to Dewey, all titles on environmental research are split up among these subjects and it is only by using full Dewey notations that users will have the possibility of accessing all classes connected with problems of environment. Retrieval using captions with search verbal search elements such as environment-(Umwelt-) and pollution will be able to overcome the constraints of discipline-based classification of subjects.

Another problem to be solved in the DNB was how to use Dewey notations for interdisciplinary documents. As Dewey was originally developed as a shelving system to allocate only one notation for a document, work was undertaken to develop rules for assigning more than one Dewey number. The approach used by the SNL in assigning documents to only one category was discussed and in the end, it was decided to take a different approach and assign up to two or three numbers to a document. This approach was chosen in order to guide German users to subjects classed in disciplines that would not be obvious according to German academic traditions or points of view. The additional title entries mentioned above were made in the DNB and also in the Austrian national bibliography Österreichische Bibliografie (ÖB) in cases where a document is interdisciplinary or could be interesting for librarians or scholars in different disciplines. These so-called Nebensachgruppen consisted only of a short entry author/title and the identification number of the title so that users can be directed to the main subject category where the complete bibliographical description, including subject headings, can be found.

The ÖB has given up the printed issues and is published only in an electronic version since 2004; so it is no longer necessary to make a distinction between main and additional entries in subject categories. If necessary the title can be found in two or three subject categories. DNB continues to be published in printed form and thereby needs to save space by distinguishing between main subject category with the full bibliographic description of the title and one or two possible short entries in additional Nebensachgruppen.

To make sure the Dewey numbers are assigned and understood correctly, a manual for classifiers as well as for clients was established. It describes the position of all subjects and the content of the classes in the Dewey arrangement of the DNB, and also topics and situations where Nebensachgruppen are allowed or useful. The manual includes an index with about 3'500 entries of search terms by topics, type of documents and genres which had been proved to be necessary for the classifying of German-language publications in the 100 Dewey subject categories.

This list should not be considered as an abridged form of the Relative Index. The so-called Hauptsachgruppe (the place of the main and full entry of the title) will always correspond to the full Dewey number used for classification according to the international DDC practice.

In a few cases, the German application of the DDC will also allow to classify with a second or third notation but as this classification is a more time-consuming process than the pure grouping of titles in subject categories, this will only be done if it seems to be absolutely necessary from the classifier's point of view and knowledge of German users' expectations. One typical case is the event celebrating the 60th anniversary of the end of World War 2. A huge number of books about the war, about air-raids on German towns, the holocaust and the liberation of the concentration camps were published in a rather short period and it became important to organise the documents more precisely. All these publications receive the DDC subject category 940 as Dewey assembles all these topics within notations in the 940.53 classes. But from a German point of view many of these topics also belong to class 943.0862 and 943.0864 under the broader subject category 943 (History of Germany). The possibility to use a second or third subject category and, for detailed classification, even add a second or even third full Dewey number makes it easier to adjust the classification according to particular literary warrant and perceived users' bibliographic needs.

Conclusion: The cooperation between three national libraries in establishing a common approach in developing access to their national bibliographies was an enriching experience. While each national library chose to adjust the classification to their particular needs and according to literary output, there was a genuine spirit toward achieving a consensus approach. The mutually influenced classification approach adopted by each library is a good basis for future development. The results achieved demonstrate the commitment toward the use of the Dewey Decimal Classification in the three countries and with the publication of the German language version of DDC22 in 2006, it is easy to foresee many more cooperative initiatives between the three libraries.

A Guide to the Dewey Decimal Classification Scheme

This library uses the Dewey Decimal Classification scheme (DDC) to arrange books and other library materials on the shelves so they may be easily retrieved. It is used in many libraries and allows items about the same subject to be shelved together.

How does the Dewey Decimal System Work?: DDC is an hierarchical number system that organizes all human knowledge into ten main categories. These are:

000 Generalities (includes computing)

100. Philosophy

200. Religion

300. Social sciences

400. Languages

500. Natural sciences and mathematics

600. Technology (applied science)

700. The arts

800. Literature

900. Geography and history

Each main category is then divided into ten sub-categories. For example:

500. Natural sciences and mathematics

510. Mathematics

520. Astronomy

530. Physics

540. Chemistry

550. Earth sciences

560. Palaeontology

570. Life sciences

580. Plants

590. Animals

Each sub-category is then also divided into ten specific topics. For example:

530. Physics

531. Solid mechanics

532. Fluid mechanics

533. Pneumatics

534. Sound

535. Light

536. Heat

537. Electricity

538. Magnetism

539. Modern physics

Each of these topics may be further divided into more specific subject areas. A decimal point is used after the first three digits to separate the specific subjects -it also makes the numbers easier to read. You will see that as the subject becomes more specific, so does the numbering. For example:

534. Sound

1. Generation of sound

2. Transmission of sound

22. Transmission of sound in solids

23. Transmission of sound in liquids

DDC at Oxford Brookes

When an item arrives in the library it is assigned a DDC number, often called the "classmark" or "shelfmark". Each of the numbers in this shelfmark has a meaning and is not assigned randomly.

For example, the book "The Royal doctors 1485-1714" by Elizabeth Furdell has been assigned the shelfmark 610.6952094205 FUR. These numerals indicate:

610. = Medical sciences

610.6 = Professions

610.69 = Medical personnel

610.695 = Specific kinds of medical personnel

610.6952 = Physicians

610.69520942 = Physicians in England and Wales

610.6952094205 = Physicians in England and Wales 1485-1603

Most items will also be assigned some letters at the end of the numerals, "FUR" in the above example. These are taken from the author's surname or the first word of the title.

Finding Items on the Shelves

The shelfmark will always have at least three numbers, followed by some letters. It is usually displayed on the spine of the item, but is sometimes placed on the front cover. Here are some examples:

361.	382.	576	599.	647.	823.
3	63	JON	935	944	914
HIG	COC	PHI	21	BAI/B	LON

The DDC system places items about the same subject at the same number. This means that once you have identified the DDC number for the subject you are interested in, you can browse the shelves at that number.

On each shelf the items are arranged in a numerical sequence from left to right by their DDC number. Where several items have an identical DDC number, the letters are used to further arrange them. For example,

361.	361.	361.	363.	363.	363.
3	32	32	35	377	377
HIG	BOR	STO	CIV	PRE	PRO

Beware of Separate Sequences

If you are looking for a specific item you should check the library catalogue and make a note of the full shelfmark (numbers and letters) and any words that appear before the shelfmark. The majority of library materials are shelved together but there are several separate sequences that are kept in different areas, but which are all indicated on the Library catalogue. Look out for sequences such as Pamphlet, Oversize, Local Collection, Short Loan, Music Scores, Quick Reference, Subject Floor Quick Reference.

Journals

Journals are also shelved in a separate section. The same DDC numbers are used, but the catalogue shows these items with a shelfmark that is preceded by a "J", and which only has one letter after the numbers. For example, the journal "Nursing Standard" has the shelfmark J 610.73 N.

And finally ... Art and Architecture materials.

When looking for items in this area you may be confused to find two alphabetic sequences at the same number. For example, general items about French architecture can be found at the shelfmark 724.90944 and have three letters after the numbers. At the end of these come works about specific French architects, at the same number 724.90944, but these have four letters after the numbers. For example:

724.	724.	724.	724.	724.	724.
909	909	909	909	909	909
44	44	44	44	44	44
FIR	PRI	ZYM	BAR/M	LEC/F	LEC/M

This happens in some other areas in the 700s, so when checking the library catalogue remember to make a note of the full shelfmark -numbers and letters.

If you have any questions or would like more help, please ask a member of library staff.

Quick Guide to Dewey Numbers used in this Library

This is only a brief guide to subjects. For more information, especially when looking for specific items, please remember to check the library catalogue.

000	**Generalities and Computing**
010	Bibliography
020	Library and Information Science
030	Encyclopaedias
040	Not used
050	Not used
060	Organizations and Museums
070	Journalism and publishing

080 General knowledge
090 Manuscripts and rare books
100 Philosophy and Psychology
110 Metaphysics
120 Epistemology, causation
130 Paranormal phenomena
140 Specific philosophical schools
150 Psychology
160 Logic
170 Ethics and moral philosophy
180 Ancient, Medieval, Oriental philosophy
190 Modern western philosophy
200 Religion
210 Theory of religion
220 Bible
230 Christianity
240 Christian moral & devotional theology
250 Christian orders and local church
260 Social and ecclesiastical theology
270 Christian church history
280 Christian denominations and sects
290 Comparative religion
300 Social sciences
310 Collections of general statistics
320 Politics
330 Economics
340 Law
350 Public administration & military science
360 Social problems and services
370 Education
380 Commerce, communications, transport
390 Customs, etiquette, folklore
400 Language
410 Linguistics

420 English and Old English language
430 German language
440 French language
450 Italian and Romanian languages
460 Spanish and Portuguese languages
470 Latin language
480 Greek language
490 Other languages
500 Natural sciences and mathematics
510 Mathematics
520 Astronomy, cartography
530 Physics
540 Chemistry
550 Earth sciences, geology
560 Palaeontology
570 Life sciences, biology
580 Plants
590 Animals
600 Technology
610 Medical sciences
620 Engineering
630 Agriculture
640 Home economics, catering
650 Management
660 Chemical engineering, food technology
670 Manufacturing
680 Manufacture for specific uses
690 Building
700 The arts
710 Planning -urban, rural, transport
720 Architecture
730 Sculpture, pottery, ceramics
740 Drawing and decorative arts
750 Painting and paintings

760	Graphic arts
770	Photography
780	Music
790	Entertainment, recreation, sport
800	**Literature**
810	American literature
820	English literature
830	German literature
840	French literature
850	Italian literature
860	Spanish literature
870	Latin literature
880	Greek Literature
890	Literature of other languages
900	**Geography and history**
910	Geography and travel
920	Biography
930	History of the ancient world
940	History of Europe
950	History of Asia
960	History of Africa
970	History of North America
980	History of South America
990	History of other areas

Introduction : Exploring the Armamentarium

In the course of their professional education, training, reading, and practical experience, many librarians and information specialists may receive little exposure to the range and diversity of library and bibliographic classification. The richness that is available includes different ways of viewing and organizing knowledge, multiple functions of classification, a variety of systems, options within those systems, different procedures for constructing and applying schemes, new means of searching schedules and classified files. Because courses in cataloguing and classification necessarily include descriptive cataloguing, subject cataloguing, and other concerns, their treatment of classification is consequently confined. Usually detailed theoretical and practical attention is given to just one or two classification schemes, with some other systems receiving shorter mention and without supporting practice work. The most-used textbooks tend to accord with the curricular emphases.

Many information professionals work exclusively in specialized areas such as technical services, reader services, or library management. Others may gain more variety according to some "dual-assignment" plan, thus becoming more aware of the difficulties of both the users and the cataloguers/classifiers at firsthand. Not only cataloguers/classifiers but all library staff members may be required or wish to contribute to decision-making on policies and practices concerning classification. If these professionals lack acquaintance with a span of solutions and are overly conditioned by those used on-site, they may be tempted to conclude too quickly that those adopted systems and procedures are inevitable and as good as can be had. They may not question enough that current local practice, use of established pseudo-standards, and so-called economized technical processing (the latter increasingly utilized partly due to competitive tendering) may repeatedly waste valuable time and energy of service staff and readers.

The intention in presenting this set of papers is to encourage fresh and wider interest in library and bibliographic classification decisions, the extent of choice, and the "best fit" of a system to local factors. It is perhaps timely to reaffirm that the arrangement and optimum navigation of the document collection and its records constitute key resources and responsibilities of the entire library staff. Their active and informed involvement in identifying user approaches, problems, and preferences is essential to any careful decision and implementation. Therefore it is hoped that the gathering of papers may help promote a more participatory propinquity or collocation of subjects, and that not only classifiers and cataloguers as such but also reader and bibliographical services staff, library administrators, and others might take part. The "Great American Library Dream" has been described as "that dream of librarians which strives to reveal to readers the subject-contents in books." But how to make that dream come true? Requirements include surveying readers' interests and behaviour, considering how successful are the local policies and procedures in force, and then confirming, adapting, adopting or fashioning apt organizations of knowledge (explicit in the form of classifications, covert in the guise of syndetic references to and from related subject access points).

Information required for making choices in classification may be said to fall into two broad kinds: external information and internal information. External information includes appreciation of the available and the emerging technical repertory-that armamentarium used to withstand and more nearly accommodate turbulent changes in knowledge and user needs. Many theories and systems, whether old or new, have some relevance for today and therefore, first or closer acquaintance with them constitute useful "new" experiences. Internal environmental information relates to the current and future functions of the particular library or information centre, characteristics of the collections, the performance and acceptability of the system in present use, and specific requirements or preferences of staff and users of various categories and levels. The individual reader must indeed "remain a 'gray' and 'ghostlike' individual until defined as to intelligence, interests, and motivation." Comparative assessment of possible solutions, including those already employed, may be made and sample trials carried out on the most promising systems. Feedback on experience with Dewey Decimal Classification and Library of Congress Classification is widely available though there is need for more hard information as to why and how libraries use the internal options of those schemes. For lesser known classifications, some degree of reality-testing may be gleaned from visits, interviews, correspondence, and reading the reports of adoptions and modifications by other libraries and centers.

This collection of papers is necessarily limited and identifies, describes, and discusses only some of the variety of options and investigative approaches. Many more are being discovered, rediscovered, written about, devised, refined, researched, and evaluated. Some schemes are highly specialized and purposefully drawn up for individual collections yet embody partially transferable thought-provoking notions, structures, and devices. Advances in technology render further enhancements and innovations certain.

The enthusiasm and cooperation of the contributors in sharing their "gifts differing" is acknowledged with thanks, as is the sustained patience and guidance provided by Dr. Ruth C. Carter, editor of Cataloguing & Classification Quarterly. Numerous arguments with former colleagues Pat Booth, James Shearer, Mary South, John Shinebourne, and Pnina Wentz always generated light rather than heat; the jury is still out on most of the issues.

The Contents List is just like any other classified arrangement in that certain contributions could have been placed equally well in other sections, clear cases for alternative location. The series or array of the sections themselves might have been ordered differently, while within each paper alternative sequencing of text would doubtless have suited certain readers better. The opening section, BASIC DESIGN CONSIDERATIONS, presents ideas and principles concerning the function, assessment, design, and construction of classifications. It is hoped that the papers therein may raise some of the initial questions for those with established library collections who are wondering whether to retain their present scheme or switch to a different system (in both cases with or without modifications). It is also hoped that those privileged and challenged to select or create a system for a quite new information centre or library will find some clarification and benefit. Some relative weighing of particular schemes is included in the section Combination Platters and Reclassification.

The next section, OPTIONS WITHIN STANDARD CLASSIFICATION SYSTEMS, covers the Library of Congress Classification and the Dewey Decimal Classifications. Because these two are used so much and emphasized in basic textbooks and consequently their general features well known, the focus of the contributed papers is on choices available in these systems. A paper considering the Library of Congress versus Dewey decision appears in the Combination Platters and Reclassification section, while a description of electronic Dewey has been placed in the last section Classification and the New Technology.

ALTERNATE CLASSIFICATION SYSTEMS are generally less well known and therefore their chief contexts, characteristics, and developments are described. This section includes classifications intended for wide adoption as well as some prepared for particular local settings. The review of reader interest classifications, which frequently co-exist with the Dewey Decimal Classification, is placed last so as to immediately precede the next section. That section COMBINATION PLATTERS AND RECLASSIFICATION covers use of multiple classifications within the same institution or even the same collection and includes also the related decision and planning of reclassification. The last section, CLASSIFICATION AND THE NEW TECHNOLOGY, features firstly a review which includes the present and potential support from our trusty "Three Musketeers"-the computer, telecommunications, and information storage technologies. A second paper provides a guide to features of electronic Dewey.

Kelley, well experienced in both classifying and readers' advisory work, investigated the contribution of classification in her day. Her holistic approach and creative skepticism may perhaps find some echo and extension in recent books by librarian Thomas Mann. Though Kelley identified many limitations she later concluded: "As I pondered thus upon the unified nature of library service, I discovered that classification could be thought of only in relation to the part it contributed to a final goal. Again it resumed a kind of central position; but this time, instead of resuming also its separate entity, it seemed to radiate throughout the structure shafts of illumination, lighting up and strengthening all library service. It seemed to me that classification could be made to reinforce the framework of our service and prevent the whole from collapsing into a formless and undirected tangle."

Today there beckons a replete repertoire available of principles, perspectives, models, applications, practices, feedback, and research results. Searchable specifications from several schemes and thesauri may be added to a record, diverse strategic paths for a literature search devised, displayed and recorded to suit group and individual preferences. The contribution of classification now and increasingly offers added value, variety, and versatility.

Taxonomy

Purpose

The purpose of this article is to describe and explain taxonomies so that a reader will appreciate how a taxonomy, as a type of information structure, can help bring order to a body of knowledge.

The article will also provide a fundamental insight into the basic uses of taxonomies. Upon completion of this chapter, a reader will appreciate the problem that taxonomies solve and the prominent features of a taxonomy. We will provide some examples that command instant recognition.

Taxonomy Background

Taxonomies are important because they bring order to a body of information or a collection of objects. Greater orderliness very often enhances one's ability to understand complex subject matter.

Neither the taxonomy term nor the concept is new. Probably the most famous use of a taxonomy was its use by the Swedish scientist Linnaeus to classify the biological world. It was one of the early successful attempts to bring order to an otherwise disorganized body of knowledge.

Even today taxonomies are very useful to break down a large entity into constituent parts that, when individually understood, help make sense of the larger whole. Quite often the "large body" that's broken down is knowledge about some thing or some subject. Taxonomies of this sort include glossaries, dictionaries and encyclopedia. Taxonomies need not embrace knowledge exclusively; they may also bring order to objects or collections of objects. For example, a listing of rifle parts categorized according to major parts of a rifle is a taxonomy. Also, listings of rifles categorized according to caliber classifications comprise a taxonomy.

Taxonomies are used by virtually everybody. Often we don't even think about it.

Precisely what are taxonomies and what are they used for?

Explanation

The following definitions and examples will expand our understanding of taxonomies.

Definitions

The following defines and also explains the origin of the term "taxonomy":

Taxonomy (from Greek taxis meaning arrangement or division and nomos meaning law) is the science of classification according to a pre-determined system, with the resulting catalogue used to provide a conceptual framework for discussion, analysis, or information retrieval. In theory, the development of a good taxonomy takes into account the importance of separating elements of a group (taxon) into subgroups (taxa) that are mutually exclusive, unambiguous, and taken together, include all possibilities. In practice, a good taxonomy should be simple, easy to remember and easy to use.

The function of a taxonomy is to classify or categorize a body of knowledge or collection of objects in a hierarchical manner. Each tier of the hierarchy "inherits" or possesses all attributes of the one immediately above -whatever those attributes might be. When one views a hierarchy from top to bottom, the matter becomes more particular and more specific the lower one goes in the hierarchy.

Advanced practitioners of information technology or knowledge representation usually refer to a body of knowledge as a "knowledge domain".

Taxonomies are especially useful for searching for specific objects in a large collection (such as a Sears catalogue) as well as for understanding concepts (such as those found in a glossary or a thesaurus).

Taxonomies may also be used to:

- Provide a controlled vocabulary for search engines.
- Delineate hierarchical relationships by means of an "IS A" relationship (*e.g.*, a sedan IS AN automobile and an SUV IS AN automobile).
- Delineate types of hierarchical relationships such as classes, subclasses, and superclasses (*e.g.*, the class "automobile" is a subclass of "motor vehicle. In turn, "motor vehicle" is a superclass of "automobile").
- Outline, catalogue, or structure a given knowledge domain.

Examples of Taxonomies

The following examples of taxonomies are discussed in order of increasing complexity and/or size:

Visualizing a Basic Example: To visualize a taxonomy, consider how a listing of American cities might appear when categorized according to a hierarchy of regions and states in the United States. The following lists just a few cities for illustration purposes.

Region	*State*	*City*
Midwest	Illinois	Chicago
		Urbana
		Springfield
	Indiana	Ft. Wayne
		West Lafayette

Contd..

Region	***State***	***City***
New England	Vermont	Montpelier
		Burlington
		Middlebury
	Maine	Portland
		Freeport
	Massachusetts	Boston
		Springfield
Southwest	California	Los Angeles
		San Diego
	Arizona	Tempe
		Phoenix

One can readily visualize the above as a hierarchical categorization where each tier goes into increasing specificity from top to bottom.

Upper tiers pass on characteristics to lower tiers. Seen from another direction, members of lower tiers inherit characteristics from upper tiers.

Suppose we were to characterize the weather of each region as follows: Midwest, hot summers; New England, cold winters; Southwest, dry air year-round. Doing so would cause each of the constituent states and cities to inherit the same characteristics. To further differentiate states, however, we could conceivably use soil characteristics as an attribute, and to further differentiate among cities we might use relative population sizes. By using attributes at each tier as we did above, taxonomies help us to "compare and contrast" between objects and concepts at different positions in the hierarchy. Very often that knowledge helps us to understand complex concepts or to identify a few particular objects among many in a large collection.

The Dewey Decimal System: The Dewey Decimal System is the world's most actively used taxonomy. It is also known as the Dewey Decimal Classification System (DDC). Its function is to categorize all areas of knowledge so that books and pamphlets may be assigned a classification number appropriate to a particular subject.

It was invented by Melvil Dewey in 1873 when he was a librarian at Amherst College. It was first published in 1876 and was quickly adopted for general use by libraries and schools across the United States. Today it is the most widely used taxonomy in the world.

The system is now maintained by classification specialists at the Library of Congress, even though the Library of Congress has its own classification system. It has had 21 major revisions since its inception. More than 100,000 new numbers are assigned annually.

The system consists of a hierarchy of numbers delineated in classes, divisions, and sections called "summaries". The word "decimal" is included in the name of the system in recognition of the role the number ten plays as a primary organizational feature: there are ten main classes; each main class has ten divisions and each division has ten sections. However, not all divisions and sections are in use.

Numbers belonging to the system must be at least three digits in length. Additional numbers can be used by adding a decimal point followed by additional numbers to the extent needed to accomplish the desired degree of classification.

The following shows how the number "636.8" is assigned to the classification of cats in the section of Animal Husbandry in the division of Agricultural and Related Technologies in the class of Technology:

600	Number from (first) summary of ten classes (*i.e.*, the class named Technology)
630	Number from (second) summary of ten divisions (*i.e.*, the division under class Technology named Agriculture)
636	Number from (third) summary of ten sections (*i.e.*, the section named Animal Husbandry)
636.7	Number representing dogs
636.8	Number representing cats

Thus, from the bottom up, the numbers for dogs and cats were created as (1) extensions of "636", the classification for Animal Husbandry which in turn was (2) an extension of "630", the classification for Agriculture which in turn was (3) an extension of "600", the classification for Technology.

To see a description of the ten classes in the first summary, click here.

To see a description of the Second Summary -The Hundred Divisions, click here.

To see a description of the Third Summary -The Thousand Sections, click here. The DDS site also has an excellent tutorial, click here.

Other Examples of Taxonomies: The Taxonomy Warehouse web site is a portal to many other taxonomies. One can investigate numerous examples by picking and choosing from those listed in the site's main interface. This is a good illustration of using a taxonomy for database search purposes.

One can also visit the Army's CALL (Centre for Army Lessons Learned) web site using the Taxonomy Warehouse or by clicking here. This site is home to a system that catalogues more than 18,000 U. S. Army terms, acronyms, and other expressions.

If other military uses of taxonomies are of interest, enter the Google search web site and perform a search using the term military taxonomy. The result will produce over 32,000 listings.

Limitations of Taxonomies

Taxonomies are a promising but incomplete means of structuring information.

More precisely, one can say that they are a necessary but not sufficient condition for adequate understanding of precise meaning. While the taxonomic categorizations and sub-categorizations enhance understanding, the lack of detail in describing objects—at each level of the taxonomy—still leaves room for ambiguity as to the precise meaning of any particular term or object.

As we will further see, combining a taxonomy with additional detail about the data or metadata, as such information is called, greatly helps to reduce ambiguity and has other benefits as well.

Conclusion: Taxonomies may not be "the ultimate" contemporary information structure, but they certainly can help reduce chaos when attempting to make order out of a body of knowledge or a collection of objects. They are simple and almost intuitive since one is encouraged early in school to use outlines (perhaps the briefest of taxonomies) when writing papers.

The taxonomy's greatest future use may be in providing foundations for other structures. Two information structures offering the greatest promise for reduced ambiguity, machine readability, and automated transfer of information are Extensible Markup Language (XML) schema and structures that use ontologies in their composition.

Universal Decimal Classification (UDC)

The Universal Decimal Classification is a system of library classification developed by the Belgian bibliographers Paul Otlet and Henri la Fontaine at the end of the 19th century. It is based on the Dewey Decimal Classification, but uses auxiliary signs to indicate various special aspects of a subject and relationships between subjects. It thus contains a significant faceted or analytico-synthetic element, and is used especially in specialist libraries. UDC has been modified and extended over many years to cope with the increasing output in all disciplines of human knowledge, and is still under continuous review to take account of new developments.

The documents classified by UDC may be in any form. They will often be literature, *i.e.* written documents, but may also be in other media such as films, video and sound recordings, illustrations, maps, and realia such as museum pieces.

UDC classifications use Hindu-Arabic numerals and are based on the decimal system. Every number is thought of as a decimal fraction with the initial decimal point omitted, which determines filing order. For ease of reading, a UDC identifier is usually punctuated after every third digit.

Thus, after 61 "Medical sciences" come the subdivisions 611 to 619; under 611 "Anatomy" come its subdivisions 611.1 to 611.9; under 611.1 come all of its subdivisions before 611.2 occurs, and so on; after 619 comes 620. An advantage of this system is that it is infinitely extensible, and when new subdivisions are introduced, they need not disturb the existing allocation of numbers.

The main categories:

0 Generalities. Informatics and Information Sciences

1 Philosophy. Psychology

2 Religion. Theology

3 Social Sciences. Statistics. Politics. Government. Economics. Law. Administration. Military. Folklore

4 Unassigned

5 Natural Sciences. Mathematics

6 Applied Sciences. Medicine. Technology

7 The Arts. Recreation. Entertainment. Music. Sports

8 Languages. Linguistics. Literature

91 Geography

92 (Auto-) Biography

93/99 History. Archeology

A document may be classified under a combination of different categories through the use of additional symbols. For example:

+	plus	Addition	e.g. 59+636 Zoology and animal breeding
/	stroke	Extension	e.g. 592/599 Systematic zoology (everything from 592 to 599 inclusive)
:	colon	Relation	e.g. 17:7 Relation of ethics to art
[]	square brackets	Algebraic subgrouping	e.g. 31:[622+669](485) statistics of mining and metallurgy in Sweden (the auxiliary qualifies 622+669 considered as a unit)
=	equals	Language	e.g. =20 in English; 59=20 Zoology, in English

The design of UDC lends itself to machine readability, and the system has been used both with early automatic mechanical sorting devices, and modern library OPACs. A core version of UDC, with 65,000 subdivisions, is now available in database format, and is called the Master Reference File (MRF). The current full version of the UDC has 220,000 subdivisions.

Universal Decimal Classification System

0	Generalities
00	Prolegomena. Fundamentals of Knowledge and Culture
004	Computer science
005	Management
01	Bibliography
02	Librarianship
030	Encyclopaedias. General Reference Works
050	Serial Publications. Periodicals
06	Organizations and Associations
069	Museums
070	Newspapers. Journalism
08	Polygraphies. Collective Works
09	Manuscripts. Rare and Remarkable Works
1	Philosophy. Psychology
101	Nature and role of Philosophy
11	Metaphysics
13	Philosophy of mind and spirit
14	Philosophical systems
159.9	Psychology
16	Logic. Epistemology. Theory of Knowledge
17	Moral Philosophy. Ethics
2	Religion. Theology
21	Prehistoric and Primitive Religions
22	Religions of The Far East
23	Religions of The Indian Subcontinent. Hinduism. Jainism. Sikhism
24	Buddhism
25	Religions of Antiquity. Minor Cults and Religions
252	Religions of Mesopotamia
254	Religions of Iran

257	Religions of Europe
26	Judaism
27	Christianity
271	Eastern church
272/279	Western Church
272	Roman Catholic church
274/278	Protestant churches
28	Islam
282	Sunnite Islam
284	Shi'ite Islam
285	Babi-Baha'i
29	Modern Spiritual Movements
3	Social Sciences
304	Social questions. Social practice.
308	Sociography. Descriptive studies of society
311	Statistics
314	Demography
316	Sociology
32	Politics
321	Forms of political organization. States as political power
323	Home affairs. Internal policy
324	Elections. Plebiscites. Referendums
327	International relations
328	Parliaments. Congresses. Representation of The people. Governments
329	Political parties and Movements
33	Economics
331	Labour. Employment. Work. Labour Economics. Organization of labour.
336	Finance
338	Economic policy. Management of The economy. Production. Services. Prices
339	Trade. Commerce. International economic relations. World economy
34	Law. Jurisprudence
341	International law
342	Public law. Constitutional law. Administrative law
343	Criminal law

343.9	Criminology
347	Civil law
35	Public Administration. Government
352/354	Levels of administration. Local, regional, central administration
355/359	Military Science
36	Safeguarding The Mental and Material Necessities of Life
364	Social Welfare
368	Insurance. Communal provision through sharing of risk
37	Education
371	Organization of educational and training system. School organization
374	Education and training out of school. Further education
378	Higher education. Universities. Academic study
379.8	Leisure
39	Ethnology. Folklore
391	Costume
392	Customs, manners, usage in private life
393	Death. Treatment of corpses. Funerals. Death rites
394	Public life. Social life. Life of The people
395	Social ceremonial. Etiquette. Good manners
398	Folklore in The strict sense.
396	Feminism
5	Mathematics and Natural Sciences
502/504	Environmental Sciences. Conservation of natural resources. Threats to The environment and protection
51	Mathematics
52	Astronomy
528	Geodesy, cartography
529	Chronology
53	Physics
54	Chemistry
548	Crystallography
549	Mineralogy
55	Earth Sciences
551.5	Meteorology. Climatology
551.7	Stratigraphy

552	Petrology
553	Economic geology
556	Hydrology
56	Palaeontology
57	Biological Sciences
572	Anthropology
573	General biology
574	Ecology
575	Genetics
576	Cytology
577	Biochemistry. Biophysics
578	Virology
579	Microbiology
58	Botany
59	Zoology
6	Applied Sciences. Medicine. Technology
61	Medicine
619	Veterinary medicine
62	Engineering. Technology in General
621	Mechanical engineering
621.3	Electrical engineering
621.38	Electronics
622	Mining
623	Military engineering
624	Civil engineering
625.1/.5	Railway engineering
625.7/.8	Highway engineering
626/627	Hydraulic engineering
628	Public health engineering
629	Vehicle engineering
63	Agricultural Sciences
630	Forestry
631/634	Farm management. Plant husbandry
635	Horticulture
636/638	Animal husbandry

639	Hunting. Fishing
64	Home Economics
641/642	Cookery
643/649	Household equipment and management
65	Management
651	Office management
654	Telecommunications
655	Printing. Publishing. Book Trade
656	Transport and Postal Services
657	Accountancy
659	Publicity. Advertising. Public relations
66	Chemical Technology
669	Metallurgy
67/68	Industries, Crafts and Trades
69	Building
7	The Arts
71	Regional Planning
72	Architecture
73	Plastic Arts
74	Drawing
745/749	Applied Arts
75	Painting
76	Graphic Arts
77	Photography
78	Music
79	Recreation. Entertainment. Games. Sport
791	Cinema. Films (Motion Pictures)
792	Theatre
793	Dance
794	Board and table games
796/799	Sport
8	Language. Linguistics. Literature
80	Philology
81	Linguistics
811	Individual languages

82	Literature
821	Literature of individual languages
9	Geography. Biography. History
902	Archaeology
903	Prehistory
904	Cultural remains of historical times
908	Area Studies
91	Geography
929	Biography
929.5	Genealogy
929.6	Heraldry
93/99	History
930	Science of history. Ancillary historical Sciences
930.1	History as a science. Theory and Philosophy of history
930.25	Archivistics. Archives. Public records
930.27	Epigraphy. Palaeography
94	General History (Subdivision by auxiliaries of place -Table 1e, time -Table 1g and ethnic grouping -Table 1f)
94(100)	History of The world
94(3)	History of The ancient world
94(4)	History of Europe
94(5)	History of Asia
94(6)	History of Africa
94(7/8)	History of The Americas
94(9)	History of Oceania, The Polar regions, Australasia, etc.

Library of Congress Classification System

In order to access the types of biological and chemical literature listed above, it is necessary to understand the arrangement of books in libraries.

Library science took a great step forward in 1876 with Mevil Dewey's introduction of his decimal classification of books. This system was adopted quickly as is or in modified form by many libraries. There are three major library book classification systems used today: Dewey, Library of Congress, and Universal Decimal Classification (UDC), a modified Dewey widely used in European libraries.

The Dewey decimal classification divided knowledge into the following nine classes plus one for general works:

000 General Works

100 Philosophy

200 Religion

300 Social Sciences

400 Languages

500 Pure Science

600 Technology or Useful Arts

700 Fine Arts

800 Literature

900 History, Geography, Biology

Each of these ten major divisions is further subdivided into a maximum of 99 subdivisions, and further divided as shown below for two classes, science and technology:

500 Pure Science

510 Mathematics

520 Astronomy

530 Physics

540 Chemistry, Crystallography, Mineralogy

541 Physical and Theoretical Chemistry

542 Apparatus and Equipment

543 Analytical Chemistry -General

544 Qualitative Analysis

545 Quantitative Analysis

546 Inorganic Chemistry

547 Organic Chemistry

548 Crystallography

549 Mineralogy

550 Earth Sciences

560 Paleontology

570 Biological Sciences

580 Botanical Sciences

590 Zoological Sciences

600	Technology
610	Medical Sciences
630	Agriculture
660	Chemical Technology

Conceived in 1895 and introduced in 1905, universal decimal classification, (UDC) and international adaptation of the Dewey decimal classification system, has been adopted by many European libraries. Considerably more detailed than the Dewey system, UDC has been used as an indexing scheme as well as document classification. Shown below are a few abbreviated divisions for two classes: science and technology.

Science

5	Natural Sciences
54	Chemistry
543	Analytical Chemistry
547	Organic Chemistry
547.2	Acrylic, Aliphatic Compounds
547.28	Carbonyl Compounds
547.284	Ketones

Technology

678	Macromolecular Materials
678.01:53	Physical Properties
678.01:536	Thermal Properties
678.06	Applications
678.06:621	Engineering
678.06:621.3	Electrical
78.4	Rubber and Natural Macromolecules

The other standard book classification, and the one which most Americans will encounter, is the Library of Congress Classification system (LC), which was also conceived and introduced in the last part of the nineteenth century. Originally designed for the Library of Congress only, LC was based on the over three million books collected at that time.

Unlike Dewey and UDC, LC is not based on a decimal system; it has 21 major classes of knowledge, and is based on the alphabetical and numerical representation for classes, as follows:

A	General Works	G	Geography
B	Philosophy and Religion	H	Social Science
C	Auxiliary Sciences of History	J	Political Science
D	Universal History	K	Law
E and F	American History	L	Education
M	Music	S	Agriculture
N	Fine Arts	T	Technology
P	Language and Literature	U	Military Science
Q	Science	V	Naval Science
R	Medicine	Z	Bibliography, Lib Sci

The first subdivisions of the 21 major classes are also indicated with capital letters, as in the following breakdown of science:

Q	Science	QH	Natural History
QA	Mathematics	QK	Botany
QB	Astronomy	QL	Zoology
QC	Physics	QM	Human Anatomy
QD	Chemistry	QP	Physiology
QE	Geology	QR	Bacteriology

Each subdivision is divided by a numerical system, as illustrated below for chemistry and chemical technology:

QD	Chemistry	QD281.86	Polymerization
QD1	Chemical Societies	QD301-319	Aliphatic Compounds
QD7	Nomenclature	QD410	Organometal Compds
QD11-18	History	QD419	Gums and Resins
QD45	Laboratory Manuals	TP	Chemical Technology
QD71-145	Analytical Chemistry	TP155	Chemical Engineering
QD81-95	Qualitative	TP977-982	Gums and Resins
QD101-142	Quantitative	TP986	Plastic Materials
QD151-199	Inorganic Chemistry	TP986.A5	Special Plastics
QD241-449	Organic Chemistry	TP986.A5.B3	Bakelite
Etc.			

Since the Library of Congress Classification System is used in every college and university library in the USA, then mastering it will apply to any college or university a student attends.

Glossary

Accession: The act and procedures involved in taking records or papers into physical and legal custody by an archival agency or manuscript repository. The purpose is to extend basic control over a collection as quickly as possible to prevent its being confused or mixed with other material in custody. 2. The materials involved in such a transfer of custody.

Acid: A substance capable of forming hydrogen ions when dissolved in water. Acids can weaken cellulose in paper, board, and cloth, leading to embrittlement. Acids may be introduced in the manufacture of library or archival material. Acids may also be introduced by migration from other materials or from atmospheric pollution.

Address: An identifier that specifies the source or destination of IP packets and that is assigned at the IP layer to an interface or set of interfaces.

Alkaline Buffer: Alkaline substances, which have a pH of over 7.0, may be added to materials to neutralize acids or as an alkaline reserve or buffer for the purpose of counteracting acids that may form in the future. A buffer may be added during manufacture or during the process of deacidification. A number of chemicals may be used as buffers, but the most common are magnesium carbonate and calcium carbonate.

APIPA : See Automatic Private IP Addressing.

Archives: The noncurrent records of an organization or institution preserved because of their continuing value; also referred to, in this sense, as archival materials or archival holdings. Or to use David B. Gracy's definition: Archives are the records, organically related, of an entity systematically maintained because they contain information of continuing value.

ARP Cache : A table for each interface of static or dynamically resolved IPv4 addresses and their corresponding MAC addresses.

ASCII (American Standard Code for Information Interchange): A standard code designed by the American National Standards Institute (ANSI) to facilitate information interchange between unstandardized data processing and communications equipment. The code, consisting of eight bits including a parity bit, can represent a character set of 128 alphabetic, numeric, and special symbols.

Automatic Private IP Addressing : A feature in Windows Server 2003 and Windows XP that automatically configures a unique IPv4 address from the range 169.254.0.1 through 169.254.255.254 and a subnet mask of 255.255.0.0. APIPA is used when the Internet Protocol (TCP/IP) component is configured for automatic addressing, no DHCP server is available, and the Automatic Private IP Address alternate configuration option is chosen.

Calendar: A chronological arrangement or list with description for each document in a collection.

Classless Inter-Domain Routing (CIDR) : A technique for aggregating routes and assigning IPv4 addresses on the modern-day Internet. CIDR expresses address prefixes in the form of an address prefix and a prefix length, rather than in terms of the address classes that CIDR replaces.

Coalition for Networked Information (CNI): Formed by ARL, CAUSE, and EDUCOM in March 1990 to "advance scholarship and intellectual productivity" by promoting the provision of information resources on existing and future telecommunications networks and the linkage of research libraries to these networks and their respective constituencies.

Colon Hexadecimal Notation : The notation used to express IPv6 addresses. The 128-bit IPv6 address is divided into eight 16-bit blocks. Each block is expressed as a hexadecimal number, and adjacent blocks are separated by colons. Within each block, leading zeros are suppressed. An example of an IPv6 unicast address in colon hexadecimal notation is 2001:DB8:2A1D:48C:2AA:3CFF:FE21:81F9.

Commission on Preservation and Access (CPA): A non-profit organization incorporated in 1988 for the purpose of fostering development and supporting systematic and purposeful collaboration in order to ensure the preservation of the public and documentary universe in all formats and to provide equitable access to that information.

Conservation: The treatment of library or archival materials, works of art, or museum objects to stabilize them chemically or strengthen them physically, sustaining their survival as long as possible in their original form. Conservation implies the restoration of an item to a state close to the original by means of physical treatment. See also preservation.

Correspondence: Letters, postcards, memoranda, notes, printed e-mail, and any other form of addressed, written communications sent and received.

Council on Library Resources (CLR): A private operating foundation based in Washington, DC, which aims to assist libraries, especially academic and research libraries, to take advantage of emerging technologies to improve operational efficiencies and services for library users.

Cubic Foot: An archival term used to describe the quantity of a collection. A bankers box, or records centre carton, holds one cubic foot.

Deaccession: The process of removing material from the care and custody of an archives, either because the material has been reappraised and found to be unsuitable for the archives, or because the legal owner has requested its return, or because it has been agreed to transfer it to another repository. Deaccessioning is a serious matter which requires careful consideration and documentation because of legal ramifications and possible donor reaction.

Default Gateway : A configuration parameter for the Internet Protocol (TCP/IP) component that is the IPv4 address of a neighbouring IPv4 router. Configuring a default gateway creates a default route in the IPv4 routing table.

Default Route : A route that summarizes all possible destinations and is used for forwarding when the routing table does not contain any other more specific routes for the destination. For example, if a router or sending host cannot find a subnet route, a summarized route, or a host route for the destination, IP selects the default route. The default route is used to simplify the configuration of hosts and routers. For IPv4 routing tables, the default route is the route with the network destination of 0.0.0.0 and netmask of 0.0.0.0. For IPv6 routing tables, the default route has the address prefix::/0.

Deposit Agreement and Instrument of Transmittal: A legal document that designates The University of Texas at Arlington Libraries as official depository for the records of a labour union, which are to be donated at scheduled intervals. The agreement permits the union to retain ownership of its records or to transfer ownership to the university. The agreement may be amended or terminated at any time by mutual consent. Both the union representative and a university representative must sign and date the agreement.

Description: The process of establishing intellectual control over holdings through the preparation of finding aids.

Direct Delivery : The delivery of an IP packet by an IP node to the final destination on a directly attached subnet.

Disposal: Removal of an item, or items, in a collection following the appraisal process.

Distance Vector : A routing protocol technology that propagates routing information in the form of an address prefix and its "distance" (hop count).

Donation: A voluntary deposit of records involving the transfer of legal ownership, as well as custody, to the archives.

Dotted Decimal Notation : The notation most commonly used to express IPv4 addresses. The 32-bit IPv4 address is divided into four 8-bit blocks. Each block is expressed as a decimal number, and adjacent blocks are separated by periods. An example of an IPv4 unicast address in dotted decimal notation is 131.107.199.45.

Double Colon : The practice of compressing a single contiguous series of zero blocks of an IPv6 address to "::". For example, the multicast address FF02:0:0:0:0:0:0:2 is expressed as FF02::2.

Ead: Encoded archival description. EAD is a nonproprietary encoding standard for machine-readable finding aids.

Educational and General Expenditures (E&G): The sum of total institutional expenditures for instruction, research, public service, academic support, student services, institutional support, operation and maintenance of plant, scholarships and fellowships, mandatory transfers, and (in recent years) non-mandatory transfers.

Encapsulation; Polyester Encapsulation: A protective enclosure for papers and other flat materials that involves placing the item between two sheets of transparent polyester film that are then sealed around all the edges. The object is physically supported and protected from the atmosphere, although it may continue to deteriorate within the capsule. It can be removed easily from the capsule by cutting one or more of the edges of the polyester. Ideally an item should be deacidified before it is encapsulated.

EUI-64 Address : A 64-bit link-layer address that is used as a basis for an IPv6 interface identifier.

Extended Unique Identifier : A link-layer address defined by the Institute of Electrical and Electronics Engineers (IEEE).

Finding Aids: The descriptive media, published and unpublished, created by establishing physical, administrative, and intellectual control over records, papers, and collections.

Global Unicast Address : An IPv6 unicast address that is globally routable and reachable on the IPv6 portion of the Internet. IPv6 global addresses are equivalent to public IPv4 addresses.

GNP Deflator: An updated version of the general price index used to adjust the U.S. gross national product (GNP) for inflation.

Guide: A descriptive list of a repository's holdings.

Higher Education General Information Survey (HEGIS): The predecessor of the IPEDS surveys of post-secondary education institutions by the National Centre for Education Statistics, U.S. Department of Education.

Host : A node that is typically the source and a destination of IP traffic. Hosts silently discard received packets that are not addressed to an IP address of the host.

Host Route : A route to a specific IP address. Host routes allow packets to be routed on a per-IP address basis. For IPv4 host routes, the route prefix is a specific IPv4 address with a 32-bit prefix length. For IPv6 host routes, the route prefix is a specific IPv6 address with a 128-bit prefix length.

ICMP : See Internet Control Message Protocol.

IEEE : Institute of Electrical and Electronics Engineers.

IEEE 802 Address : A 48-bit link-layer address defined by the IEEE. Ethernet and Token Ring network adapters use IEEE 802 addresses.

IGMP : See Internet Group Management Protocol.

Illegal Address : A duplicate address that conflicts with a public IPv4 address that the ICANN has already assigned to another organization.

Indirect Delivery : The delivery of an IP packet by an IP node to an intermediate router.

Interface : The representation of a physical or logical attachment of a node to a subnet. An example of a physical interface is a network adapter. An example of a logical interface is a tunnel interface that is used to send IPv6 packets across an IPv4 network.

Internet Control Message Protocol (ICMP) : A protocol in the IPv4 Internet layer that reports errors and provides troubleshooting facilities.

Internet Control Message Protocol for IPv6 (ICMPv6): A protocol in the IPv6 Internet layer that reports errors, provides troubleshooting facilities, and hosts ND and MLD messages.

Internet Group Management Protocol (IGMP) : A protocol in the IPv4 Internet layer that manages multicast group membership on a subnet.

Internet Protocol (IP) : For IPv4, a routable protocol in the IPv4 Internet layer that addresses, routes, fragments, and reassembles IPv4 packets. Also used to denote both IPv4 and IPv6 sets of protocols.

IP : Features or attributes that apply to both IPv4 and IPv6. For example, an IP address is either an IPv4 address or an IPv6 address.

IPv4 : The Internet layer in widespread use on the Internet and on private intranets. Another term for IP.

IPv6 : The Internet layer protocols of the TCP/IP protocol suite as defined in RFC 2460. IPv6 is gaining acceptance today.

LAN segment : A portion of a subnet that consists of a single medium that is bounded by bridges or Layer 2 switches.

Lignin: A component of the cell walls of plants that occurs naturally, along with cellulose. It is largely responsible for the strength and rigidity of plants, but its presence in paper and board is believed to contribute to chemical degradation. It can be, to a large extent, removed during manufacture. No standards exist for the term "lignin free," and additional research is needed to determine the precise role of lignin in the durability and permanence of paper.

Linear Feet: 1. A measurement for descriptive and control purposes of shelf space occupied by archives, records, or manuscripts. For vertical files (records filed on edge), the total length of drawers, shelves, or other equipment occupied is calculated; in the case of material filed horizontally (flat or piled up), the total vertical thickness is used. Linear feet, except for card indexes, may be equated with cubic feet on a one-to-one basis for descriptions of textual records. 2. A measurement for descriptive and control purposes of length of film, tape, or microfilm. (Usually expressed as feet.)

Link State : A routing protocol technology that exchanges routing information consisting of a router's attached subnet prefixes and their assigned costs. Link state information is advertised upon startup and when changes in the network topology are detected.

Link-local Address : A local-use address with the prefix of FE80::/64 and whose scope is the local link. Nodes use link-local addresses to communicate with neighbouring nodes on the same link. Link-local addresses are equivalent to Automatic Private IP Addressing (APIPA) IPv4 addresses.

Local Address : An IPv6 address identified by the prefix FC00::/7. The scope of a Local address is an organization. Local addresses are reachable from other sites in an organization, but not from the IPv6 Internet.

Longest Matching Route : The algorithm used to select the routes in the routing table that most closely match the destination address of the packet being sent or forwarded.

Loopback Address : For IPv4, the address 127.0.0.1. For IPv6, the address 0:0:0:0:0:0:0:1 (or::1). Nodes use the loopback address to send packets to themselves.

Manuscript: A handwritten, typed, or electronically reproduced document or communication.

Marc Formats: The Library of Congress developed the MARC formats in the late 1960s for communication of bibliographic information in machine-readable form. These MARC (for Machine-Readable cataloging) formats identify bibliographic data for computer recognition and manipulation. In the mid-1970s as variations were developed, the formats used by the Library of Congress became known as "LC-MARC formats." Since the early 1980s, however, LC-MARC formats have come to be referred to as "USMARC formats" because they are standards for MARC records in the United States.

MARC: Derived from "machine-readable cataloguing," U.S. MARC is a standard for representation and communication of bibliographical and related information in machine-readable form.

Materials and Binding: Materials are expenditures for items purchased in a given time period, usually a fiscal year, to be added to a library's collections, including books (monographs), periodicals and other serials, microforms, audiovisual materials, and other library materials; also sometimes includes expenditures for electronic searching and other modes of access to information that is not added to library collections in traditional ways. Binding is expenditures for contract binding, usually by commercial binders.

Multicast Address : An address that identifies zero or multiple interfaces and is used to deliver packets from one source to many destinations. With the appropriate multicast routing topology, packets addressed to a multicast address are delivered to all interfaces identified by the address.

Multicast Listener Discovery (MLD) : A set of three ICMPv6 messages that hosts and routers use to manage multicast group membership on a subnet.

Name Resolution : The process of resolving a name to an address.

Neighbour : A node that is connected to the same subnet as another node.

Neighbour Cache : A cache maintained by every IPv6 node that stores the IPv6 address of a neighbour and its corresponding MAC address. The neighbour cache is equivalent to the ARP cache in IPv4.

Neighbour Discovery (ND) : A set of ICMPv6 messages and processes that determine relationships between neighbouring nodes. Neighbour Discovery replaces ARP, ICMP router discovery, and the ICMP Redirect message used in IPv4.

NetBIOS : See Network Basic Input/Output System.

Network : Two or more subnets that are connected by routers. Another term for network is internetwork.

Network Address Translator (NAT) : An IPv4 router that translates addresses and ports when forwarding packets between a privately addressed network and the Internet.

Network Basic Input/Output System (NetBIOS) : A standard API for user applications to manage NetBIOS names and access NetBIOS datagram and session services.

Neutral: Having a pH of 7; neither acid nor alkaline.

Next-hop Determination : The process of determining the next-hop address and interface for sending or forwarding a packet, based on the contents of the routing table.

Node : Any device, including routers and hosts, which runs an implementation of IP.

Online Computer Library Centre (OCLC): A not-for-profit organization serving over 15,000 member libraries worldwide, OCLC provides services such as cataloguing copy, interlibrary loan transactions, and retrospective conversion of bibliographic records. It has a bibliographic database currently in excess of 24 million unique bibliographic titles and 500 million items. It has expanded its services into reference, public services, and publishing.

Open Shortest Path First (OSPF) : A link state-based routing protocol for use within a single autonomous system. An autonomous system is a portion of the network under the same administrative authority.

Oral History Deed of Gift: A legal document transferring ownership of a taped interview from the interviewee to The University of Texas at Arlington Libraries, Special Collections Division. The deed of gift must be signed and dated by both the donor (interviewee) and the interviewer and by a university representative. Restrictions may be placed by the donor on the use of the interview.

Original Order: The order in which records and archives were kept when in active use. The principle of original order requires that this order be preserved or reconstructed, unless it is clear that there was no order or that the records had been accumulated haphazardly.

OSPF : See Open Shortest Path First (OSPF).

Other Operating Expenditures: Any expenditures other than those for materials, binding, and salaries and wages, from a library's budget during a given time period.

Packet : The protocol data unit (PDU) that exists at the Internet layer and comprises an IP header and payload.

Path Vector : A routing protocol technology that exchanges sequences of hop information that indicate the path for a route. For example, BGP-4 exchanges sequences of autonomous system numbers.

Permanent/Durable Paper: A term generally applied to pH neutral papers.

Personal Papers: The documents accumulated by an individual or a family.

Polyester: A common name for the plastic polyethylene terephthalate. Its characteristics include transparency, colorlessness, and high tensile strength. Polyester is useful in preservation because it is chemically stable. Commonly used in sheet or roll form to make folders, encapsulations, and book jackets. Its thickness is measured in mils. Common trade names are Mylar by DuPont and Mellinex by ICI.

Prefix Length Notation : The practice of expressing address prefixes as *StartingAddress/PrefixLength*, in which *PrefixLength* is the number of high-order bits in the address that are fixed.

Preservation: Activities associated with maintaining library, archival, or museum materials for use, either in their original physical form or in some other format. Preservation is considered a broader term than conservation. See also conservation.

Private Addresses : IPv4 addresses that organizations use for private intranet addressing within one of the following address prefixes: 10.0.0.0/8, 172.16.0.0/12, 192.168.0.0/16.

Processing: The operations performed on materials to make a collection available for use.

Public Addresses : IPv4 addresses that are assigned by the ICANN and that are guaranteed to be globally unique and reachable on the IPv4 Internet.

Records: All recorded information, regardless of media or characteristics, made or received and maintained by an organization or institution in pursuance of it legal obligations or in the transaction of its business.

Request for Comments (RFC): An official document that specifies the details for protocols included in the TCP/IP protocol suite. The Internet Engineering Task Force (IETF) creates and maintains RFCs for TCP/IP.

Research Libraries Group (RLG): A not-for-profit membership corporation of over 120 libraries, archives, historical societies, museums and other institutions devoted to improving access to information that supports research and learning.

Research Libraries Information Network (RLIN): Owned and operated by RLG, RLIN serves the information access and management needs of its member institutions as well as individuals worldwide. It contains over 55 million bibliographic records.

Retrospective Conversion: The process of converting bibliographic records from print to a machine-readable format.

RFC : See Request for Comments (RFC).

RIP : See Routing Information Protocol (RIP).

Route Determination Process : The process of determining which single route in the routing table to use for forwarding a packet.

Route Summarization : The practice of using address prefixes to summarize the address spaces of regions of a network, rather than using the routes for individual subnets.

Router : A node that can be a source and destination for IP traffic and can also forward IP packets that are not addressed to an IP address of the router. On an IPv6 network, a router also typically advertises its presence and host configuration information.

Router Advertisement : For IPv4, a message sent by a router that supports ICMP router discovery. For IPv6, an IPv6 Neighbour Discovery message sent by a router that typically contains at least one Prefix Information option, from which hosts create stateless autoconfigured unicast IPv6 addresses and routes.

Router Discovery : A Neighbour Discovery process in which a host discovers the local routers on an attached subnet.

Routing Information Protocol (RIP) : A distance vector-based routing protocol used in small and medium sized networks.

Routing Protocols : A series of periodic or on-demand messages that contain routing information that is exchanged between dynamic routers.

Routing Table : The set of routes used to determine the next-hop address and interface for IP traffic sent by a host or forwarded by a router.

Salaries and Wages: All monies paid in salaries and wages from the library's budget during a given period of time before deductions for all staff paid.

Series: File units or documents arranged in accordance with a filing system or maintained as a unit because they relate to a particular subject or function, result from the same activity, have a particular form, or because of some other relationship arising out of their creation, receipt, or use. Also known as a record series.

Site-local Address : A local-use IPv6 address identified by the prefix FEC0::/10. The scope of a site-local address is a site. Site-local addresses are equivalent to the IPv4 private address space. Site-local addresses are not reachable from other sites, and routers must not forward site-local traffic outside the site.

Solicited-node Multicast Address : An IPv6 multicast address that nodes use to resolve addresses. The solicited-node multicast address is constructed from the prefix FF02::1:FF00:0/104 and the last 24 bits of a unicast IPv6 address. The solicited-node multicast address acts as a pseudo-unicast address to efficiently resolve addresses on IPv6 links.

Sorting: The process by which manuscripts are physically divided into appropriate alphabetical, chronological, numerical, subject, or other groups. Less frequently used with archives, except when restoring them to their original or intended order.

Static Routing : The use of manually configured routes in the routing tables of routers.

Subnet : One or more LAN segments that are bounded by routers and that use the same IP address prefix. Other terms for subnet are network segment and link.

Subnet Mask : The expression of the length of an address prefix for IPv4 address ranges in dotted decimal notation. For example, the address prefix 131.107.0.0/16 in subnet mask notation is 131.107.0.0, 255.255.0.0.

Subnetted Address Prefix : Either a new IPv4 address prefix that is the result of subnetting an IPv4 address prefix or a new IPv6 address prefix that is the result of subnetting an IPv6 address prefix.

Subnetting : The act of subdividing the address space of an IPv4 or IPv6 address prefix.

Subseries: An aggregate of file units within a record series readily separable in terms of physical class, type, form, subject, or filing arrangement.

Supernetting : The obsolete use of route summarization to assign blocks of Class C address prefixes on the Internet.

TCP : See Transmission Control Protocol.

TCP/IP : See Transmission Control Protocol/Internet Protocol (TCP/IP).

Textual Records: The term usually applied to manuscript or typescript, as distinct from cartographic, audiovisual, and machine-readable records and archives.

Total Library Expenditures (TLE): The sum of expenditures for materials, binding, salaries and wages, and other operating expenditures during a given period of time.

Transfer of Title: A legal document transferring ownership of a body of papers from one entity to another. The transfer of title must be signed and dated by the donor and by a university representative.

Transmission Control Protocol/Internet Protocol (TCP/IP) : A suite of networking protocols, including both IPv4 and IPv6, that are widely used on the Internet and that provide communication across interconnected networks of computers with diverse hardware architectures and various operating systems.

Unicast Address : An address that identifies a single interface and is used for delivering packets from one source to a single destination. With the appropriate unicast routing topology, packets addressed to a unicast address are delivered to a single interface.

Unspecified Address : For IPv4, the address 0.0.0.0. For IPv6, the address 0:0:0:0:0:0:0:0 (or::). The unspecified address indicates the absence of an address.

Upper-layer Protocol : A protocol above IP that uses IP as its transport. Examples of upper-layer protocols include Internet layer protocols such as the Internet Control Message Protocol (ICMP) and Transport layer protocols such as the Transmission Control Protocol (TCP) and User Datagram Protocol (UDP).

User Datagram Protocol (UDP) : An unreliable, connectionless Transport layer protocol that runs on top of IP.

UV Filter: A material used to filter the ultraviolet (UV) rays out of visible light. Ultraviolet radiation is potentially damaging to library, archival, and museum objects. More UV is present in sunlght and fluorescent light than in incandescent light. Removing UV radiation from storage, use, and exhibition spaces will reduce the rate of deterioration of library materials stored there.

Variable Length Subnet Masks (VLSMs) : The use of different subnet masks to produce subnets of different sizes.

Variable Length Subnetting : The practice of using variable length subnet masks.

Volume: A physical unit of any printed, typewritten, handwritten, mimeographed, or processed work, contained in one binding or portfolio, hardbound or paperbound, which has been catalogued, classified, and made ready for use. (The study follows the definition used by ARL.)

Volumes Added Gross: The volumes catalogued by a library during a given period, usually a fiscal year. Not to be confused with acquisitions, although sometimes considered a surrogate for them.

Windows Sockets : A commonly used application programming interface (API) that Windows applications use to transfer data using TCP/IP.

Zone ID : An integer that specifies the zone of the destination for IPv6 traffic. In the Ping, Tracert, and Pathping commands, the syntax for specifying a zone ID is *IPv6Address%ZoneID*. Typically, the *ZoneID* value for link-local addresses is equal to the interface index. For site-local addresses, *ZoneID* is equal to the site number. The *ZoneID* parameter is not needed when the destination is a global address or a Local address and when multiple sites are not being used.

Bibliography

Alefeld, G. and J. Herzberger: *Introduction to Interval Computations,* Academic Press, New York, 1983.

Alfred Aho, John Hopcroft, and Jeffrey Ullman: *Data Structures and Algorithms*, Addison-Wesley, 1983.

Amoroso, E.: *Fundamentals of Computer Security Technology*, Prentice Hall, Englewood Cliffs, 1994.

Aparac-Gazivoda, T & K, Dragutin: *Wounded Libraries in Croatia*, Zagreb, Croatian Library Association, 1993.

Ashley, J., M. Flickner, J. Hafner, D. Lee, W. Niblack, and D. Petkovic: *Proceedings of the International Conference on Management of Data (SIGMOD)*, ACM Press, 1995.

Bag, A.K.: *Science and Civilization in India*, New Delhi, Navrang, 1985.

Beaumont, Jane: *Make Mine MARC (MARC 21): A Manual of MARC Practice for Libraries*, Westport, Beaumont, 2001.

Brichford, Maynard J.: *Archives and Manuscripts: Appraisal and Accessioning*, Chicago, Society of American Archivists, 1977.

Buchanan, B.: *Theory of Library Classification*, London, Bingley, 1979.

Budd, John: *CEO Credibility: The Management of Reputation*, Turtle Publishing, 1993.

Byrne, Deborah J.: *MARC Manual: Understanding and Using MARC Records*, Englewood, Libraries Unlimited, 1998.

Center, Allen & Jackson, Patrick: *Public Relations Practices : Managerial Case Studies and Problems*, Prentice-Hall 1990.

Chan, L.M.: *Library of Congress Subject Headings: Principles and Application*, Colo, Libraries Unlimited, 1995.

Chepesiuk, Ron: *Winthrop College Archives and Special Collections: A Manual of Policies and Procedures,* South Carolina: Winthrop College, 1978.

Clack, Doris Hargrett: *Authority Control: Principles, Applications, and Instructions*, Chicago, American Library Association, 1990.

Comaromi, J.P.: *Dewey Decimal Classification and Relative Index: Devised by Melvil Dewey*, Albany, Forest Press, 1989.

Danton, J. Periam: *The Dimensions of Comparative Librarianship*, Chicago, American Library Association, 1973.

Duckett, Kenneth W.: *Modern Manuscripts: A Practical Manual for Their Management, Care, and Use*, Nashville, American Association for State and Local History, 1975.

Duff, I. S. and J. Koster: *The Design and Use of Algorithms for Permuting Large Entries to the Diagonal of Sparse Matrices,* SIAM J. Matrix Analysis and Applications, 1999.

Gentle, James E.: *Random Number Generation and Monte Carlo Methods*, Springer-Verlag New York, 1998.

Golub, G. and C. Van Loan: *Matrix Computations*, Johns Hopkins University Press, Baltimore, 1996.

Gorman, Michael and Paul W. Winkler: *Anglo-American Cataloging Rules*, Chicago, American Library Association, 1988.

Hammer, R. M. Hocks, U. Kulisch, D. Ratz: *C++ Toolbox for Verified Computing I. Basic Numerical Problems,* Berlin-Heidelberg, Springer, 1995.

Harvey, John F. & Carroll, Frances Laverne: *Internationalizing Library and Information Science Education,* Connecticut, Greenwood Press, 1987.

Johnson, B.L.C.: *Development in South Asia*, Harmondsworth, Penguin, 1983.

Kahan, W.: *Accurate Eigenvalues of a Symmetric Tridiagonal Matrix*, Computer Science Dept., Stanford University, 1966.

Kahn, Miriam B.: *Disaster Response and Planning for Libraries,* Chicago, American Library Association, 1998.

Karypis, G. and V. Kumar: *A Fast and High Quality Multilevel Scheme for Partitioning Irregular Graphs*, SIAM Journal on Scientific Computing, 1998.

Kearfott, R.B.: *Rigorous Global Search: Continuous Problems,* Dordrecht, Kluwer, 1996.

Khanna, J.K.: *Colon Classification,* New Delhi, Ess Ess Publications, 1986.

Kirkpatrick, S., and Stoll, E.: *A Very Fast Shift-Register Sequence Random Number Generator*, Journal of Computational Physics, 1981.

Kruckeberg, Dean & Starck, Kenneth: *Public Relations & Community: A Reconstructured Theory*, Greenwood, 1988.

Kumar, P.S.G.: *Introduction to Colon Classification,* Nagpur, Dattsons, 1987.

Lambrecht, Jay H.: *Minimal Level Cataloging by National Bibliographic Agencies*, New York: K.G. Saur, 1992.

Langridge, D.: *Approach to Classification: for Students of Librarianship*, London, Bingley, 1973.

Lesly, Philip: *Lesly's Handbook of Public Relations and Communications*, AMACOM, 1991.

Marcella, R. and Newton, R.: *A New Manual of Classification*, Aldershot, Gower, 1994.

Markey, K.: *The Online Catalogue: Developments and Directions*, London, Library Association, 1989.

Middleton, Kent & Chamberlin, Bill: *Law of Public Communication*, Longman, 1994.

Mitchell. J.: *Dewey Decimal Classification and Relative Index: Devised by Melvil Dewey*, Albany, Forest Press, 1996.

Mortimer, Mary: *Learn Descriptive Cataloging*, Lanham, Scarecrow Press, 2000.

Neumaier, A.: *Interval Methods for Systems of Equations,* Cambridge, Cambridge University Press, 1990.

Parkhi, R.S.: *Decimal Classification and Colon Classification in Perspective,* New York, Asia Publishing House, 1964.

Paul S. Adler and Terry Winograd: *Usability : Turning Technologies into Tools*, Oxford University Press, 1992.

Rahman, Abdur: *Science and Technology in Indian Culture: A Historical Perspective*, New Delhi, National Institute of Science, Technology and Development Studies, 1984.

Raju, A.A.N.: *Decimal Universal Decimal & Colon Classification,* Delhi, Ajanta Publications, 1984.

Ranganathan, S.R.: *The Five Laws of Library Science,* Bangalore, Sarada Ranganathan Endowment for Library Science, 1988.

Robb, Peter G.: *Dalit Movements and the Meanings of Labour in India*, Delhi: Oxford University Press, 1993.

Routledge, Paul: *Terrains of Resistance: Nonviolent Social Movements and the Contestation of Place in India*, Westport, Praeger, 1993.

Rowley, J.E.: *Organising Knowledge: an Introduction to Information Retrieval*, Aldershot, Gower, 1987.

Saraswathi, T.S., and Baljit Kaur: *Human Development and Family Studies in India: An Agenda for Research and Policy*, New Delhi, Sage, 1993.

Seitel, Fraser P.: *The Practice of Public Relations*, Macmillan, 1994.

Serge Abiteboul, Sophie Cluet, and Tova Milo: *Proceedings of the Nineteenth International Conference on Very Large Databases*, Dublin, Ireland, 1993.

Taylor, Arlene G.: *The Organization of Information,* Englewood, Libraries Unlimited, 1999.

Taylor, Arlene G.: *Wynar's Introduction to Cataloging and Classification,* Westport, Libraries Unlimited, 2000.

Vatuk, Sylvia: *American Studies in the Anthropology of India*, New Delhi, Manohar, 1978.

Wynar, B.S.: *Introduction to Cataloguing and Classification*, Englewood, Libraries Unlimited, 1992.

Index

D

E

F

G

H

I

L

M

N

O

P

R

S

T

U

❖❖❖